New interventions for children and youth

New interventions for children and youth
Action-research approaches

ROBERT N. RAPOPORT

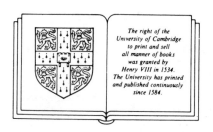

The right of the
University of Cambridge
to print and sell
all manner of books
was granted by
Henry VIII in 1534.
The University has printed
and published continuously
since 1584.

CAMBRIDGE UNIVERSITY PRESS

Cambridge
New York   New Rochelle   Melbourne   Sydney

Published by the Press Syndicate of the University of Cambridge
The Pitt Building, Trumpington Street, Cambridge CB2 1RP
32 East 57th Street, New York, NY 10022, USA
10 Stamford Road, Oakleigh, Melbourne 3166, Australia

First published 1987

Printed in the United States of America

Library of Congress Cataloguing-in-Publication Data
Rapoport, Robert N.

New interventions for children and youth.

Includes bibliographies and index.
1. Problem children—Services for—United States—
Case studies. 2. Juvenile delinquents—Services for—
United States—Case studies. 3. Action research—
United States—Case studies. I. Title.
HV741.R36 1987 362.7′4′0973 87–23860

British Library Cataloguing in Publication Data
Rapoport, Robert N

New interventions for children and youth:
action-research approaches

1. Child Welfare–United States
I. Title
362.7′95′0973 HV741
ISBN 0-521-34122-1

Contents

Acknowledgments

Many people have helped with the task of completing this book and I wish to thank them collectively for the interest and support they have shown. The staff and Board of the William T. Grant Foundation have contributed many thought-provoking comments as well as material support. Of the friends and colleagues with whom I have discussed aspects of the work, I want to mention particularly Bernard Barber, Sotiris Kitrilakis, Barbara Laslett, Eric Trist, Dorothy and Leon Lipson, and Rhona Rapoport. Marian Harrison provided superb secretarial support.

Something more than a simple word of thanks is due the principals in the action-research projects that form the basis for the ten case studies described in this book. Allowing me in – partly as a foundation executive and partly as a curious anthropologist – and allowing their experiences to be made public took courage and a high degree of professional dedication. The discussions I had with them, at workshops, in their offices, at the field sites, doubtless had some effect on the eventual picture, but we tried to keep this, as well as the glossing that often occurs in scientific journals and monographic reports, to a minimum. For their helpful cooperation I wish to thank the following: David Fanshel of Columbia University on the research side, and Alfred Herbert of the Lower East Side Family Unit on the agency side; Michael Phillips of Fordham University on the research side, and Daniel Kronenfeld and Verona Middleton-Jeter of the Henry Street Settlement's Urban Family Center on the agency side; John Clabby and Maurice Elias of Rutgers University on the research side, and Tom Schuyler of the Middlesex County Schools, N.J., on the action side; Frank Riessman and Andrew Humm of the City University of New York on the research side, and the New York public schools on the action side; Barbara Falsey of New York University and Hunter College on the research side, and Maryann Hedaa and Jack Flannagan of Urban Adventures on the agency side; Jane Knitzer of the Institute for Child and Youth Policy Studies and Bank Street College on the research side, and Howard Levine of the New York Bar Association on the action side; Robert Emery of the University of Virginia on the research side, and Judge Zehler and Cookie Scott of the Albemarle County Courts on the action side; Sally Merry and Ann Marie Rocheleau on the research side, and Sandra Wixted and Elizabeth Vorenberg of the Massachusetts Advocacy Center on the action side; Alvia Branch and Jim Riccio of the Manpower Demonstration Research Corporation (MDRC) on the research side, working with MDRC operations staff and a national network of action agencies; and Irma Hilton and Claudette Kunkes of Yeshiva University on the research side, and Loraine Henricks and A. Therese Nowlan of The Door on the action side.

There were others involved, as the case studies make clear, and they, too, deserve sincere thanks for their support.

Passages of quoted observations and data that do not bear references to published materials come from interviews, workshop discussions, and project reports. Drafts of the text have been reviewed with all participants, who have given their consent to publication here. However, I retain responsibility for any deficiencies in analysis or interpretation of data used.

R.N.R.   1987

1 Social invention and action-research

Over a decade ago, in an address to the British Social Science Research Council on the relationship between research and social action, Daniel Patrick Moynihan expressed concern for the lessons to be learned from the disappointing experiences with large-scale programs of the 1960s and with the possible contributions of action-research. Citing the American Social Science Research Council's response, he said

> The difficulty we . . . face in solving our problems is not will but knowledge. We want to eliminate poverty, crime, drug addiction and abuse; we want to improve education and strengthen family life, but we do not know how. Traditional measures are no longer good enough. Very different ones must be sought, invented, tried on a small scale, evaluated and brought closer to perfection. (1970, p. 4)

In this book we look at ten projects that represent new approaches to the mental health problems of children and youth. We call them "social inventions" because they represent departures from previous, inadequate ways of dealing with the problems. The projects described all attempt to meet the goals Mr. Moynihan speaks of, in relation to the needs of children as they develop ways of coping with the stresses of modern life. Rather than directly tackling the large-scale sources of inequality, prejudice, social conflict, and turbulence or concentrating on the specific problems of individuals, these projects address characteristic problems of children and youth in adapting to the society in which they must live. The projects are working collaborations between an action system operating in the community and a social science researcher. In working conceptually and interactively with researchers, the program operators seek to do more than "tinker" with the problems. They inform their interventions with an analysis of the nature of the social and psychological processes involved, and in so doing they plant the seeds for more widespread and enduring changes.

The term *social inventions* may be misleading because, unlike technical inventions, social inventions lack the sense of being entirely new. Although all inventions, technical as well as social, are based on previously

1

known elements, social inventions tend to be more reiterative. A mental health policy for one billion people in China would be, to be sure, different from a mental health policy for the United States (Lin and Eisenberg, 1985). But despite the differences of scale and of cultural context, the familiar ideas, roles, and organizational structures serve in new combinations to tackle the problems involved.

The mental health problems faced by young people are complex and not readily resolved through the established, traditional methods of the biomedical disciplines alone. Social and behavioral factors play a crucial role, particularly in relation to health problems following early childhood. The Institute of Medicine in the United States and similar organizations elsewhere have recognized the importance of adding approaches involving multidisciplinary collaboration to the basic research of the established biomedical disciplines (Institute of Medicine, 1981). In contrast with the traditional biomedical approaches, social interventions emphasize sociocultural elements, such as new concepts, social structures, and organizational arrangements, rather than technical elements, such as pharmacological products or electronic equipment. As for their associated research efforts, whereas traditional biomedical approaches have drawn on the findings and styles of work of the physical sciences, the new approaches are more likely to draw on the methods of the social and behavioral sciences. This departure from tradition requires adaptation to diverse methodologies and styles of work. Rather than conducting research in a laboratory where the particular variables under observation can be manipulated for the purposes of the experiment, the new approaches seek to incorporate the natural settings in which people function. The aim of this book is to learn from examining these "experiments of nature" in which practitioners have evolved collaborative relationships with social and behavioral scientists to solve mental health-related problems.

With the new kinds of interventions will come a better understanding of how they can be developed and widely applied. The challenge is considerable, raising many questions and issues of how to develop research approaches appropriate to new situations without abandoning the canons of "normal" scientific method. How do these new approaches – "social inventions" – evolve generally, and how can research be a means for developing new interventions? What kind of collaboration is required, if any, and what are the problems of creating the appropriate team structure, of communicating, and of resolving conflict between practitioners and scientific researchers?

The laboratory sciences, while expressions of scientific method *par excellence,* do not in themselves define what is scientific. The same canons of scientific method may require different approaches to gather social and behavioral data and to interpret the findings (this is true in the natural sciences but is sometimes forgotten by social scientists in their quest for scientific credibility). The cases reported in this book represent the action-research approach, emphasizing an interactive collaboration between the practitioner and the researcher. (Cf. Rapoport, 1985; Kelly, 1986; Schenshul, 1985.) While this may seem an obviously desirable arrangement and widely used, it is in fact relatively rare, far from universally accepted, and by no means based on a unified conceptual model. On the one side there are practitioners who believe that research in their fields is superfluous and possibly disruptive. On the other side are researchers who shun work in action agencies, seeing the arrangement as imposing dissonant demands, having uncongenial norms and power structures, and entailing a loss of the rigor and control required for scientific progress.

The projects that will be described were developed by practitioners and researchers who emphasized mutual advantages to working together: the development of service innovations and the advancement of scientific knowledge. The case studies are a mixed bag of projects in the children's mental health field which received foundation and government support in the early 1980s. They are examined for what they seem to show in a rather general sense about contemporary efforts to improve social interventions for children and youth. In each case there are specific issues that relate to particular people and problems, but there are also nonspecific or generic issues which relate in a broader sense to children and young people coping with stress. A broken home, for example, may be prominent in the background of a given teenage disturbance such as truancy, but along with it may be a number of other stress factors, such as poverty, overcrowded housing, and the experience of disadvantage and discrimination variously operating in the background of specific truants. Equally, broken homes may give rise to other forms of disturbance or to no disturbance at all, and under some circumstances, it may be a background factor to socially desirable outcomes, such as artistic creativity or a social service orientation.

The multiple-causality, multiple-problems model is represented in Figure 1-1.

Interventions are devised sometimes at antecedent (causal) and sometimes at outcome (problem) stages. They may be directed at any level: personal, familial, or socioeconomic. Using public health as a model,

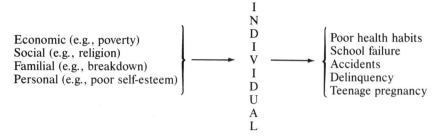

Figure 1-1. *Multiple-causality, multiple-problems model*

(Adapted from Haggerty, 1987)

antecedent interventions are preventive in orientation and are analogous to inoculation; outcome measures are treatment-oriented and are analogous to sanitation procedures.

In relation to the task of developing new social interventions for children, three themes are recurrent in this book. How do inventions arise and take form as new intervention? What is the role of action-research in developing such interventions? And how can participation in these processes contribute to increasing knowledge about children's capacity to cope with the stresses of modern life? Following a description of the invention process itself – in both technical and social fields – and the action-research approach, the individual projects will be introduced and discussed.

The invention process

The basic distinction between *technical* and *social invention* is that the former is made of tangible materials – nuts and bolts, pumps and valves, machines, silicon chips, electrical circuits, and the like – while the latter is made of people in social relationships, who behave according to shared values, role conceptions, and organizational principles. Each system has an associated set of sciences, themselves social inventions.

Technical and social systems are interdependent, but they function differently. The technical order advances stepwise as devices are invented to do something better, faster, more efficiently. Its progress is linear, reflecting ever-increasing capacity to harness forces of nature. While this advance is punctuated by spurts associated with technological revolutions and paradigmatic shifts, its direction is ever upward. Most aspects of the social order, in contrast, change by making new arrangements of the same elements. In art, family and neighborhood life, and religion, change is more like a kaleidoscope than a ladder. Art has changed, but modern art is not discernibly more pleasant or expressive than primitive art; only its technical apparatus is superior. Families have more household technology than previously, but there is no indication that the core intimate relationships in the household are improving. Gender roles have changed significantly, but the changes are not cumulative in the same way technological changes are. Modern neighborhoods have more material goods than tribal ones, but the quality of human relationships is not discernibly better. Modern churches, mosques, and synagogues incorporate new technologies (e.g., sound amplification) but the religions of orthodox Christians, Jews, or Muslims remain very similar to those of their preindustrial ancestors.

Inventions range from small improvements to "breakthroughs." Breakthroughs are inventions that create something radically different – the horseless carriage; the propellerless (jet) airplane. *Improving inventions* involve fine-tuning of the same form (e.g., a new wing shape or engine location on a jet aircraft). There are also *incorporative inventions,* or "reinventions" created by adapting something from another culture or setting to the requirements of a different environment – antibiotics for treating primitive villagers; computers for farmers. Although breakthroughs occur in social inventions (e.g., the therapeutic community concept to reform psychiatric hospitals), they tend to be less frequent and less spectacular. Social inventions are more likely to involve the rearrangement of familiar elements in a new situation and thus to have the character of reinventions. The issues of developing them are largely the same as those of inventions generally.

Early studies of invention emphasized the powerful and often unanticipated social consequences of technological advances, rather than the process of overcoming impediments to inventing. Ogburn's classic study of the motorcar is an example. Initially developed as a kind of toy for the well-to-do, the motorcar only later came to be used as a utilitarian means of transport for the masses. What impressed Ogburn (1922) was the unanticipated range of new social developments that it entailed. Although it has added immeasurably to the enrichment of the life of people of all ages, the motor car has also produced air pollution, traffic congestion, crippling, and death. In his later work, Ogburn gave more recognition to the reciprocal processes in invention: the social values and institutions that were affecting the occurrence of inventions as well as the new technical products that were affecting society.

Traditional social studies have also highlighted the importance of inventive individuals. The invention process is generally thought of as one in which an inventive individual works alone or with a few assistants in a workshop-laboratory. The new devices which are created are tried out "in the field," successively debugged, and then widely disseminated (Rein, 1983). Many inventors have indeed worked in this way. In the past they may have been supported by politicians or warlords wanting improved weaponry, as was Leonardo da Vinci. Sometimes they were entrepreneurs seeking profits, such as Ford, Goodyear, McCormick, Gillette, and Eli Whitney. But there have also been salaried scientists, hired by large corporations. Vladimir Dworkin, who invented the iconoscope from which television was developed, was hired by RCA and ascended the corporate ladder to become an executive and continued to create new ideas and products for the company. Sometimes support has come from philanthropic funds, or from universities. Barbara McClintock, a Nobel prizewinner, developed breakthroughs in the study of maize genetics in university laboratories.

Research conducted for one purpose may be applied to others. Examples are seen in the spin-offs from space research, or in wartime. Research and development, though spoken of together as though they were a single activity, are in fact distinct. Derek de Solla Price has likened the interaction between science and technology to a dance, with the partners sometimes closer, sometimes farther from one another. Each, however, is indispensable to the other, and the two enterprises have grown in parallel.

In the technical field there has been an enormous increase in inventions, reflected in the number of patents, which has risen from 600,000 in 1900 to millions now on file. Two major changes in the process of invention have accompanied this increase. First, proportionately fewer patent applications are by individuals filing patents for their own devices. A greater proportion of inventions are the products of industrial laboratories like RCA, Bell Laboratories, or other large-scale teams like the National Aeronautics and Space Administration. Schnookler has found that of 61 major inventions of the twentieth century, about half came from corporate R & D establishments. Second, there is the growth of professional roles specifically directed at invention through the research and development process. The *laissez faire* attitude to lone individuals is now partially supplanted by the purposeful creation of goal-directed teams to seek out new ideas and transform them into desired products. The dominant image now is not of the eccentric, maverick inventor working on his own, but of the professional team systematically developing new ideas in the context of an organization, which is geared to translating the ideas into workable products.

Though inventions or discoveries may occur in small scale, even marginal, settings of academic or social life, their development is another matter. The requirements for developing such innovations usually include large cash injections and an efficient industrial organization. This money may come from government grants or from corporate investment. In either case, a commitment from the top and an organizational philosophy favoring innovation is required. A recent survey by the Japanese Ministry of International Trade and Industry looked at "significant inventions since World War II." The survey found that in the fifties and sixties Britain produced the highest proportion of significant inventions (55 percent), with America trailing at 22 percent and Japan a mere 6 percent. But because they differed sharply in the degree of economic and organizational commitment they were prepared to put into developing them, there were obvious consequences. Inventiveness alone is not enough. This is further highlighted in a study by the RAND Corporation of 140 cases in which new technology was introduced into public agencies during the same post-World War II period. The study found that the effective use of an innovation depends on what the RAND team called the "innovative environment" (Yin et al., 1976).

It should not be assumed that all innovation is desirable and all resistance to change undesirable. Donald Schon cites valid organizational reasons for resisting innovation, such as the cost of changing may exceed what can be recovered, and the disruption entailed in abandoning a tried and true method for an unknown one may realistically involve too great a risk for the organization to absorb. Organizations have a responsibility for system maintenance as well as adaptation to change, and often it is only when there is a threat to survival itself that an organization is willing to disrupt the stable state (Schon, 1966).

Economics is a key element in technical inventions. Habbakuk (1962) has detected a tendency for inventors to concentrate on problems related to scarcity, and Schnookler (1962) has shown that inventors concentrate where there are perceived economic payoffs. However, "throwing money at problems" does not automatically produce results, and in the human services sector, the economic payoff element is less directly relevant. Even in the technical fields, many inventive individuals are not primarily motivated by the wish to accumulate money for themselves. Those from wealthy backgrounds may be like Sir Humphrey Davy, inventor of the miner's safety lamp, who is quoted as saying, when urged to take out a patent, "I never thought of doing such a thing. My sole object was to serve the cause of humanity, and if I have succeeded, I am amply rewarded." James Watt, Samuel Morse, and Alexander Graham Bell expressed similar sentiments. Thomas Edison, although very successful in achieving economic payoffs, ploughed much of his income back into research and development.

Much of invention occurs out of a primal sense of curiosity: to see how something works or could be made to work better. Scientists and technologists are also motivated by the wish for recognition – by winning a prize, or by having their names immortalized. Another motivation for businessmen like Ford or Hoover who hitch their wagons to a technological star is to build an organization. According to Schumpeter (1982), the wish to "build one's own kingdom" is a key motive in entrepreneurship; it is the drive for autonomy, to be one's own boss, to exercise control over one's time and activities, to "run one's own show," to create a monument. According to one successful modern high-technology innovator, people like himself seek market leadership not for the economic gain *per se,* but to be able to attract the top talent and have the resources to "trailblaze new frontiers" (Ray Stata, cited by Clifford and Cavanagh, 1985, p. 44; also cf. Botkin, Dimanescu, and Stata, 1984).

Robert Merton (1973) has demonstrated that when a society or field is "ready," that is, with a sense of need, a receptive environment, and an appropriate level of groundwork, many inventions become almost obvious, and multiple independent inventions occur. Patents and copyrights are designed to protect and motivate genuine inventors by assuring that they are rewarded, and when a society is "ready," an invention can be extremely rewarding for the patent-holder (for example, McCormick with his reaper, Glidden with his barbed wire, Dupont's nylon). But sometimes innovators have gone unrecognized because they were one of the nonpatented "multiples." And it is common for inventors to encounter resistance, even if they obtain a patent. Garnsworth, a major figure in the development of television, has described how a professor told him four reasons why his ideas would never work. His original papers on transistors met with complete indifference from colleagues. Max Planck's biographical description of his professors' indifference to his attempts to contact them to discuss his ideas on thermodynamics is a classic instance. Chester Collier, who invented the Xerox copier, had the basic idea in 1937 and approached over 20 firms for support to develop it; none showed any interest. Finally, in 1944, Batelle bought the idea, but sold it 12 years later to the Haloid Company of Rochester, New York, still not appreciating its potential. Many scientists, like Robert Oppenheimer, have emphasized the importance of open-mindedness in the invention process and noted its frequent absence.

Even when there is an open-mindedness in principle, breakthroughs do not always happen rationally. Often, as in the case of Alexander Fleming, a semi-fortuitous discovery is made and then not followed through until sometime later, when a new enthusiasm and a new talent (in this case, that of Howard Florey) are injected into the situation. Sometimes, as in the case of Pasteur's discoveries of immunization, both the achievement of scientific goals and the development of practical applications come about through nonrational *and* rational factors combined.

Pasteur developed a theory that microbes vary in virulence according to the environments in which they ferment. He discovered semi-accidentally how to attenuate the virus when he found on returning from holiday that the cultures he had left unused had weakened in the interim. His formal report did not mention this but only that by allowing a longer interval of time between successive inoculations he was able to obtain a method for decreasing the virulence, achieving a mild case of the disease which "preserves from the deadly disease." The happy accident illustrates how chance favors the prepared mind, but what happened subsequently was highly systematic and purposeful. Pasteur worked first in the laboratory to establish that anthrax microbes could be attenuated by heating them in culture to a specific temperature (42° – 44° C). He then conducted a classic field trial:

On May 5, 1881, twenty-four sheep, one goat and six cows were injected with an attenuated anthrax strain. On 31 May, a fully virulent culture was injected into all 31 vaccinated animals, and twenty-nine unvaccinated. By 2 June, all the vaccinated animals were still healthy, while by the evening of that day all the unvaccinated sheep were dead and the unvaccinated cows were ill. (Harre, 1981, p. 103)

The result was a triumph for Pasteur, whose factory manufactured and sold great quantities of the vaccine.

Just as innovative ideas and practices emerge out of mixtures of rational and non-rational elements, so do resistances to innovation, as Francis Bacon long ago observed. Preconceived ideas often block the capacity to absorb innovations. Even after Copernicus published *De Revolutionibus* and his new concepts were formally accepted, most astronomers of the day felt more comfortable with the accepted way of thinking, that the sun revolved around the earth. Thomas Kuhn (1957) conceptualized this in terms of paradigms that impose a structure on what is perceived and what is rejected. The history of science and technology has many examples both of eagerness to embrace new ideas and of resistance. Bernard Barber (1961) noted that like other people, scientists experience a fear of newness and may additionally be blinded by specialization. They show the same clubbiness and the same tension between generations as do other social groups. Dael Wolfle goes so far as to say that fundamental and sweeping innovations cannot be thoroughly grasped until a new generation has grown up, with the new ideas in their bones, so to speak, unhampered by preceding modes.

Building on new knowledge requires determination and a high level of motivation, whether for economic payoff or other reasons. Many scientific and technological innovations have occurred through cross-fertilization and "lateral" thinking, rather than by a straight-line, goal-oriented process. Guttenberg conceived his ideas for a letter press through observing the way wine was pressed; Kepler evolved his ideas for a theory of gravitation by a loosely drawn analogy with the role of the spirit in the Holy Trinity. The mighty Einstein, who was a school failure, wrote in a child's autograph book:

A thought that sometimes makes me hazy,
Am I, or are the others, crazy? (Cited by Baker, 1976)

In summary, there are many patterns of motivation and environmental conditions affecting invention, and how they interplay seems to be crucial: between science and technology in developing inventions, and between the innovators and their environment in disseminating the innovation. Disseminating an invention requires a favorable socioeconomic and political climate and the capacity to build appropriate organizations (Nelson and Yates, 1978). Technical inventions, though often arising through the "lateral" interests of peripheral persons or agencies, feed into a mainstream of cumulative development with measurable increments over time. How do social inventions compare?

Social invention

Recent reviews of the social science literature confirm that social inventions are in some ways comparable to scientific discoveries and technical inventions. Karl Deutsch and two associates (1971) identified 62 "advances" in social science between 1900 and 1971, and noted that, like technical inventions, they were the product of a deliberate effort to improve some kind of human enterprise through scientific method. And like technical inventions, they often encountered resistance, and generally took 10 to 15 years to become established even after their merit was recognized. However, social phenomena are particularly prone to the ups and downs of fashion. To determine whether innovations in the social sciences endure in the manner of discoveries in the physical sciences, Daniel Bell examined the list to assess continuities. He found that most of the advances identified by Deutsch had endured, but that more recent ones differed in character from earlier ones. Those that preceded the development of sophisticated quantitative methodology in the social sciences, (e.g., Weber's theory of bureaucracy, Lenin's theory of the one-party organization and revolution, Freud's theory of psychoanalysis) were qualitative, while later ones (decision theory by Anatol Rapoport; stochastic models by J. S. Coleman; econometrics by Tinbergen) have been mostly quantitative in style. An exception is Levi-Strauss's structuralism.

As in technological R & D, there has been a movement toward team effort, and a mutually productive interplay between theory and practice. Bell noted, however, that social innovations have tended to be culture-bound and therefore require more reinvention for adaptation to diverse settings than is generally true for technological inventions.

Explicit attempts to relate advances in social theory to the development of new social interventions, particularly in the public service fields, have been disappointing. William Foote Whyte (1982), among others, has called for a massive effort to encourage social inventions to solve contemporary human problems. His own experience is primarily in the industrial field. George Fairweather (1972) has urged a similar effort, basing his formulations on his experiments in mental hospital settings.

One of the characteristics of social inventions is their volatility. An invention may begin as a concept directed at solving an individual's problem in a school or clinical setting, and develop into a large-scale policy or program or school of therapy. Or it may be directed initially at a specific role relationship, for example, the parents' disciplinary practices toward the child, and end up as a set of organizing principles for educational institutions or community intervention programs. An invention may arise in one setting and be incorporated in a different way elsewhere: the French *educateur* role as adapted into American school settings as "teacher counselors" (Hobbs, 1982); or the industrial mediation and arbitration procedures as adapted to the resolution of family disputes (Folberg and Taylor, 1984). At the organizational level of intervention, the invention of the "therapeutic community" as a way of helping returned prisoners of war to adapt to civilian life was reapplied to the reform of the custodial mental hospital system, the remotivating of "work-shy" unemployment cases, the resocialization of delinquents, and as a "mediating structure" for ex-hospital patients and others in transition from one set of institutional settings to another (Jones, 1953; Woodson, 1981). Furthermore, changes in environmental demands and in prevalent modes of problem-definition can result in institutions which were innovative becoming outmoded or merely routine (Pearse and Crocker, 1947; Geiger, 1985; Gordon, 1978/80).

Inventions occurring at one level may spread to other levels either through *expansion* (from the individual clinical level to a large-scale development) or through *devolution* (from large-scale national programs, such as Head Start, down to local practice). Gellner (1985) has recently analyzed the history of psychoanalysis as an international social movement that grew from the clinical ideas of an individual practice. The parent-education movement is also an example of how an innovation may escalate from a small-scale, practice-based effort to a large-scale social movement (cf. Spock, 1946; Jaffe, 1973; Segal, 1983).

Great sums of money have been spent on large-scale efforts to develop solutions for major problems in the wake of depression and wartime exigencies. Under the New Deal and Great Society programs, projects were promulgated to provide jobs, improve race relations, develop a sense of community, improve housing, expand education, prevent delinquency, and promote mental health. In many of these programs there was social science participation.

In the educational field, for example, studies by the RAND Corporation (Berman and McGaughlin, 1978) and Abt Associates (Abt, 1977; Rosenblum and Louis, 1981) contributed to the understanding of issues involved in adapting innovative educational programs to various local conditions. Working in conjunction with the National Opinion Research Center, RAND selected 293 projects in 18 states representing communities with federal grants for implementing innovations in school programs under ESEA Title I, 1974. Among their conclusions were the following:

- Money alone does not assure implementation.
- Enthusiasm in the project director is important in getting a project started, but implementation and continuation depend on grass-roots rank-and-file support.
- Durable changes in systems into which innovations are introduced depend on follow-through activities that are not automatically incorporated into innovations: training, technical assistance, problem-solving discussion groups, and sharing decision-making with teachers.

Expansion and devolution involve different issues. The incorporation of large-scale ideas into local practice requires a degree of reinvention (Larsen and Agarwala-Rogers, 1977); while the "bottom-up" approach requires the mobilization of a different order of administrative skills and resources. Available data suggest that neither a "top-down" nor a "bottom-up" approach is unequivocally effective (Rosenblum and Louis, 1981). Factors affecting the success of either approach include the *capacity* of those who are to use an innovation (Datta, 1978), their awareness of the importance of developing resource networks (Emrick, 1977), and the influence they may bring to bear on ecological factors (Emery and Trist, 1973; Bronfenbrenner, 1979; Perrow, 1979; Travers and Light, 1982).

George Fairweather (1972) reviewing the issues in placing therapeutic community units in mental hospitals (lateral dissemination of an innovation) stresses the importance of an outside disseminator who is active in engaging the cooperation of inside persons and groups in the potential adopting agency.

All inventions confront the issue of how they are to be sustained. Technical inventions link more readily to business and commerce, where they tend to be developed with an economic investment orientation, and sustained if they are profitable. In the behavioral field there are some inventions which are investment-oriented and market-based, for example, in the leisure and entertainment, personnel management, advertising, and public-relations fields. But those described in this book are in the not-for-profit field and are supported primarily by government, universities and philanthropic foundations. They operate on a budget rather than a balance sheet. They are what Peter Drucker (1985) terms "public service" agencies, which are particularly resistant to innovation and, as noted earlier, tend to look for new ways of doing things only when faced with catastrophe or when mandated to from outside. Drucker pointed to some notable exceptions – the Catholic Church, the Girl Scouts of America, and the American Academy for the Advancement of Science – all of which developed constructive innovations in adapting to their changing environment. In all of these cases he emphasized the importance of entrepreneurship in the transformation of a good idea into a viable new organization or product.

The kinds of social inventions which are described in the projects presented in this volume are relatively modest in their aspirations, both in terms of immediate goals and envisioned changes. They involve grassroots, piecemeal changes rather than large-scale utopian ones.

The action-research relationship

There is no rule that says researchers and social intervention agencies must collaborate. There are many action agencies which are convinced of the value of what they are doing, based on practice experience and the continued demand for their services, and have no need for research. They are able to create new services based on experience and conviction. However, many new interventions arise out of what Rein (1983) calls "practice worries," where the problems are much more apparent than are possible solutions. The practitioner may, at this point, seek the collaboration of a researcher. In other instances, there may be a new intervention which seems valuable to its proponents, but which may be of questionable value objectively, particularly if choices must be made in a situation of scarce resources. The kind of research which has frequently been sought, and is sometimes mandated in such a situation, is program evaluation.

Whichever way the researcher becomes involved in an action program, there will be differences in viewpoints and ways of working between the researcher and the practitioner, and tensions can be expected to arise. Lees (1976) notes that the requirements of a research design may run counter to the requirements of an innovative action agency. In addition, service innovators characteristically proceed from a sense of conviction that what they are doing is good and right, whereas researchers characteristically adopt a skeptical stance, requiring evidence before drawing conclusions on which an intervention would be based. (Also see Halsey, 1972; Lees and Smith, 1975.)

Some researchers are strongly motivated to use their scientific knowledge and skills to help action agencies, while recognizing that there are many situations which may not merit this help. Also, as Robert Kahn said, the seeking-to-help motive does not always go hand-in-hand with the motive of truth-telling; nor does the activity of practical problem-solving always make a contribution to basic science. Action-research, as here defined, emphasizes the potential reciprocity in certain situations where the two goals – helpful/practical and basic/scientific – may overlap:

Action-research aims to contribute both to the practical concerns of people in an immediate problematic situation and to the goals of social science by joint collaboration within a mutually acceptable ethical framework. (Rapoport, 1970)

A number of contemporary social scientists subscribe to this orientation (Clark, 1976; Price and Politser, 1980; Argyris, Putnam, and Smith, 1985; Snowden, Munoz, and Kelly, 1979).

The term action-research came into current use just prior to and just after World War II. The concept on which it was based, the quest for an integral connection between social research and social intervention, goes back to the early days of social science. Early anthropological work was developed hand in hand with the work of missionaries and colonial administrators. Freud's invention of psychoanalysis evolved in a dialectic between what was being taught in academic settings and what he dealt with in his own practice. Piaget's research on child development and his educational innovations also went hand in glove. Indeed, only recently has the gulf between action and research increased, with the differentiation and specialization of the academic disciplines. Partnerships increased in wartime between research-oriented action agencies and application-oriented researchers, stimulated by the national emergency, and produced a body of work in the social sciences which was acknowledged to be useful both to the conduct of the war and to the growth of scientific knowledge. Psychologists were engaged in a range of activities from personnel selection to therapy (e.g., Murray, 1938; Grinker and Spiegel, 1945; Main, 1946; Bion, 1961; Jones, 1953). Anthropologists analyzed enemy morale and helped with strategic work (Bateson and Mead, 1941; Benedict, 1946; Leighton, 1949).

Alexander Leighton and a team of social scientists studied the camps in which Americans of Japanese descent were interned following Pearl Harbor. Although the issue of a mutually acceptable ethical framework was and still remains problematic (many people felt that the internment policy was morally wrong), Leighton and his team contributed to our understanding of what is now called "governance," and arguably they helped to ameliorate the plight of the internees (Leighton, 1946). Samuel Stouffer and his colleagues made surveys of American soldiers which were useful to army administrators and also became milestones in the methodology of sociological research (Stouffer, 1949). Many social scientists who worked in close collaboration with the authorities during the war returned afterwards to the mainstream of academic pursuits and became part of a momentum of interest in multidisciplinary approaches. Multidisciplinary units were formed, such as the Department of Social Relations at Harvard and the Department of Human Relations at Yale. The growth of action-research can be understood in this context.

The term *action-research* was actually coined prior to the war, and was used in two settings: first by John Collier (1945), then Commissioner for Indian Affairs under Roosevelt, and then by Kurt Lewin. Collier saw the American Indian situation as a vast natural laboratory which could be useful to anthropologists for testing hypotheses about social change, and also useful to the Indian Service as a basis for policymaking. At that time, Sol Tax and some of his anthropology students at the University of Chicago had developed a similar approach which they called "action anthropology." It failed to flourish, however, partly because of countervailing trends in the academic field, and partly because there was a national shift in priorities away from treating the Indians as a special ethnic group.

The approach taken by Kurt Lewin, in contrast, flourished in several settings, of which three will be described. They had in common several basic ideas:

- The conviction that research and action could be linked for mutual benefit.
- A close interactive relationship between researchers and action agencies based on overlapping values.
- Use of programs with a recurring cycle from formulation and design through program implementation, evaluation, feedback, and dissemination.

Each setting emphasized different combinations of these basic ideas. One subgroup at the University of Michigan's Institute of Social Research is associated with such names as Ronald Lippitt, Stanley Seashore, John French, and, more recently, Richard Price. Their distinctive characteristic is an emphasis on methodological rigor and a quasi-experimental design, even when working in the community or industrial context. A second group, based in the National Training Laboratories, is group-dynamics-oriented and is associated with Warren Bennis and Edgar Schein, among others. It is concerned with demonstrating the relationship between personal development and group process. A third group was based at the Tavistock Institute in London, and is associated with such names as A. T. M. Wilson, Eric Trist, and Adam Curle (1952); Elliot Jacques (1952); and Harold Bridger (1983). This strand of work is psychoanalytically oriented and has produced work which is clinical in character. Social and organizational dynamics underlying the presenting problems are analyzed in terms of covert processes. Interpretations are made in the style of a psychotherapist and the implications of the new insights are worked through collaboratively. Their method was sometimes called "sociotherapy" because it sought to improve the functioning of social systems. Their motto in the early days was "no research without therapy and no therapy without research." The work of the Tavistock group also contained elements of systematic quasi-experimental research and was concerned with theory-development as well as practical results (cf. Emery and Trist, 1973, and Sofer, 1961).

There are other strands, some – as Nevitt Sanford has pointed out – looking very much like action-research, but under other names: operational research (Lawrence, 1966); social engineering (Freeman et al., 1983); action-learning (Revans, 1982; Morgan and Ramirez, 1983); participatory research (Brown and Tandon, 1983; Tharp and Gallimore, 1982); a learning process approach (Korten, 1980); the experimenting society (Campbell, 1981); social experimentation (Riecken and Boruch, 1974); social intervention (Seidman, 1984); cooperative learning (Reason and Rowan, 1981); and action learning (Argyris et al., 1985). Heller (1986) distinguishes between action-research (in which the emphasis is on fact-finding as a guide to action), and research-action (in which the emphasis is placed on the action, from which scientifically valid learning is expected).

The achievements and lessons of action-research are recorded in several publications. One book summarizes the recent accomplishments centering on the Tavistock group (Clark, 1976), and another centers on the work of the Michigan ISA complex (Price and Politser, 1980). Most recently, a number of experts in the child and family research area have reviewed its history and prospects in those fields (Rapoport, 1985). In all this certain themes have become widely recognized.

- Action-research is an approach that seeks to learn from action situations and to gain new knowledge. It operates through a cycle of planning, intervention, evaluation, feedback, and dissemination for as long as there is something to contribute. In this it contrasts with research, which focuses on specific variables measured with instruments to test hypotheses geared to specific disciplinary interests.
- Action-research involves the collaboration and interaction between members of different systems – one geared to goals of action, the other to goals of knowledge. It is intrinsically multidisciplinary and multisystems-oriented.
- Action-research upholds an interest in process as well as structure – in *how* a phenomenon works as well as whether it works, and with what *might* be as well as what is.
- In action-research, evaluation is treated not only as a summative statement, but also as a formative element, which in itself requires specific skills and techniques.
- Action-research is a demanding method and has many pitfalls as well as exciting potentials. Researchers may become marginal to their parent disciplines. In their partnership with intervention agents, they may be in conflict over the approach to change, and feel isolated from the kind of colleague supports available in academic institutions. However, these tensions may have a synergizing effect. (Kelly, 1976; Price and Burke, 1985)

During the postwar years in which action-research flourished, there were many massive social science oriented action programs which enjoyed public support and which subsequently suffered troubles. There is much that can be learned from them.

In the heyday of Great Society programs of the fifties and sixties, there was considerable interplay between public policymakers and social scientists. Federal support for the social sciences increased from $30 million annually to over $500 million (SSRC Bulletin, September, 1983), and in the foundation world, the Ford Foundation alone spent close to $40 million on the behavioral sciences between 1951 and 1956. Much of this money went into action-oriented programs, many with research components.

Some of the Great Society social experiments were predominantly economic (e.g., the Negative Income Tax Experiment). Others had major social or psychological dimensions, such as Head Start and the School Desegregation Programs.

In the eight-year span of the Kennedy-Johnson administration there were many attractive concepts available as ideals to guide the various action programs. Researchers and action agents could agree on the desirability of ideas such as opportunity, community, and coordination. But in some of the urban programs what actually occurred was rioting, conflict, and political assassination. These social disturbances cannot be said to have been the fault of the social scientists, but the concepts and methods that social scientists made available were clearly inadequate to solve practical problems on this scale; and for the researchers the negative outcomes were a shock, contributing to their withdrawal to less-trying, less-exposed arenas of work.

Harold Gerard (1983) reviewed the School Desegregation Program in these terms. The policy was conceived and developed with the participation of top social scientists. Gerard argues that the historic Supreme Court Decision to desegregate the schools, in Brown vs. Board of Education 1954, was influenced by a collusion between the rhetoric of politicians and the utopianism of academic social science theorists. Academics agreed that segregation was psychologically harmful and that it produced inequalities of opportunity. However, data to support the action proposition that merging racially segregated school populations would remedy these deficiencies was very thin. Merging was expected to remove the psychological stigmatization that went with separation. In addition, merging was expected to foster a "lateral transmission of values." In other words, the achievement orientation of whites would rub off onto blacks, providing them with motivation to overcome inequalities. Gerard observed that research evaluations have not vindicated the hypotheses – school desegregation has not achieved as great an increase in minority interaction as expected, nor has it greatly improved minority achievement values and self-esteem (Gerard, 1983). Gerard identified four flaws in the assumptions of the experts:

> That there would be firm and consistent endorsement of the program by those in authority;
> That there would be an absence of competition among the representatives of the different groups;
> That equivalence of positions and functions would exist in the de-segregated setting;
> That inter-racial contacts would be of the type that fostered learning about one another as individuals. (Gerard, 1983, p. 870)

This set of conditions was virtually nonexistent as a total package and was often contravened by conditions oriented in the opposite direction. For example, black self-esteem was actually found to diminish in many desegregated classroom situations because of such factors as teacher prejudice or unfavorable experiences of direct competition with whites. After a detailed dissection of flaws in the underlying assumptions, Gerard concluded that

social scientists were wrong in the belief that change would come easily. There were so many resistances to overcome, many of which should have been anticipated, but many of us were blinded by our ideology into thinking that we could have utopia in one fell swoop of mandated busing. Simply mixing children in the classroom and trusting to benign human nature could never have done the trick. . . . What I am questioning here are the assumptions underlying the belief that school desegregation as implemented in the typical school district will be an instrument to achieve that end. (Gerard, 1983, p. 875)

Stuart Cook (1984), one of the social science experts who participated in the original formulations of the desegregation program, has criticized Gerard's analysis on the basis of his own research. In a more recent and more modest action-research project in Denver, he demonstrated that what is crucial is the *mode* of introduction and incorporation of a school desegregation program. In situations where the program is explained and the cooperation of participants actively solicited, there is a greater chance for success. A new key concept that emerged from this is "cooperative interdependence" (Cook, 1984). On the basis of this, he urges social scientists to remain engaged in action efforts rather than abandoning projects after encountering difficulties.

Anthropologists and specialists in area studies experienced another set of difficulties. When John Collier envisaged an Indian Service with policies informed by the best anthropological minds of the country, he had the backing of the country's top administrators. Some of the leading academics were also enthusiastic, having set up new programs following the war: Lloyd Warner and his colleagues at Chicago, Clyde Kluckhon and his colleagues at Harvard, the Leightons at Cornell, and Spicer at Arizona were among them. But because of the change of Indian Service policy, the Indian Service studies of personality development in several tribal groups, while of interest to academics, were of little help in formulating policies toward the Indians. This was a case where, contrary to stereotypes, applied social research had more value for science than for action. George Stocking (1979), in his history of anthropology at the University of Chicago, notes that the collaboration with the Bureau of Indian Affairs also suffered when there were clashes over the ownership and control of the data. Further difficulties emerged after an experimental foray into "action anthropology" by the students of Sol Tax, who tried to combine field research with the Fox Indians with active efforts to promote tribal development. Many Fox Indians did not appreciate the effort and even attacked it, and despite the agreement by all on "the right to make mistakes," the young anthropologists were not especially skilled at practical problem solving or achieving political consensus (Gearing, Netting, and Peattie, 1960).

Even more disturbing were the experiences of Project Camelot, in which anthropologists and other Latin America specialists clashed with the military establishment over the uses of research data in a highly politically charged area of the world (Horowitz, 1967; Sjoberg, 1967). Research in third-world countries tended to be confused with covert military activity, and researchers concluded that they should distance themselves from action agencies. Stocking noted that anthropologists had come to believe that they should concentrate on academic concerns and "insist on the need to maintain a separation between academic research in the social sciences and mission-oriented activity under government control."

A prominent type of social action-oriented research in this period was not what Stocking called "mission-oriented," but more evaluation-oriented. Classically, the program evaluator, like the basic researcher, emphasized the detached role of the researcher. Although some evaluation researchers, like Peter Rossi and Howard Freeman, have been effective communicators, others have been so detached that their work has been disowned by the action agency and has tended to reinforce the tension between agency personnel and researchers. As S. M. Miller (1983) notes, evaluation studies have typically been weak theoretically, making it difficult to apply the information to other situations.

Another criticism of the classic program-evaluation approach is it tends to cast the social action program into the mold of an "independent variable" in the traditional experimental model (Schwarz, 1981). But action programs are generally based not on a single hypothetical proposition but on an amalgam of ideas derived from a range of experiences and hopes, and on preliminary impressions of efficacy, economy, and viability. There is a mistaken tendency to discount an entire program when the outcomes are "not proven statistically," as in the case of the Head Start program. The program was based on the observation that some groups of children were seen to have intellectually deficient preschool environments which reduced their chances of success in school. It was reasonable to expect that a program to enrich preschool intellectual inputs should improve school performance. But initial evaluations showed equivocal results and the program was branded a failure. In the long run, data on the effects of Head Start showed some clear gains, but because government policymakers required a relatively quick assessment, the short-term information had an unwarranted and damaging effect. Scientific standards for assessing such complex processes require a breaking down of the issue into parts, a review of findings at each stage, and further study and multivariate analyses to determine which elements contribute to observed effects and which might be altered to strengthen overall effects (Zigler and Valentine, 1979). Schwarz (1981, p. 19) argues that

The reason these colossal efforts failed was that they did *not* break the long sequence from input to desired result into modest chunks or cycles, did *not* provide for a collaborative approach to negotiate them incrementally, did *not* incorporate research to help across bridges and hurdles, did *not* arrange for a feedback at each step of the way.

Some studies which did use the kind of approach that we are advocating had more success. The Ypsilanti studies, for example, demonstrate the value of a program of action-oriented research in terms of many of the principles of action-research enumerated above (Schweinhart and Weikart, 1986). Researchers found that, as in the initial program evaluations of Head Start, IQ advantages gained by children in the program tended to blur over time. However, by following through and taking into account other factors, they were able to make formulations more complex than "proven" or "not proven." They found that individual responses varied greatly, and that high educational achievement persisted in many cases. By following through from their initial Perry Preschool Project, in which economically disadvantaged children attended a Piaget, cognitive-oriented program and were compared with a control group that did not, and staying with the program after its initial evaluation, they concluded that the original "cultural deficit" model was inadequate. A new more effective model, in terms of both scientific explanation and practical action, became what they called a "cultural difference" model. This model could accommodate the variation actually present in the populations while retaining a rigorous methodological format. In the most recent report of results of their 20-year follow-up studies, the Ypsilanti group have been able to quantify not only IQ and school achievement variables, but use of social services and eventual earning power through job placement. These variables are particularly powerful in communicating the utility of research to policy issues.

While some of the difficulties experienced at the action-research interface have stemmed from imprecise methodology, the opposite extreme of elegant quantitative methodology is no panacea. S. M. Miller and his colleagues (1983) note that even where there is a highly developed formal methodology, as in the econometrics modeling field, the use of flawed data will produce erroneous results. By using proxy data and pyramiding assumptions from them, econometricians have been able to perform complex numerical manipulations and report crisp and concise findings. Even when couched in such qualifying terms as "suggestive" and "one of many considerations," their style tends to imply precision and therefore is often accepted as definitive. Miller's suggestion is to use qualitative analysis rigorously executed to counterbalance this tendency.

Other difficulties with action-research arose from studying sophisticated populations, often including people in positions of power. These people, with their own observations and point of view, had the power to attack or suppress the work if they did not like the results. A researcher must be skilled and strong to defend against this type of reaction, but project management skills are often dismissed as not part of the social science methodology. Daniel Patrick Moynihan (1969) has emphasized the importance of such skills in handling problems arising from cultural gaps between activists (politicians, judges, advocates, policymakers, managers, and administrators) and academic researchers (professors, theoreticians, methodologists). When collaborating with activists, many academics suggest theoretical solutions to problems without having reliable or relevant information and experience; they thus expose themselves to justifiable criticism. Moynihan stresses that researcher involvement in social and political processes requires both adequate data and adequate communication skills.

In Britain, similar large-scale experiments were tried and similar difficulties encountered, as in the Community Development and Educational Priority projects (Lees and Smith, 1975; Halsey, 1972). In the urban planning field, Peter Hall (1980) analyzed what went wrong with a series of "great planning disasters." These enterprises had contained research, but they were beset by a complex of economic and political factors which overrode any contribution the research could have made to keeping them within originally planned time frames and budgets.

Henry Riecken (1983) sums up the problem of this era as springing from the convergence of a number of factors: resistance to change, suspicion that social scientists were ideologues in disguise, and controversy surrounding many of the results even among social scientists. Researchers, in addition, whatever the scientific merits of their findings, were inept at meeting political arguments. Riecken suggests that social scientists should equip themselves to consider both intellectual *and* political issues.

Recently a number of indicators have suggested the time is right to attempt to forge new collaborative links between researchers and action agencies. First, human services workers are dissatisfied with the common-sense approach. Rein (1983) refers to this kind of dissatisfaction as "practice worries" – feelings of malaise and anxiety about clients' problems and of the need for new solutions. In the teenage pregnancy field, pediatrician Elizabeth McAnarney (1984) argues that while there are many factors possibly relevant to teenage pregnancy, uncertainty remains as to how to act on them appropriately. Gaining further knowledge and expertise calls for a multidisciplinary approach, with better communication and coordination of effort among the various participants, particularly in this case, as the weight to be given to specific factors is continuously changing with changes in the roles of women, in demographic patterns, and in conceptions of family life. McAnarney argues that even if all of the relevant factors for prevention cannot be controlled, it is still possible to equip young women who become parents prematurely to act more wisely with their next child. Even this more limited aim requires an improved knowledge base and improved services working in tandem.

Second, there is a renewed sense of dissatisfaction with certain kinds of academic social science research which have become too removed from human life issues (Sarason, 1981; Hymes, 1974). S. B. Sarason makes the point that post-World War II psychologists had a number of naive misconceptions, the failure of which has brought frustration and disillusionment to their discipline. One of the problems was a shallow optimism, which was bound to yield disappointment. Another was the tunnel vision of the monodisciplinarian that fortified the false polarity between the individual and society, which was bound to lead to inadequate formulations for the world of policy and action. Finally, there was the grandiosity that made cloistered academics imagine that they understood the turbulent world of politics and social change. But this should not mean that an action-oriented role for the psychologist of the future should be avoided. More attention should be paid to interrelations with the other institutions of society, including business and industry; better links should be forged between the disciplines; and there should be a much more sophisticated appreciation of conflict and dysfunction in society, as well as orderliness, equilibrium, and harmony.

Third, academics find themselves in the paradoxical situation of having increased capacity to handle complex methodological problems and, simultaneously, decreased opportunities to exercise these skills in conventional academic settings.

The field of community psychology has attempted to forge new collaborative relationships that incorporate these methodological skills on an interdisciplinary basis (Sarason, 1972, 1977; Snowden, Munoz, and Kelly, 1979; Susskin and Klein, 1985; Rappaport, 1977). Similar efforts are under way in educational and organizational research (Argyris, Putnam, and Smith, 1985).

Finally, there is the knowledge learned from earlier action-research. Francis Sutton (1982), reviewing the Ford Foundation's development programs, noted that although the earlier assumption of unalloyed rationality of intervention agencies now seems naive, this does not justify the abandonment of the principle of human rationality. Similar observations underlie Peter Hall's retrospective analysis of the "Great Planning Disasters," and Moynihan's retrospective analysis of the Great Society Programs.

Experience with action-research has led to several conclusions:

1. Action-research, an approach which flourished briefly following the Second World War, and then went into eclipse, has been and is still potentially useful in fostering the invention and development of new solutions to human problems.
2. This is an auspicious time to reexamine the potential contribution of action-research to solving some of today's enormous array of social problems affecting children – family discord, alienation from schooling, adolescent troubles with premature/unwanted pregnancy, and delinquency offenses.
3. The approach calls for an interactive collaboration between researchers and action agencies. It seeks not only to help with specific practical problems of service provision, but also to contribute to scientific knowledge by utilizing the action situations as windows on social processes not ordinarily accessible to academic researchers.
4. Action-research is a family of approaches, rather than a single model. At its core is a cycle of collaboration between researcher and action agency (see pages 16 and 17 of this text).
5. The most effective point of application in the current social, political, and economic situation is with small-scale pilot or exploratory enterprises seeking piecemeal solutions, rather than with grand utopian programs.
6. To succeed, scientists must review lessons from earlier action-research experience and generate new principles to suit the special issues and challenges of the 1980s (Rapoport, 1985).

Case-study approach

The small-scale projects which we are now able to examine need not be seen as "mere tinkering." Real problems of contemporary life can be engaged and analyzed on a small scale, keeping in mind their potential generic or large-scale relevance. Our purpose in presenting the case studies is to examine some of these propositions in greater detail. The case study method, which we use in presenting these projects, has a long and productive history in anthropology, history, law, clinical psychology, and organizational analysis. Benjamin Paul's (1955) book of cross-cultural case studies has served generations of researchers and practitioners in the public health field. There has been a tendency among those favoring more controlled experimental designs to see case studies as primarily useful for exploratory purposes. However, there has recently been considerable interest in the distinctive value of qualitative analysis of case studies and in the improvement of methodology associated with them (Miles and Huberman, 1984; Campbell, 1981; and Yin, 1985), so that more persuasive conclusions can be drawn from them. Kai Erikson's analysis of the Buffalo Creek Disaster (1976) demonstrated this in a single case study. His conclusions about how an overwhelming physical disaster can produce a loss of community as well as of property has had a profound effect on both practical and theoretical spheres. The relevance of the Buffalo Creek experience for communities generally is widely accepted. Bromley (1986) has amassed instances where case studies have contributed to psychological knowledge in ways that experiments do not; but he warns that while case study accounts need not be undisciplined, their resemblance to everyday commonsense analysis makes it easy to slip into errors and unrecognized assumptions.

Peter Szanton (1981) has used case vignettes productively in his consultative research for government agencies. The National Academy of Sciences study groups have used case vignettes in analyzing the application of social science to various fields (Hayes, 1981; Travers and Light, 1982). Bernard Barber (1987) has developed case studies in policy analysis, based on the work of "effective social scientists." In Europe, Phyllis Willmott and Susan Mayne (1983) have analyzed seven cases where a specific innovation – family day care centers – were introduced as part of an action-research program to combat poverty.

The cases of action-research examined here relate to a range of social inventions. The form and the function of the inventions vary, but they share an attempt to develop social innovation. They are not large-scale (type IV) programs, nor do they seek explicitly to produce radical change in the sociopolitical system. They are all affected by the current decentralization process in government, making their focus on small-scale innovations both more necessary and more widely relevant.

The cases are grouped by the social systems involved – families, schools, law courts, communities. Not all systems are included; nor have we attempted to document all recognized circumstances giving rise to new interventions. We have not included studies of the work systems, of catastrophes such as wars or depressions, or of many of the myriad critical life events affecting child development. Nevertheless the new interventions presented are broadly typical of contemporary efforts to develop more effective public service systems for children. The goals of each project described are to improve services *and* to increase knowledge about young people's developmental processes. Ideally, the action-research collaboration enhances both goals through a synergistic effect; our purpose is to examine what happens in actuality.

In using the case-study method, we seek to maximize the advantages of qualitative analysis of real-life experience while avoiding some of the recognized pitfalls, in particular, the pitfall of over-specificity, which has been mentioned in connection with many program evaluations, and the pitfall of over-subjectivity, which has been noted in connection with qualitative research. Each case has been presented in terms of its generic as well as its specific aspects. A systematic format has been used for data-gathering and analysis to avoid over-subjectivity, and the write-ups have undergone several rounds of review by participants in the projects and by external authorities (cf. Glaser and Strauss, 1967; Stenhouse, 1977).

New interventions for competence building

The developing child confronts an expanding range of stresses daily, weekly, monthly, annually, and throughout his or her lifetime. Healthy functioning depends on the child's capacity to cope with these stresses. Social interventions facilitate the development of a coping capacity in children and ameliorate the factors which put them at risk.

Research on children's development of a capacity to meet the stresses of modern life has been receiving increased attention in the past decade (Garmezy et al., 1983). This capacity requires cognitive competence (White, 1959), vigor, and goal-directedness in the context of interpersonal and social relationships (Foote and Cottrell, 1955; Sullivan, 1964; Jahoda, 1958). Cognitive skills need to be applied to tasks of coping with barriers and resistances of various kinds, functioning in social roles and planning realistically in relation to social situations (Baumrind, 1973). The development of such capacities involves not only the prevention or avoidance of psychopathology (Achenbach and Edelbroch, 1981) but also the development of a degree of resistance or imperviousness to stress without sacrificing the sensitivity necessary to sustain social roles and relationships (Clausen et al., 1968; Bandura, 1986). The influences contributing to the mentally healthy developing person emanate from various levels – biological, psychological, social, and cultural – and in different life sectors, including school, home, work, and community (Bronfenbrenner, 1979).

Self-conscious interventions specifically directed to children are absent from the lists of social inventions cited above, although the theories of Freud and Piaget are obviously relevant. This is partly because, as Philippe Aries (1962) has pointed out, the concept of childhood as a distinctive phase of life is recent. De Mause (1974) argues that societies have always recognized childhood, but earlier orientations were more callous, even brutal, and it is only recently that attention has centered on improving the lot of children. Haggerty and his colleagues (1975) observe that medical concerns with child development have only recently shifted from the reduction of communicable diseases. A new range of problems has arisen which are not solvable by traditional biomedical approaches alone and are often not presented to doctors directly. This "new morbidity" consists of behavior problems, which reflect the increased stress in modern life. Dealing with these problems requires addressing the issues that give rise to and sustain their life-styles. The new emphasis is toward encouraging competence and self-sufficiency. In the various fields concerned with children, there are different implications. In certain legal and fiscal proceedings children are explicitly seen as incompetent, and this incompetence model has informed many social interventions for children since Victorian times. Foundling homes, orphanages, adoption societies, and settlement houses were based on this model and children were grouped with indigents, disabled people, and other people defined as socially incompetent. In such settings, a paradigmatic change is required. Examples of how this has been occurring are seen in some of the children's associations founded in the Victorian era (e.g., the Boy Scouts and Girl Scouts, the YMCA and YWCA, Boys' and Girls' Clubs). Many such organizations began as church-based movements concerned with protecting the child from the moral perils of an expanding industrial society. More recently the emphasis of these and of newer organizations has been on cultivating personal strengths through education and interests that will engage them with the larger society (Macleod, 1983).

While some of the recent social interventions for children have been based on social science theories, most have been pragmatic, common-sense adaptive responses to social changes. New roles (e.g., Big Brother, Big Sister, den mother) use kin terms to replace or supplement absent or defective family relationships. Other new interventions at a more complex organizational level (e.g., Child Watch) constitute replacements for traditional community and neighborhood controls weakened in the course of urbanization.

Modern interventions for children's mental health tend to be part of the public service sector, developed by public policymakers and practitioners. Although there is a commercial interest in innovation in relation to children and youth – as in the fields of fashion and entertainment – these are not the areas of focus here. There are also interventions which purport to be altruistic, but are suspect in their actual impact, such as some cult groups (Enroth, 1977). We are concerned with public service activities whose purpose is to facilitate the development of competence in children and youth and whose actual impact is being subjected to scientific assessment.

Relevant interventions have occurred at different levels, and an examination of their characteristics indicates two distinct strategies: deficit correction and competence building. Table 1-1 illustrates the two strategies at the different levels.

Both strategies continue to be used, but there has been a shift in emphasis from deficit correction toward competence building. There are several reasons for this. In our complex modern society, identifying all the deficits that need treatment is an overwhelming task. In addition, the traditional epidemiological model seems no longer able to identify specific etiological factors directly linked to subsequent disorders (Coelho et al., 1974; Schulberg and Killilea, 1982).

Within each level of intervention, there are the different theoretical orientations of the practitioners and researchers involved. For example, the emotional inoculation theory of Janis (1958) has been very influential among those who emphasize the importance of affective factors in determining individual behavior. For those stressing the importance of cognitive elements, the emphasis tends to be on formal teaching (Bandura et al., 1977; Jessor and Jessor, 1977). For those who emphasize social factors, the social-sanitation strategy is prominent, with its emphasis on creating more healthy settings (Sarason, 1972, 1977; Caplan, 1974). And within each level are variations as to how radical a change is sought. For example, a relatively limited goal (however resistant the subject may be) is to change a specific behavior such as smoking or eating fatty foods (cf. Bandura, 1986). A more radical goal is to change the individual's basic personality structure or life-style.

Issues

New social interventions generally arise in response to perceived need (Rein's "practice worries"), where there is expected benefit (Schnookler, 1962), and where competent entrepreneurial leadership is available (cf. Drucker, 1985). However, there are forces which may block such changes: the "fear of innovation" (Schon, 1966); the operation of countervailing interests which override the merit of the innovation (Miles and Huberman,

Table 1-1. *Levels and strategies of intervention*

	Intervention strategy	
Intervention level	Therapeutic (deficit correction)	Preventive (competence building)
Individual	Psychotherapy	Health education
Intimate social setting	Family therapy	Home-building services
Wider social network	Multiple-impact therapy	Boys and girls clubs

1984); the momentum of large-scale social evolutionary forces (Quigley, 1979); or the conservative social equilibrating forces of "cultural lag" (Ogburn, 1920; Young, 1983). We want to know how these various factors combine to affect the development of new social interventions for children and youth. From the answers we wish to learn to devise better ways to solve the pressing problems today's children face.

Action-research is only one method for studying innovations. Some new interventions are not accessible to collaborative project work, and others may evolve productively on the basis of what is already known from basic social science or practice experience without the need for further formal research. In still other cases, the close involvement of the researcher so biases the operation of the innovation that it becomes difficult to judge the relevance of the findings to other situations.

But practitioners can facilitate access to many situations, some so new that engagement in their development is the only way to gain knowledge about them – to learn through doing (Morgan and Ramirez, 1983). Properly conducted, the scientific gains through involvement in a new intervention program can have advantages which the more classic experimental research models lack, particularly in developing new paradigms for understanding social change processes (Kessel, 1979; Argyris, Putnam, and Smith, 1985). Cooperative work on a mutually interesting topic often serves to break down the barriers between practitioners and researchers (Reason and Rowan, 1981).

Each academic discipline concentrates on increasing understanding of a particular dimension of child development. But the development of a capacity to cope with contemporary life stresses is an intrinsically multidimensional process. This makes the multidisciplinary action-research approach particularly relevant. However, it also raises a problem in relation to how the findings of an action-research project may be combined with the knowledge base of specific disciplines. And because of this some research results may be neglected. If, however, the new understandings

Come to be widely accepted, they may contribute to new paradigms for understanding children – paradigms unlikely to emerge in the context of monodisciplinary academic research. In the cases that follow we try to shed light on ways to avoid falling into the worst-case trap and to discover what produces the best results.

References

Abt Associates. 1977. *Children at the Center.* Cambridge, Mass.: Abt Associates.

Achenbach, T. M., and Edelbroch, C. S. 1981. Behavioral problems and competencies reported by parents of normal and disturbed children aged four to fourteen. Monographs of the Society for Research in Child Development 46, serial 188.

Argyris, C.; Putnam, R.; and Smith, D. McC. 1985. *Action Science.* San Francisco: Jossey-Bass.

Aries, P. 1962. *Centuries of Childhood.* New York: Knopf.

Baker, A. 1976. *New and Improved: Inventors and Inventions That Have Changed the Modern World.* London: British Museum.

Bandura, A. 1986. Self efficacy mechanism in physiological activation and health-promoting behavior. In *Adaptation, Learning and Affect,* ed. by J. Madden et al. New York: Raven Press.

Bandura, A.; Adams, N. E.; and Beyer, J. 1977. Cognitive processes mediating behavioral change. *Journal of Personality and Social Psychology* 35:125–139.

Barber, B. 1961. Resistance by scientists to scientific discovery. *Science* 134, no. 3479.

Barber, B. 1987. *Effective Social Science.* New York: Russell Sage Foundation.

Bateson, G., and Mead, M. 1941. Principles of morale-building. *Journal of Educational Sociology* 15:206–220.

Baumrind, D. 1973. The development of instrumental competence through socialization. In *Minnesota Symposium on Child Psychology,* vol. 7, ed. by A. D. Pick. Minneapolis: University of Minnesota Press.

Benedict, R. 1946. *The Chrysanthemum and the Sword.* Boston: Houghton Mifflin.

Berman, P., and McGaughlin, M. 1978. *Federal Programs Supporting Educational Change.* Santa Monica, Calif.: Rand Corporation.

Bion, W. R. 1961. *Experiences in Groups, and Other Papers.* London: Tavistock Publications.

Botkin, J.; Dimanescu, D.; and Stata, R. 1984. *The Innovators: Rediscovering America's Creative Energy.* New York: Harper and Row.

Bridger, H. 1983. Northfield revisited. In *Bion and Group Psychotherapy,* ed. by M. Pines. London: Routledge.

Bromley, D. E. 1986. *The Case Study Method in Psychology.* New York: Wiley.

Bronfenbrenner, U. 1979. *The Ecology of Human Development: Experiments by Nature and Design.* Cambridge, Mass.: Harvard University Press.

Brown, L. D., and Tandon, R. 1983. Ideology and political economy in inquiry: Action research and participatory research. *Journal of Applied Behavioral Science* 19(3): 277–294.

Campbell, D. T. 1981. Getting ready for the experimenting society. Introduction to *Social Experiments: Methods for Design and Evaluation,* ed. by L. Saxe and M. Fine, vol. 131. Beverly Hills, Calif.: Sage.

Caplan, G. 1974. *Support Systems and Community Mental Health.* New York: Behavioral.

Clark, A. 1976. *Experimenting with Organizational Life.* London: Plenum.

Clausen, J. A., ed. 1968. *Socialization and Society.* Boston: Little, Brown.

Clifford, D. K., and Cavanagh, R. E. 1985. *The Winning Performance: How America's High Growth Midsize Companies Succeed.* London: Sidgwick & Jackson.

Coelho, G.; Hamburg, B.; and Adams, J. (eds.). 1974. *Coping and Adaptation.* New York: Basic Books.

Collier, J. 1945. The United States Indian Service as a laboratory of ethnic relations. *Social Research,* pp. 275–276.

Cook, S. 1984. The 1954 social science statement on school desegregation: A reply to Gerard. *The American Psychologist* 39(8): 819–831.

Datta, L. 1978. Damn the experts and full speed ahead: An examination of the cases against directed development and for local problem-solving. Unpublished data. Washington, D.C.: National Institute for Education.

de Mause, L. 1974. The evolution of childhood. *History of Children Quarterly* 1(4): 503–575.

Deutsch, K.; Platt, J.; and Senghaas. 1971. Conditions favoring major advances in the social sciences since 1900: An analysis of conditions and effects of creativity. *Science* 171: 450.

Drucker, P. 1985. *Innovation and Entrepreneurship.* London: Heinemann.

Emery, F., and Trist, E. L. 1973. *Towards a Social Ecology: Contextual Appreciation of the Future in the Present.* London: Plenum.

Emrick, J. 1977. *Evaluation of the National Diffusion Network.* Menlo Park, Calif.: Stanford Research Institute.

Enroth, R. 1977. *Youth, Brainwashing and the Extremist Cults.* Exeter: Paternoster.

Erikson, K. 1976. *Everything in its Path: Destruction of the Community in the Buffalo Creek Flood.* New York: Simon and Schuster.

Fairweather, G. W. 1972. *Social Change: The Challenge to Survival.* Morristown, N.J.: General Learning Press.

Folberg, J., and Taylor, A. 1984. *Mediation.* San Francisco: Jossey-Bass.

Foote, N. N., and Cottrell, L. S. 1955. *Identity and Interpersonal Competence.* Chicago: University of Chicago Press.

Freeman, H. E.; Dynes, R. R.; Rossi, P. H.; and Whyte, W. F. (eds.). 1983. *Applied Sociology.* San Francisco: Jossey-Bass.

Garmezy, N.; Rutter, M.; et al. 1983. *Stress, Coping and Development in Children.* New York: McGraw-Hill.

Gearing, F.; Netting, R. McC.; and Peattie, L. 1960. *Documentary History of the Fox Project, 1948–1959.*

Geiger, H. J. 1985. Community health centers. In *Reforming Medicine,* ed. by V. W. Sidel and R. Sidel. New York: Pantheon.

Gellner, E. 1985. *The Psychoanalytic Movement.* London: Paladin.

Gerard, H. B. 1983. School desegregation: The social science role. *American Psychologist* 38(8): 869–877.

Glaser, B. G., and Strauss, A. L. 1967. *Discovery of Grounded Theory.* Chicago: Aldine.

Gordon, J. 1978/80. *Caring for Youth: Essays on Alternative Services.* Washington, D.C.: National Institute of Mental Health.

Grinker, R., and Spiegel, J. P. 1945. *Men Under Stress.* New York: McGraw-Hill.

Habbakuk, H. J. 1962. *American and British Technology in the 19th Century.* Cambridge: Cambridge University Press.

Haggerty, R. J. 1987. Behavioral pediatrics: A time for research. *Pediatrics.*

Haggerty, R. J.; Roghman, K. J.; and Pless, B. (eds.). 1975. *Child Health and the Community.* New York: Wiley.

Hall, P. 1980. *Great Planning Disasters.* Harmondsworth: Penguin.

Halsey, A. H. (ed.). 1972. *Educational Priority.* London: HMSO.

Hamburg, B., and Lancaster, J. (eds.). 1985. *School-Age Pregnancy.* New York: Aldine.

Harre, R. 1981. *Great Scientific Experiments.* Oxford: Oxford University Press.

Hayes, C. D. (ed). 1981. *Making Federal Policy Affecting Children.* Washington, D.C.: National Academy of Sciences.

Heller, F. 1986. *Uses and Abuses of Social Science.* Beverly Hills, Calif.: Sage.

Hobbs, N. 1982. *Troubled and Troubling Child.* San Francisco: Jossey-Bass.

Horowitz, I. L. 1967. *The Rise and Fall of Project Camelot: Studies in the Relationship Between Social Science and Practical Politics.* Cambridge, Mass.: MIT Press.

Hymes, D. (ed). 1974. *Reinventing Anthropology.* New York: Random House.

Institute of Medicine. 1981. *Research on Stress and Human Health.* Washington, D.C.: National Academy Press.

Jacques, E. 1952. *The Changing Culture of a Factory.* London: Tavistock Publications; New York: Dryden.

Jaffe, D. 1973. Transition, people and services. *Journal of Applied Behavioral Science* 9(213): 199–217.

Jahoda, M. 1958. *Current Conceptions of Positive Mental Health.* New York: Basic Books.

Janis, I. 1958. *Psychological Stress.* New York: Wiley.

Jessor, R., and Jessor, D. 1977. *Problem Behavior and Psychosocial Development.* New York: Academic Press.

Jones, M. 1953. *The Therapeutic Community.* New York: Basic Books.

Kahn, R. 1986. Comments on Kelly. *American Journal of Community Psychology* 14(6): 591–594.

Kelly, J. G. 1976. Synergy: Making it happen. In *Synergy '76,* ed. by B. Boldt et al. Eugene, Oreg.: Center for Leisure Studies.

Kelly, J. G. 1986. The ecology of research collaboration. Paper presented at American Psychiatry Association Symposium, Washington, D.C.

Kessell, F. 1979. Research in action settings: A sketch of emerging perspectives. *International Journal of Behavioral Development* 2:185–205.

Korten, D. C. 1980. Community organization and rural development: A learning process approach. *Public Administration Review* 40:480–511.

Kuhn, T. S. 1957. *The Copernican Revolution.* Cambridge, Mass.: Harvard University Press.

Larsen, J. K., and Agarwala-Rogers, R. 1977. Reinvention of innovative ideas: Modified? Adopted? None of the above? *Evaluation* 4:134–140.

Lawrence, J. R. (ed). 1966. *Operational Research and the Social Sciences.* London: Tavistock Publications.

Lees, R. 1976. *Research Strategies for Social Welfare.* London: Routledge and Kegan Paul.

Lees, R., and Smith, G. 1975. *Action Research in Community Development.* London: Routledge and Kegan Paul.

Leighton, A. 1946. *The Governing of Men.* Princeton, N.J.: Princeton University Press.

Leighton, A. 1949. *Human Relations in a Changing World.* New York: Dutton.

Lin, T., and Eisenberg, L. (eds.). 1985. *Mental Health Planning for One Billion People: A Chinese Perspective.* Vancouver: University of British Columbia.

Macleod, D. 1983. *Building Character in the American Boy: The Boy Scouts, YMCA and their Forerunners, 1870–1926.* Madison: University of Wisconsin Press.

Main, T. F. 1946. The hospital as a therapeutic institution. *Bulletin of the Meninger Clinic* 10:66–70.

McAnarney, E., and Schrieder, C. 1984. *Identifying Social and Psychological Antecedents of Adolescent Pregnancy.* New York: William T. Grant Foundation.

Merton, R. 1973. *The Sociology of Science.* Chicago: University of Chicago Press.

Miles, M., and Huberman, M. 1984. *Qualitative Data Analysis.* Beverly Hills, Calif.: Sage.

Miller, S. M.; Kelleher, P.; and Kelleher, C. 1983. Lesson drawing. Unpublished paper. Dublin.

Morgan, G., and Ramirez, R. 1983. Action learning: A holographic metaphor for guiding social change. *Human Relations* 37(1): 28.

Moynihan, D. P. 1969. *Maximum Feasible Misunderstanding.* New York: Free Press.

Moynihan, D. P. 1970. The role of social scientists in action research. *Social Science Research Council Newsletter,* London.

Murray, H. L. 1938. *Exploration in Personality.* New York: Oxford University Press.

Nelson, R., and Yates, D. 1978. *Innovation and Implementation in Public Organizations.* Lexington, Mass.: Heath Books.

Ogburn, W. F. 1922 and 1950. *Social Change.* New York: Viking.

Paul, B. (ed). 1955. *Health, Culture and Community.* New York: Russell Sage Foundation.

Pearse, I. H., and Crocker, L. H. 1947. *The Peckham Experiment.* London: George Allen and Unwin.

Perrow, C. 1979. *Complex Organization.* Glenview, Ill.: Scott, Foresman.

Price, R., and Burke, C. 1985. Youth employment. In *Children, Youth and Families: The Action-Research Relationship,* ed. by R. N. Rapoport. New York: Cambridge University Press.

Price, R., and Politser, P. 1980. *Evaluation and Action in the Social Environment.* New York: Academic Press.

Quigley, C. 1979. *The Evolution of Civilizations.* Indianapolis: Liberty.

Rapoport, R. N. 1970. Three dilemmas in action research. *Human Relations* 23(6): 499–513.

Rapoport, R. N. (ed.). 1985. *Children, Youth and Families: The Action-Research Relationship.* New York: Cambridge University Press.

Rappaport, J. 1977. *Community Psychology, Values and Research.* New York: Holt, Reinhart and Winston.

Reason, P., and Rowan, J. (eds). 1981. *Human Inquiry: A Sourcebook of New Paradigm Research.* New York: Wiley.

Rein, M. 1983. *From Policy to Practice.* London and New York: Macmillan.

Revans, R. 1982. *The Origins and Development of Action Learning.* London: Chartwell-Bratt.

Riecken, H. W. 1983. The national science foundation and the social sciences. *Social Science Research Council (SSRC) Items,* New York.

Riecken, H. W., and Boruch, R. F. 1974. *Social Experimentation: A Method for Planning and Evaluating Social Intervention,* New York: Academic Press.

Rosenblum, S., and Louis, K. Seashore. 1981. *Stability and Change: Innovation in an Educational Context.* New York: Plenum.

Sarason, S. B. 1972. *The Creation of Settings and the Future Societies.* San Francisco: Jossey-Bass.

Sarason, S. B. 1977. *Human Services and Resource Networks.* San Francisco: Jossey-Bass.

Sarason, S. B. 1981. *Psychology Misdirected.* New York: Free Press.

Schenshul, J. J. (ed.). 1985. Collaborative research and social policy. *American Behavioral Scientist* 29(2): 131–264.

Schnookler, J. 1962. *The Rate and Direction of Inventive Activity.* Princeton, N.J.: Princeton University Press.

Schon, D. 1966. The fear of innovation. In *Uncertainty in Research, Management and New Product Development,* ed. by R. M. Hainer, S. Kingsbury, and D. B. Gleicher. Conover-Mast.

Schulberg, H. C., and Killilea, M. (eds.) 1982. *The Modern Practice of Community Mental Health.* San Francisco: Jossey-Bass.

Schumpeter, J. 1982. Cited by M. Casson in *The Entrepreneur.* Oxford: Martin-Robertson.

Schwarz, P. 1981. Throwing science at problems. Paper prepared for the William T. Grant Foundation Conference on Action Research, New York, June 8.

Schweinhart, L. J., and Weikart, D. P. 1986. *Young Children Grow Up: The Effects of the Perry Pre-school Program Through Age 15*. Ypsilanti, Mich.: High Scope Foundation.

Segal, J. 1983. Utilization of stress and coping research. In *Stress Coping and Development in Children*, ed. by N. Garmezy and M. Rutter. New York: McGraw-Hill.

Seidman, E. (ed.). 1984. *Handbook of Social Interventions*. Beverly Hills, Calif.: Sage.

Sjoberg, G. 1967. *Ethics, Politics and Social Research*. Cambridge, Mass.: Schenkman.

Snowden, L. R.; Munoz, R. F.; and Kelly, J. G. (eds.). 1979. *Social and Psychological Research in Community Settings*. San Francisco: Jossey-Bass.

Sofer, C. 1961. *The Organization from Within: A Comparative Study of Social Institutions Based on a Socio-Therapeutic Approach*. London: Tavistock.

Spock, B. 1946. *Baby and Child Care*. London: New English Library.

Stenhouse, L. 1977. Case study as a basis for research in a theoretical contemporary history of education. Centre for Applied Research in Education, University of East Anglia.

Stocking, G. 1979. Anthropology at Chicago: Tradition, discipline, department. University of Chicago Library.

Stouffer, S. 1949. *The American Soldier*. Princeton, N.J.: Princeton University Press.

Sullivan, H. S. 1964. *The Fusion of Psychiatry and Social Science*. New York: Norton.

Susskin, E., and Klein, D. C. (eds). 1985. *Knowledge Building in Community Psychology*. New York: Praeger.

Sutton, F. X. 1982. Rationality, development and scholarship. *SSRC Items* 36(4).

Szanton, P. L. 1981. *Not Well Informed*. New York: Russell Sage Foundation.

Tharp, R., and Gallimore, R. 1982. Inquiry process in program development. *Journal of Community Psychology* 10:103–118.

Travers, J. R., and Light, R. J. 1982. *Learning from Experience: Evaluating Early Childhood Demonstration Projects*. Washington, D.C.: National Academy Press.

White, R. W. 1959. Motivation reconsidered: The concept of competence. *Psychological Review* 66:297–333.

Whyte, W. F. 1982. Social inventions for solving human problems. *American Sociological Review* 47(1): 1–13.

Willmott, P., and Mayne, S. 1983. *Families at the Centre*. London: Bedford Square Press.

Wilson, A. T. M.; Trist, E. L.; and Curle, A. 1952. Transitional communities and social reconnection: A study of civil resettlement of British prisoners of war. In *Readings in Social Psychology*, ed. by G. E. Swanson et al., 2nd ed. New York: Holt.

Woodson, R. L. 1981. *A Summons to Life: Mediating Structures and the Prevention of Youth Crime*. Cambridge, Mass.: Ballinger.

Young, M. 1983. *The Social Scientist as Innovator*. Cambridge, Mass.: Abt Associates.

Yin, R. 1985. *Case Study Research*. Beverly Hills, Calif.: Sage.

Yin, R., et al. 1976. A review of case studies of technological innovation in state and local services. RAND Corporation, Santa Monica, Calif.

Zigler, E., and Valentine, J. (eds.). 1979. *Project Head Start*. New York: Free Press.

2 Families

Families provide the fundamental interventions affecting children's development. They are the social and psychological crucible within which the child's personality is shaped and the foundation is laid for subsequent competences *and* problems. Families are varied in their structures and processes: internally in the way households are organized and externally in the way they are linked to others. But at a given time and place, some family forms are more prevalent, some more valued (Rapoport et al., 1977), and some more troubled (Skynner and Cleese, 1983; Minuchin, 1984).

In recent decades there have been some dramatic trends in family life within the developed countries, affecting specific family experiences and also the prevailing conception of the family as a social institution. These changes have brought new problems and have determined to some extent the kinds of social interventions which have evolved (Sussman and Steinmetz, 1986). Families are now generally smaller. There are a great many more single-parent families, and changes in the conceptions of men's and women's roles have led to a much greater participation by women in the economy, and therefore to the growth of dual-worker families. With a more permissive attitude toward sexuality and an earlier age of menarche, there has been an increase in births occurring outside marriage. The emphasis on the right to individual self-fulfillment and a more secular and facilitative attitude toward marital dissolution have resulted in a greater number of divorces. Divorces increasingly include couples with children as well as those in the earliest childless phase of marriage, as previously. These changes have stimulated the development of a number of social interventions, including day-care nurseries.

Many of the changes have occurred painfully and with considerable disruption, pending new interventions devised to prevent or ameliorate the distress. There has been an increase in detected family violence, and with it, a range of new social interventions such as the "women's shelter" in response. The increased rate of child neglect and abuse has brought interventions in the fields of foster care and parent education. There is a

35

large amount of costly and psychologically damaging litigation over custody following marital dissolution. Whole new fields of mediation and conciliation procedures have arisen to deal with some of these problems (Folberg and Taylor, 1984). "No-fault" divorce is a new intervention to ameliorate some of the stresses caused by earlier procedures, but recent research has shown that inequities remain, and these have their own psychological complications (Weitzman, 1985).

Women tend to face a much greater drop in economic standards following divorce than men, and in youthful one-parent households headed by women, there tend to be a high number of children. These facts have contributed to the observation that children now outrank all other subcategories living in poverty. This situation is stimulating a new effort to invent social and economic supports for families in this position (Moynihan, 1985).

Children, dependent on their families during their formative years, are both protected and vulnerable. Although recent research has introduced many qualifiers and exceptions, the general conviction of clinicians and others is that early experiences are disproportionately influential (Brim and Kagan, 1980). And while the parent-child relationship is unquestionably a reciprocal one, children are limited in the degree to which they can alter their environments while they live in the parental home. Nor can the replay the circumstances of their birth and infant experience. They can, however, learn to deal with the problems they have inherited, and to develop ways to cope with prospective stresses. Much of this learning takes place in relation to the family, if not in the actual home, and can hopefully be facilitated by social inventions for children now being developed in the family field.

The focus in family research

In a review of the research-action relationship in the family field, McCubbin and his colleagues (1985) have identified three arenas: family policy, family therapy, and applied research on family stress and family wellbeing. The first, associated with large-scale programs, is outside the scope of the current volume. The second, family therapy, has spawned a number of new interventions, often emanating from the clinical experience of charismatic practitioners, ideologically dedicated to their particular approach. Any action-research that has resulted has been in the nature of "fine-tuning" established positions rather than developing new interventions based on the research findings. This is not an intrinsic limitation of the family therapy field, and it is likely that future action-researchers in this field will be able to form an effective, synthesized approach. It is in the area of family-stress research that the most relevant action-research approaches have occurred, despite political and other difficulties tied to the project's environment (McCubbin et al., 1985). The link between social disorganization and individual psychopathology has been reaffirmed. But rather than seeking correlations between static family states and psychopathology rates the contemporary approach to family research seeks to study the processes whereby some individuals emerge unscathed (or even strengthened) from circumstances identified as stressful while others are harmed. Understanding how families and individuals in their family contexts cope and how they could be helped to cope better are considered equally important to establishing correlations between family type and psychopathology (Rutter and Garmezy, 1983).

In other words, a research focus on family *process* has been developed to supplement the rather more static concepts such as "family cohesion" or "marital satisfaction." David Olson and his colleagues (1983), for example, have studied one thousand American families and gone beyond a simple charting of distributions of family satisfaction and its correlates. They found that family satisfaction and family cohesion are affected by the way coping strategies are developed and used. Strategies that draw on available support resources are more effective than those that emphasize other values, such as living in a high-status neighborhood or driving an impressive car ("keeping up appearances"). Other processes for inducing family cohesion include "reframing" (i.e., redefining the stressful events as manageable) and "passive appraisal" (i.e., balancing active behavior with reflective analysis values). This contrasts with the more static view that what happens in the family is immutably determined by a set of antecedent variables. Deliberately cultivating these coping capacities and strategies can decrease a family's vulnerability and reduce the impact of stressful events on its members. They are, in effect, crucial intervening variables between stress and outcome (cf. McCubbin et al., 1980). Olson and colleagues note further that there is no uniformly applicable formula, but that different coping strategies are called for at different stages of the life cycle and for different types of families.

Obviously many, perhaps most, families can organize effective coping strategies without special assistance and are able to function reasonably effectively in accomplishing family tasks of socialization, intimacy, and social control. Others, however, break down on one or more of these functions or encounter trouble in other areas – school, work, or the community (Bronfenbrenner and Cochran, 1985).

Action-research approaches have been considered particularly useful in helping to develop appropriate interventions (Rapoport, 1985). The two case studies to be presented in this chapter illustrate new interventions designed to help families cope with the consequences of stress when unable to do so by themselves. The Lower East Side Family Union (LESFU) was organized in New York City to strengthen family structures in families at risk of having their children removed and placed in foster homes. The second case study is of a special learning group treating children from violent families sheltered in the Henry Street Urban Families Center in New York City.

Case study: A family services brokerage

The Lower East Side Family Union (LESFU), a special unit for multi-problem families, was established in 1972 as a social service brokerage for at-risk families whose low educational level and ethnic heterogeneity made it difficult for them to link with social service agencies in time to prevent a family breakdown. The LESFU model was developed as a pioneering prevention-oriented method aimed at reducing the need for foster care, while at the same time it dealt with fragmentation and inaccessibility of services. The action-research project was initiated by Alfred Herbert, LESFU director, who recognized the need for an evaluation of the model's continuing application in a changing social context. The research collaborator was David Fanshel, professor of social work at Columbia University. The project commenced in 1982 and was completed in 1985.

Background

LESFU was established with the stated purpose of preventing unnecessary placement of children away from their families. Many children who suffer the loss of their families and are taken into foster care have a history of inappropriate or distorted care. At placement they display a variety of problem behaviors, such as poor school performance, delinquency, moodiness or depression, and unmet health needs. A public uproar in the late 1960s and early 1970s ensued over the escalating demand for public facilities to shelter children and over the inefficient and deteriorating quality of existing child-care services. The Citizen's Committee for Children of New York (CCC) most rigorously expressed the sense of crisis surrounding foster care and provided the visionary solution which became LESFU. The CCC addressed the local situation in 1971 by publishing a monograph called *A Dream Deferred;* it diagnosed the problem and proposed a solution. The "dream" expressed in earlier publications (*Babies Who Wait*, 1960; *Protecting New York City's Children*, 1962) envisioned an adequate system of care for needy children that would address the following problems:

> Overwhelming needs of thousands of homeless, destitute children waiting for other than temporary care
>
> Poor existing services: insufficient volunteers, overlapping private services, and inefficient public services
>
> Public confusion over changes in the political regime

The situation was brought to a head in 1970, and in their publication the CCC stated:

> We have seen the inadequate public welfare system fail families, year after year. It provides neither the wide and intensive spectrum of services to the vulnerable nor the cash grants necessary to support a sound family structure. As the City and State ignored the warning that the number of abused, abandoned and neglected children would thus inevitably increase, the population in the City's shelters rose to incredible peaks, only to explode into crisis. Not just once. But again and again. The result has always been: overcrowding, crisis, outcry, census brought down through emergency placement programs. . . . Inevitably, when the glare of publicity and public outrage dims, an uneasy calm settles until the next time. (1971, p. 1)

In calling for a new solution, the CCC argued that, dedicated though the staff of the child-welfare units might be, the long-term interests of children called for a new system of services designed under a *new model* of service provision. The new model consisted of a number of elements previously in existence, but scattered and often unrealized except in theory:

- The new service should be a *family service,* based on the "mission of helping families to do their job and cope with emergencies," rather than seeking substitute care for children.
- The material needs of families are a necessary, if sometimes not sufficient, condition for promoting adequate family living. "The community must not offer counseling, guidance, placement, or treatment as substitutes for basic protection" (p. 22). At the same time, family services must include assistance to families in coping with their handicaps or life crises in housing, finance, and health care.
- Primary responsibility for working with families should be assigned to locally based family service social workers. The new agency would not have a bureaucratic central headquarters or provide facilities that agglomerated large numbers of cases in order to reduce censuses of children in need of care. Rather, it would have outposts in neighborhoods and work with schools, settlement houses, health stations, hospitals, and housing projects where it can be accessible and understand rather than merely provide material help.
- A central task would be to work with and seek to integrate the diverse

public and voluntary services, to eliminate overlapping goals and to reach target populations more effectively.
- Planning of the agency would be based on cost-effectiveness studies, and monitoring used to ensure continued improvement and further planning and development.

Finally, the CCC recommended "flexibility and experimentation" (p. 40) in assessing the practicability of a new venture.

The CCC was under the chairmanship of James Dumpson; the executive director was Trude Lash. Bert Beck, then director of the Henry Street Settlement as well as a member of the task force which drafted *A Dream Deferred*, took a lead in urging other agencies to form a program on the Lower East Side that would serve as a demonstration project for the changes being called for. In his initial planning proposal, submitted in 1971 to the City Human Resources Administration, Beck outlined the approach of the new service:

- Decentralization of services
- Teamwork in service delivery
- Emphasis on family support service systems
- Community involvement
- Career ladders for community residents and paraprofessionals as well as professionals
- Public-private collaboration through the use of contracts

There was, in addition, an emphasis placed on the ethnic subcultures and the intention to form a union of families.

In the larger context of the project, few experiments of the kind proposed existed, though the expressed ideals were widely recognized. Seen as part of the larger field of research and training on crisis intervention and preventive mental health for families, the proposal fit well with emergent trends in the mental health field. The work of Gerald Caplan, for example, stressed many of the same principles. Services should be de-bureaucratized; interventions should be client-centered and based on stressful life events. There should be multidisciplinary collaboration between the medical and allied professionals and lay persons involved in the natural networks and informal ecological support systems of persons at risk. The rhetoric then was of preventive intervention, crisis intervention, and intensive (integrated, coordinated, united) services (cf. Caplan, 1964; Shulberg and Kilellea, 1982).

In the same decade – the seventies – several similar programs came into being. Under the general heading of "intensive services to families at risk," they represented similar responses in different settings to the assumed shortcomings of foster-care systems. Inappropriate placement or no placement, exacerbation of family disturbance, and high costs of child relocation all contributed to the pressures. Many of these programs aimed at *not* removing children from troubled homes but rather working with their families to help them cope with their difficulties and keep their children. The underlying philosophy was that children generally do better in their own family homes, and that each family's problems have to be understood individually. Even a dysfunctional family could have high significance for a child and could be valued as an important personal resource. These programs provided professional diagnostics and interventions, giving parents appropriate help and guidance to cope constructively with their problems. (A similar project in another part of the country was ISFAR [Intensive Services to Families at Risk] evaluated by S. A. Rosenberg, G. A. McTate, and C. C. Robinson of the University of Nebraska Medical Center.)

The United States Children's Bureau conducted an evaluation of several of these new programs and found that their common features were associated with similar results. In all programs, experimental groups did better than controls, and most clients welcomed the help they were offered. However, a number of residual problems were noted. First, there was the question of how much of the observed success was due to the designation of these programs as exemplary innovative efforts, the familiar "Hawthorn effect" (Gerschenson, 1983). Then there were technical issues relating to the relevance of specific methods for specific family types. Some of these issues formed the basis of the LESFU study.

The social intervention

The specific intervention constituted in LESFU was what subsequently became known as the "LESFU model" of family service, based on certain values and assumptions about families (Weissman, 1978). It emphasized *deficient community resources and supports* (such as unemployment, poor housing, and poor coordination of services) as causes of family disorganization and breakdown. In contrast, previous models had stressed personal deficiency factors, such as genetic weaknesses or neuroses.

LESFU was set up initially with a grant from the Foundation for Child Development to explore the feasibility of a neighborhood-based children and family service. Trude Lash, then executive director for the CCC, became a staff social science consultant to the foundation and devoted a good part of her energies to the task of setting up LESFU. A full-time staff worker was hired, and with Beck as chairman of the board and executive director, the establishment of LESFU was assured. Commitments were secured from seven different foundations, and at the same time Beck and Lash were appointed heads of Governor Carey's task force on social services. Both of these developments had indirect as well as direct benefits.

There was very little controversy over the formation of LESFU, with its initial goal of keeping families together. Social workers who participated in the plan liked the way it was based on their ideals of rationality and cooperation. An important element at this time was that the founders of LESFU "confronted daily the tragedies and waste of family breakdown" (Weissman, 1978, p. 22). This was not a theoretical exercise for them; they were deeply involved in trying to help with the troubles that they all deplored but felt individually too weak to tackle. They also shared some general values of the social work profession, for example, the minimization of bureaucratic barriers to service, the constant effort to improve the effectiveness of existing service systems, and the encouragement of individuals and groups to express themselves and meet their own needs.

Nevertheless, it took two years to develop the service system. LESFU began formal operations in 1974, but it was not until 1976 that the agency can be said to have been established to the point of having a functioning, organized staff. There was an administrator, a social work consultant, and local teams of residents who had significant roles as social work associates, homemakers, and housekeepers. Based in a Lower East Side house, the service delivery pattern expressed the LESFU philosophy of the need for local participation; being neighborhood based they were able to give practical assistance and coordinate efforts through the use of contracts with the clients.

At the same time, problems began to emerge. There were ambiguities in staff roles and about local community participation and problems in creating a working team and of securing financial support. A fundamental cleavage in priorities developed between those who emphasized service orientation to specific clients and those who emphasized preventive orientation, directed at the larger population of vulnerable families in the local community. The service orientation favored concentrating on families most in need of help, even if the outlook for successful resolution of their problems was in doubt. The preventive orientation wanted to spread resources more broadly to head off the development of intractable family problems in a client population more responsive to the interventive effort.

In relation to finances, it became clear that there was a problem in the gap between intention and the capacity to follow through and to demonstrate results to funding sources. Research was always a part of the intention and would have helped to serve the need to validate the program with continuous feedback derived from monitoring and evaluation. But there was no provision for a researcher on the staff, little attention to developing concepts which were systematically researchable, and no research instruments built into the initial procedures. The term "research" was used in the initial stages of LESFU; Beck conceptualized the initial period as a kind of research "pretest," in which staff experiences would be used to develop indices of the high-risk qualities of clients. But this was a loose usage of the term, with no measures built into the initial procedures to assess even key concepts underlying the model, such as family disorganization.

A step was taken in 1975 to sharpen the research agenda. Funds were secured from the state to develop indices which would not only be of value in LESFU's work to reduce the public costs of family breakup but would also help to serve more general interests in the field. Research consultants stressed the importance of developing and using indices that were reliable and could be applied in other settings. However, the familiar issue of priorities arose, of research versus service to families and children.

A study by Weissman (1978) was commissioned in order to put these issues into perspective. Weissman's study records the history of LESFU's development, analyzing some of the problems encountered in translating ideas into action. His project, described as a "social history," is primarily oriented to the concerns of social work administrators. His concluding chapter elaborates the often unrecognized complexities in such catchwords as "coordination," around which initial consensus is often achieved in program design and planning. The social history analysis provided the staff with a number of behavioral science concepts, which allowed problems to be identified for further work in developing the use of the model and the contract it contains. Two of the concepts were role strain and subcultural differences. *Role strain* is conflict occurring because of incompatible demands between or within organizations involved in working out the family agreements. *Subcultural differences* arise when a requirement is accepted as reasonable in one subculture on the Lower East Side but rejected as unreasonable in another. For example, signing a contract agreement in some settings implied a lack of faith in another person's word. Gender role differences are another example. In some settings husbands resented their wives entering into separate contracts, whereas in others it was accepted without difficulty. The social history provided an ethnographic input which was important in developing the organization's self-conception.

The following year, 1979, the Foundation for Child Development published a paper by Beck called *The Lower East Side Family Union: A*

Social Invention. It was apparent that the early research experience contributed to his capacity to make a much clearer statement about what the invention was. Beck listed 14 points which he described as practices that, taken together, constituted the LESFU model:

1. The incorporation of a *union* of family organizations in such a way that it is independent of any of the organizations with which it must work to develop support systems for families.
2. The development of *local teams,* each of which is responsible for the functioning of the union in a particular area. Typically, the team leader is a person with a graduate social work degree, but the bulk of the team is made up of social workers and homemakers, drawn from the neighborhood and trained on the job.
3. The recognition of the importance of *culture* as a behavior determinant. One team was predominantly black, and each team was composed of people who could relate to the local area's dominant ethnic groups.
4. The use of formal *written contracts* with each of the major organizations servicing the area.
5. The use of *public-service employees* on the staff as a demonstration of the public recognition being given to the innovative approach.
6. The use of an *initial assessment period* to engage the cooperation of family members in an expression of cooperative agreement in the form of a written contract.
7. The giving of *practical help by homemakers* to avoid the removal of children from the parental home.
8. The use of homemakers as *role models and parent educators* as well as emergency supports in family crisis.
9. The use of *neighbors or nearby relatives* for short-term placement of children when their welfare is at risk in the immediate home.
10. The provision of modest *funds* to meet family emergency financial needs.
11. The development of an *evaluation system* to assess goal attainments as mutually sought by the family, the union staff, and the local service providers.
12. The use of LESFU staff to obtain *information* on the family directly, rather than reliance on third-party reports.
13. A system of *in-service training* to ensure continuing staff development.
14. *Research.* The work of the social historian to report through participant observation an account of the development of the innovation was a tangible example but by no means the only type of research that might be applicable.

Beck acknowledged that many of these items could be found elsewhere, but that their combination was unique and constituted the social invention. It was seen as a proactive approach to the tangle of problems that have beset social workers in their attempt to help multiproblem families, that is, the conflicting goals and practices of service providers and families most in need of service.

At this stage Beck is quoted as having said, "Even if they don't always do it according to the model, they know what the model is and can describe it." Weissman allowed that the model had been internalized by LESFU staff, but that the amount of time and effort necessary to make it work had been grossly underestimated in idealized statements of the model's design. By analyzing and clarifying what was involved, the intention of making it a model for other efforts throughout the country might be more feasible.

This social intervention seems to have taken form under the following conditions:

> Public uproar against rising costs and inefficiency in child care services.
> A redefinition of foster care placement as undesirable for many children.
> The emergence of a public service advocacy group which had been monitoring the child welfare system and was able to provide a new model to improve the situation.
> The participation of an innovative social entrepreneur who was able to lead and mobilize like-minded social workers within his or her area to plan a new center as a workable response.
> A favorable funding situation for development, with launching grants from a private foundation and operational support from public bodies on the basis of the conviction that keeping families together meant savings for the public purse through providing an alternative to foster care.
> Cost effectiveness of the new program; whereas a child in foster care was estimated to cost $5,000 to $40,000 a year at the time, depending on the type of care, LESFU's preventive work cost about $1,500 per year per family, or less than one quarter of even the lowest estimate of foster care. Both estimates were imprecise because of various hidden costs, but the ratio is nevertheless impressive (Weissman, 1978).
> The recent completion of research into the problem. An ethnographic analysis, termed a "social history," contributed to the sense of an organizational identity, to the identification of key concepts such as role strain and subcultural variation, and to the formulation of critical issues in the organization's functioning.

The need for further research came to the fore based on three factors: the staff's positive experience in the historical/ethnographic research, the external pressure to have evaluation studies as the funding of LESFU shifted toward greater reliance on public support, and the anticipation that stringency in public spending would lead to more emphasis on programs oriented to prevention. There was, therefore, a confluence of past elements, current requirements, and future potentials.

The action-research project

By 1981 LESFU had achieved national recognition as a significant innovation and had obtained financial support from a wider range of funding bodies. It was chosen as an exemplary program in a set of "promising practices" in services to families by the Administration for Children, Youth, and Families (1981). It was included among the service providers selected by the New York State Council on Children and Families as a program demonstrating creative development.

Describing its situation as having moved from "demonstration to institutionalization," LESFU recognized that a new type of behavioral science research input was now necessary for further development. Alfred Herbert, who had become LESFU director in its establishment phase, sought support for an evaluation study. In his initial application he wrote that "the primary goal of [the proposed] study is to learn how the Family Union Service program can affect family functioning." Five elements of the work were to be evaluated:

1. The component phases of the LESFU practice model: who goes through which phases, and what difference it makes to outcome
2. Length of time spent in each phase as well as factors differentiating families with long versus short stays in each phase
3. Service provider involvement and the effect of different combinations of service provision on the outcome for families
4. Differential relevance of the family's ethnic background
5. Factors affecting the development of a family self-support system

The Robert Sterling Clark Foundation and the William T. Grant Foundation jointly provided support for the research undertaking. David Fanshel agreed to take responsibility for the research. With his position as professor in the School of Social Work at Columbia and his wide experience and prestige in the child-welfare field, his participation made it possible to involve young researchers working on their dissertations. This in turn allowed specific processes in the operation of the LESFU model to be studied more closely. Fanshel emphasized the fact that he was interested in the project precisely because it provided more than an opportunity for a simple evaluation of effects of services. Useful as such evaluations are (see Jones, Neuman, and Shyme, 1976), the LESFU project provided an opportunity to learn more about the development of a viable preventive service delivery system, rather than simply a study of whether or not it worked. Furthermore, it afforded a deeper understanding of the issues generated by a complex and troubled urban environment.

Research design. The original design called for experimental and control groups. This had to be modified in the face of the realities of the field investigation. The plan had been to identify local at-risk families known to protective service agencies and to involve a randomly selected half of the at-risk families in LESFU services, while the other half would be tracked as unobtrusively as possible. However, this was not feasible because resources became stretched to their limit in following the users of agency services.

Families were to be assessed initially and after one year, using a multi-phase assessment system with scales for physical well-being, emotional well-being, family satisfaction, role allocations, goals, values and beliefs, and decision making. LESFU model variables included distribution of risk factors among families, attitudes of families toward service involvement, self-reported family needs and problems, family composition, employment history, and type and frequency of contact with relatives.

Overlapping areas of interest were defined and written into the grant proposal. Five areas of interest both to academics and action agency workers were identified:

1. Systematic information about how a conceptual model of practice is set in operation for different kinds of families
2. Systematic information on processes involved in bridging the historic gap between research and practice in the social work profession
3. Gathering of information on a number of practice areas of interest both to service providers and researchers in the child-welfare areas, including contracting, prevention, practice theory and technique, ethnicity, and service delivery
4. Data to serve as a basis for replication of the LESFU model
5. A summative evaluation of the proposition that the LESFU intervention improved family functioning.

Of these, the last has been the most problematic, because of the lack of a control group. Part of the task of forging the collaboration centered on clarifying the degree to which the validity of the method would be "proven" and the degree to which the improved family functioning could be demonstrated to lead to children's improved mental health. It was accepted that the project would contribute to these expectations but not provide definitive proofs.

The project was guided by a conceptual orientation rather than a theoretical one in the formal sense, though Fanshel refers to his interest in developing a "theory of social work practice." Research in social work departments is generally more oriented to psychological than to sociological concepts, and psychoanalytic theory has been very influential. In this case, however, the conceptual orientation was one which assumed a multifactorial relationship between early and later experiences in child development (i.e., a life-span developmental orientation), and which also assumed a constellation of socioenvironmental influences. Perhaps this

orientation is best understood in contrast to that governing the eth-
nographic/historical study.

Although not avoiding qualitative analysis, Fanshel also sought to identify and isolate risk factors, which could then be tested for their statistical
linkage to outcome factors through the use of multivariate analysis. The
previous LESFU study had acknowledged cultural variation in the clientele; the present study sought to identify specific elements in the different
cultures and assess what difference they made in the operation of the
model. Thus, the kind of statements which might be expected to emerge
would not be confined to such generalizations as "The model works well
in some cases, not so well in others, but is useful as an overall guide."
Rather, the study would state that in the operation of the model, case types
A, B, and C tended to abort after a certain stage, while case types D, E,
and F followed it through all of the phases.

In the course of this study the concern with methodology intensified
and issues of systematization of agency data led to concrete steps to
improve the management information system.

Course of the project. This is a project in which an action-research
method was induced by coupling an independent researcher with the
agency which had initiated an application to fund an evaluation study.
David Fanshel was known to the LESFU director and was a leading
academic figure in the field, and was thus approached to take on the
research role.

An action-research workshop was convened by the Grant Foundation in
September 1982 to discuss progress in developing the action-research
collaboration. Herbert presented a brief statement on LESFU history,
noting three key elements in the background of the unit's wish to become
involved in action-research:

> The unit had a history of positive experience with research.
> The unit needed to be evaluated if it was to sustain credibility in further
> applications for financial support.
> There was an expectation that preventive intervention programs would be
> important in the future, and the project would contribute to developing
> the model in this direction.

Fanshel outlined his own reasons for wishing to become involved. As a
professor in a leading school of social work he welcomed the chance for
first-hand, active involvement in the lives of people living in socially
debilitated neighborhoods. He considered that the project could contribute to closing the gap between academic and agency perspectives of
family problems. He characterized his early exploration as an "eye-

opener" and "very sobering" and considered it salutory to the proper concern of social work to confront the human devastation taking place on such a large scale, what he termed the "urban catastrophe." As a mature scholar with much experience in the field of foster care, he had come to the conclusion that preventive work was crucially important.

Fanshel raised eight questions at the early stage of working out a research design with the LESFU team:

1. What are the implications of studying cases that, according to the descriptions of some LESFU staff, come from "the bottom of the barrel" in terms of trouble and need? Included are many chronic and intractable problem families – "tough cases." How does this affect discussing evaluation of results with them? In psychotherapy, there is a negative correlation between the degree of psychopathology and the expectation of improvement. Does this hold for social problem families?

2. What expectations are realistic for the persistence of any changes that may occur? If public responsibility requires that the team avoids "throwing money at problems," is this the best use of the funds? If sustaining changes requires a long-term investment, how long is it reasonable to expect supports to be provided before self-sufficiency is possible?

3. How much does the effect of the LESFU service model depend on its specific charismatic leadership, its specific history as an innovating unit, its specific skills and experience? How much of client change is due to the model guiding LESFU? How much involves generic influences that cut across a variety of service models?

4. What evaluation strategy is reasonable to hold the interest and involvement of a staff that works under difficult, often discouraging, conditions? A focus on client variables helps deflect anxiety, but it does not help staff to self-evaluate, which is necessary if they are to improve. How can an evaluation scheme be developed in which the emphasis is on proof that the agency is moving in the right direction, rather than that it has found a "magic cure," that it "works"?

5. How should the researcher interpret claims of the agency's uniqueness by the media? While the emphasis on innovation highlights special elements in the LESFU model, there is no doubt that much or all of this has been done before, and to ignore this would be failing to learn from prior experience. Also, to do so would be failing to give an appropriate orientation to proper dissemination and wider application of the program. How can innovative aspects be acknowledged while recognizing generic features.

6. What is the relevance of ethnic subcultures on family functioning, and how does this affect the application of the LESFU model? Are Puerto Rican one-parent families different, for example, from Chinese, black, or white ethnic one-parent families at the same socioeconomic level, and what consequences do the differences have in relation to preventive interventions?

7. How can the vulnerability of those involved in the project be approached, both on the side of the agency being evaluated and the research team?

8. Given all the difficulties, what benefit is it reasonable to expect from the

project: service lessons? scientific information? methodological findings? skill training?

Fanshel also held workshop/seminars at Columbia to discuss methodological and conceptual issues arising in the project. One of the problems experienced in the early stages and underlying the issues posed was what might be called the evaluator's dilemma. As an academic social work professor, Fanshel had become accustomed to reports on services which distill positive points. Proponents of services tend to emphasize their services' advantages and achievements. Seeing the whole picture had a disturbing effect on him in comparison to the academic accounts, which tended not to include "backstage" elements and difficulties. The researcher had the problem of how to analyze and present the flaws and deficiencies, as well as achievements, constructively, that is, without harming his collaborators.

A problem for the researcher who is more closely involved with the ongoing work is how to handle situations in which the agency personnel are themselves experiencing crises and need help. Trained not only as a researcher but as a social worker, the researcher feels pressured to get actively involved. Members of the team may seek to enlist direct help and support of the researcher. If there is tension between the person seeking help and the agency team leader, delicate problems of ethics and tactics may arise for the researcher, who must maintain a partnership with the agency as a whole.

Another problem for the researcher lies in working with a unit which is committed to a particular philosophy. As with many innovations, the LESFU model required ideological commitment. It had to be embraced as "a good thing" if a team member was to become immersed in the demanding job. If a member becomes disillusioned and demoralized, having encountered resistances and failures intrinsic in such agency work, there may be considerable hostility expressed toward the model or the agency. The researcher must handle this without becoming too personally involved.

Discussions held both within and outside LESFU helped to clarify the researchers' dilemmas in the participant-observer role. They also helped to formulate specific questions about the LESFU model and brought to the fore alternative ideologies based on perceived shortcomings of the model (e.g., direct counseling rather than brokering).

In the course of execution of the research, Fanshel found that the LESFU sample of 160 families in a sequence of three research efforts (two debriefing interviews with the social work associates and interviews with the clients) and an analysis of the data stored in the agency's management information system absorbed much of the project's resources and precluded a study of the contrast group. Preliminary exploration of what would be entailed in garnering such a group was not encouraging, and the conditions under which a sample would be built raised questions about the wisdom of going in this direction. Such a group could hardly serve as a substitute for a true control group, and studying such clients would likely muddy the waters. The exclusive focus upon the client group was seen as valuable in its own right, providing informative details of the experiences of the clients in the service system and permitting internal analysis that would portray the differential experiences of subgroups.

Difficulties with realization of the original research design is a feature of action-research that warrants scrutiny. Among the vicissitudes encountered by the investigators was the fact that the flow of clients into the agency was much slower than predicted from past agency statistics, and it took almost a year to build up the sample. There was also a resource issue of the need for repeated data-gathering excursions over time, which made the venture much more costly than the original budgetary planning had anticipated.

Methodological issues arose related to ethnic cultures. There was an explicit interest in cultural factors of families in the sample that helped shape client expectations about how to use services as a way of dealing with family problems. However, the social work staff who were Chinese expressed strong reservations about asking the kind of questions about family life required in the client interview protocols when Chinese clients were the subjects. This was an attitude shared by the Chinese graduate student who carried out a second round of interviews with the Chinese subjects for his doctoral dissertation study. Similarly, discussion with the research associate who was of Puerto Rican background about social support systems among Puerto Rican families revealed different points of view affecting his approach to the research issues in focus. The topic was help-giving among the subject families, with the research requiring a consideration of the possibility of relatives having a negative influence on children, potentially draining family resources, and undermining the functioning of parents as well as the reverse.

On the whole, Fanshel was impressed with what these researchers, who came from the ethnic groups being studied, had to offer the project by way of gaining access to staff and clients, and in interpreting the outlook of clients from a cultural perspective. On the other hand, experience showed that the ethnic factors could introduce problems of maintaining detachment and objectivity. The ethnic-identified research investigator may need to be assisted by an unaffiliated colleague who might have less of an emotional investment in the formulation of a particular perspective on the research issues.

The issue of how to handle personal feelings and values, the counter-transference issue, was felt by experienced as well as novice researchers. Fanshel himself felt the need to deal with his own feelings about the behavior observed in client families:

I have to bear in mind that many of the clients come from third world countries where child bearing begins at very young ages. The fact of a teen-ager becoming pregnant may not be defined by family and friends as catastrophic. As a white, middle-class professional, I need to be cautious about imposing my definition on the situation when it is at variance with how the relevant community feels about the phenomenon. I am aware, however, that these pregnancies entrap the young women involved in overwhelming responsibilities under formidable conditions of adversity. I am also conscious of the fact that with the marvelous advances made by the women's movement in recent years in dealing with the oppression of women, Hispanic lower class women such as we find in our sample, have largely been bypassed in the struggle for change. These larger societal issues are so much more powerful in shaping the lives of women than what can be offered in hands-on assistance when the family is beleaguered by problems.

He notes that the principle of freedom of choice to which he holds ignores the fact that people are not equally ready to make responsible choices. "Women are being launched into maternal careers at the worst times in their lives for this."

To produce a meaningful study while being aware of the importance of larger political issues as well as technical issues is a challenge to the researcher, when developing estimates of the efficacy of the agency's model.

I had a lifetime career of trying to account for the performance of agencies given a specific task, such as reconstituting broken families or trying to provide substitute housing arrangements, and always being aware that they have such little control over the causal elements in the situation. . . . Much of what we are being asked to evaluate and hold ourselves accountable for is a result of massive failures of the society.

He dealt with this problem by focusing on the task at hand, though trying not to lose awareness of the larger professional and personal commitments. In seeking to relate the specific data to more general issues, risking premature generalizations, he took the position that a good action-researcher must be both "smart and wise": smart in making tightly controlled use of the empirical data, and wise in relating it judiciously to broader experiences and issues.

Fanshel indicated that action-researchers found themselves in a characteristic dilemma in which they anticipated the possibility that they would have negative results requiring them to criticize persons and agencies with whom they had developed intimate association. He dealt with this issue by rehearsing best-case and worst-case scenarios with his action colleagues. In the best-case scenario, the honest and hard-working efforts of these dedicated people with their difficult family cases show significant and distinctive positive effects. In the worst-case scenario, they do not; the model does not work, is inefficiently applied, or is wrong for the problem. Fanshel calls this the worst-case scenario because he likes and respects the people he is working with. Also, as the money was granted to the project on the basis of its innovative elements, it would be disappointing to find it does not work, notwithstanding the scientific value of the findings. On the one hand, if he is reluctant to report bad news he could be accused of being coopted. He was assured that the grant was not given on a condition that he get positive findings; negative findings can play a constructive role in developing interventions. But they can be problematic in the relationship involved. Indigenous community-based workers, for example, are doing what they do because they want to try to help others. If they are told that their efforts make no significant difference, their morale may be affected.

The early anxieties of the researcher, then, were in three categories: technical (how to evaluate the data), field-relational (how to handle the action-research relationship), and prospective (how to deal with the implications of possible results).

On the action side, the director in this instance did not experience the commonly observed distrust of the researcher. He knew the researcher and trusted his integrity. Nor did the action agency fear that the researcher would not understand their problems – he manifestly did, though his academic status made him a little abstract and possibly not as much in touch with the concrete situation as they were. The principal anxieties were around what he would find. They knew perfectly well that agencies tend to put their best face forward in the constant scramble for funds and support, while de-emphasizing the heavy load of disappointment and frustration. Just how would the picture look when put into an objective set of tabulations and how would it be handled?

Other problems current during the research occupied much of the director's energies: administrative and financial issues in the struggle for survival of the agency; and turnover of personnel with attendant requirements for training and supervision. The demands made by the research were, in this context, somewhat peripheral.

Results

The tenth anniversary of LESFU in May 1985 provided an occasion for the research project to feed back preliminary results prior to the completion of a formal report. Fanshel, in a paper entitled "Early Findings from a Study of Families at Risk Known to the Lower East Side Family Union" gave an account of how he became involved with the study, what its preliminary findings were, and what he saw as the implications of the work.

Of the four ethnic groups served – white, Chinese, Hispanic, and black – the Hispanic is the largest, comprising some 60 percent of the 160 cases studied. Chinese (18.1 percent) and blacks (14.4 percent) followed, with the residual group of whites and "others" accounting for the balance. The family structures of these different groups, as well as their cultural characteristics, showed important variation.

In the vast majority of cases, the pivotal unit forming the household was the mother and child. Of the 160 cases there were 4 which had no child only because the mother was pregnant. Only a quarter of the family households were composed of husbands and wives living together in the conventional manner, usually in a self-contained apartment with few outsiders present. Mothers living alone with their children constituted 37.5 percent of the sample, with a further 20 percent being made up of mothers and children living with another adult. (Some were mothers living with boyfriends, but the majority were young mothers still living in their parental homes.) In 17.5 percent of the households, there was no mother present.

In a vast majority of cases, the presenting problems involved material conditions: housing, finance, neighborhood, and practical problems of establishing service entitlements, such as Medicaid and food stamps. School-related and child-behavioral problems were also prominent, mentioned by about a quarter of the cases, with a range of other personal and interpersonal problems following.

The types of problems emphasized varied with the ethnic groups. The Chinese give more attention to human relations problems (60 percent) while blacks gave this less emphasis (37 percent), emphasizing the more tangible problems. Blacks were also more prone to reveal demoralization of "being fed up with life" as a precipitating element, with nearly half mentioning this.

More than a third of the parents expressed concern for their children – that they were not doing as well in school as expected, that they might be taken away. Chinese were particularly strongly represented in this group.

Fanshel sums up this part of the findings as follows:

Material needs of life, obviously, loom large. Concern for the welfare of the children is also fairly paramount. The clients as parents and as human beings carrying on under stressful conditions – often demoralized and confused in carrying out their responsibilities – present a picture of vulnerability that requires a full panoply of service interventions. (1985, p. 18)

In seeking to understand what processes were at work in the referral, treatment, and rehabilitation of these client families, Fanshel emphasized the importance of the questions which went beyond simply assessing outcome effects. Looking at changes reported according to the type of problem presented, he found that of those who listed housing as the salient problem, over half indicated that their problem was better on follow-up, and about one-third credited LESFU's efforts for achieving the improvement. Of those reporting financial problems, almost three-quarters reported these problems as better at the time of the client interview, with nearly two-thirds crediting LESFU's efforts. Similarly, where parenting problems were reported, almost three-quarters reported improvement, with nearly two-thirds crediting LESFU (e.g., by helping to arrange daycare). School problems showed a very similar distribution: nearly three-quarters indicated an improved situation, and nearly two-thirds acknowledging LESFU's help. In the area of family relationship problems, 57 percent of the clients who mentioned them indicated improvement, and virtually all attributed their improvement to LESFU. These problems included spouse conflict and violence and better ways of coping.

Fanshel acknowledges the general tendency in follow-up studies of service provision is for clients to show improvement, and that possibly it is related to a response tendency on the part of clients to express appreciation for service. He notes, however, that these clients were a particularly difficult sample, and that the improvements reported were greater than one might expect from the findings of earlier studies. Also, the wide range of problems and the specificity of client descriptions of how they were helped were impressive. Finally, the fact that similar information emerged from analysis of the management information forms, client interviews, and all other sources of data provided support in relation to the validity of the figures.

An important element in the findings had to do with the family's field of consciousness regarding its collapse, which might possibly necessitate foster-care placement. While about half of the parents acknowledged that foster-care placement of their child was a risk if they were not able to solve their problems, they also saw other risks as important: mental health, juvenile delinquency, behavior problems, and abuse and neglect of the child. They acknowledged, as did the welfare professionals and the legislature, that foster care would be a highly undesirable outcome, but they saw it as one among many. The LESFU staff saw the realistic risks of placement as a salient factor in only about 20 percent of the cases. They were much more concerned with the manifest malfunctioning of the families and the harm it could do the children than the possibility of complete collapse of the family.

Because of the researchers' interest in process as well as outcome, an examination was made of how the families thought about their experience of coping with various problems faced; financial, administrative (e.g., housing), parental. The findings documented the great diversity of problems experienced against a background of near-universal acceptance of a positive image of family life and of children. Examples of the problems encountered by parents were inexperience (particularly among youthful parents); discipline and handling of acting-out problems, such as juvenile delinquency among adolescents (especially among blacks); bitterness and the feeling that life had turned out badly for them; drugs; mental health problems; and educational failure.

The study documented the wide variety of referral sources and agency contacts experienced by clients, and the importance of the agency's brokerage or advocacy efforts in helping clients to find the appropriate help and entitlements. On the other hand, there is little doubt that the actual working of the agency has become much more complex than was envisaged ten years ago, partly because its own outreach activities have drawn a more mixed bag of clients, and partly because new kinds of agencies have grown up and become relevant as a broader array of issues has emerged in the social setting. Perhaps the most important of these is the new emphasis on preventing abuse in the family and other pathological and dysfunctional behaviors. Fostering, meanwhile, has receded into a less prominent concern both for clients and the public.

Just over half of the cases were closed on a planned basis and with mutual consent. Chinese clients were highest in this (74 percent), with Hispanics second (54 percent) and blacks lowest (39 percent).

The researchers concluded that the model is only partly applicable. Payoff does not depend on clients going "all the way" with the model. The model serves as a heuristic device, giving the agency a sense of thrust and coherence.

The raison d'etre for the agency has changed in emphasis from its inception. The initial focus on avoiding foster care has been eclipsed by a more recent emphasis on preventing family disturbance and child abuse.

Serendipities were experienced in two areas of this project's results, one quantitative, the other qualitative. The quantitative one relates to the management information system. The research team was impressed by the potential utility of a quantifiable management information system for research, but at the same time they recognized that the system left in place by an earlier administrative consultancy was very crude. They used the available information to gather baseline data about the client families being studied and simultaneously drew up new guidelines that would help develop analytic procedures for extracting more adequate data from this potentially valuable source in future. Fanshel and Finch have become involved in a broader effort to develop this kind of information technology in a variety of social service settings.

The qualitative serendipities are seen in the thesis projects of the ethnic field workers. Alvelo's study of 40 Puerto Rican families and Li's study of Chinese families contribute to our general knowledge about ethnic factors in families at risk as well as about the focal task of the project, the functioning of the LESFU model.

Discussion

In the action-research approach used here, two members of the same profession collaborated, but in different roles. Both are social workers, but Herbert is an agency director and Fanshel an academic.

The use of the action-research paradigm rather than a classical evaluation design made it incumbent on them to go beyond simple statistical statements of the agency's impact. They have additionally discussed *process,* and examined variant cases as well as those representing the central tendencies of success (or failure) of the model. Fanshel expressed the view that one of the most important implications of the study, from the point of view of a theory of practice, is the need to counteract the simplistic assumptions underlying most policy (that a method works or it does not work, and that a good new service must carry out feats of dramatic innovation).

Legislation misses its mark when it poses definitions of service in terms of completely resolving problems of distressed people who are chronically dysfunctional. I see as my mission the articulation of the basis for continued support for services directed at these problems, with a clear picture of the gains and limitations – but also attaching to the gains considerable value as expressed by the client. These consist of many small acts which collectively are impressive, though the professional community may not particularly emphasize their importance. This kind of service is full of such small humanitarian acts, rare to come by in the larger society, and I would like to convey their worthwhileness.

In other words, small things may make big differences to families in need, and these should not be disregarded in the attempt to show outstanding achievement in order to gain support for or disseminate a method.

This finding is relevant to Fanshel's theory of practice. Indicators of success are crucial for such a theory, and sometimes success is simplistically taken to mean removal from someone's lists, whether the social service agency, the courts and prisons, or the psychiatric case load. Fanshel notes that the LESFU study indicates how success can mean getting *onto* lists people who have not been able to find their way, or to understand their entitlement. The brokerage concept of LESFU's work is thus still relevant however much the substantive focus may have shifted from fostering to family disturbance in general. Effective service should be built, the team concludes, on a specific understanding of the responsiveness of family problems to specific interventions (e.g., practical assistance, counseling, and advocacy).

In systematizing the data on management information systems, Fanshel and his colleagues further developed a technique long known to them, but not anticipated to be a key element in this project. The need for this kind of competence is in demand for improving data available for decision-making in social service agencies. As in LESFU, the demands of providing service tend over a period of time to override the development of coherent information systems. Fanshel has been impressed with the power to present such information made possible through modern information technology:

There is informational chaos in many agencies. Huge programs operate without the benefit of organized information. . . . There are no studies of how this can be introduced into a service agency and then used in decision-making.

The LESFU case provided a further spur to developing this capacity, and Fanshel and his colleagues have continued to refine and apply it.

The case also illustrates the kaleidoscopic character of the social intervention process. LESFU, like many other social service agencies, continually readapts approaches which have been known and used for a long time. Part of the innovation lies in the novel application of familiar elements in new situations. For example, giving practical help – the "hands on" approach – is very old, but helping non-English-speaking Chinese clients by taking them to the appropriate agency offices is new, as is the whole package of family intervention procedures designed to enhance their competence in a range of situations. It is the way in which a familiar technique is applied and combined with others that comprises the innovation. Similarly, the use of untrained local people as family visitors is old –

preprofessional – but it is a useful innovation in a situation where professional services are in short supply, sometimes difficult to get to because of bureaucratic barriers, and sometimes out of touch with local culture. The research findings on the importance of informal local supports is particularly important currently with the reduction of formal services.

An issue which emerged through the action-research approach (that is, taking an interest in process and approaching the research in a collaborative spirit) is how to sustain the continuity of staffing. A "front-line" agency like LESFU takes on difficult cases in a highly stressful environment with sparse resources. It is established and kept functioning by charismatic leadership. However, the exhausting demands of the ongoing work and the need continuously to justify the activity provide stresses that are not systematically acknowledged or handled. Obviously agencies need to be monitored to ensure that they remain effective, but there is also a need to develop ways of avoiding staff burn-out and disturbance. One contribution of the present research is the realization that when a case does not comply in every detail with the model, it is not necessarily a failure. Knowing this helps to reduce some of the tension that tends to characterize agencies with high expectations and formidable tasks.

The scientific value of the LESFU study extends beyond the assessment of a particular experiment to the consideration of generic issues facing agencies serving families of poor and ethnically disadvantaged groups. Service delivery is reconceptualized as a problem-solving process rather than as a substantive package of activities with finite content and boundaries.

Case study: The empathy development group

This social intervention is a special remedial group for children from violent homes. It aims to develop their empathic capacity. The need for such an intervention is suggested in research and clinical experience, which has shown that defective empathy development is a critical intervening variable in the intergenerational perpetuation of violence. The specific project was initiated by Michael Phillips, professor in the Fordham University School of Social Work, in collaboration with Daniel Kronenfeld, at the time director of the Henry Street Settlement's Urban Families Center. Scheduled for 18 months, the project commenced in January 1983. Subsequently, Verona Middleton-Jeter became director of the Urban Families Center, and Kronenfeld became executive director of the Henry Street Settlement.

Background

Recent research has indicated the problem of family violence to be more widespread than had been recognized and it is probably growing (Gelles and Straus, 1979; Straus et al., 1980; Finkelhor et al., 1981). This increase seems to be pandemic in developed industrial countries and has been analyzed by lawyers and social scientists as reflecting societal as well as personal stress factors. In 1973 a Senate subcommittee introduced legislation in the United States directed at reducing family violence (Child Abuse Prevention Act), and in Britain a parliamentary committee on violence in marriage was established during the same period with subsequent Acts passed aimed at improving the legal remedies available to victims of family violence (Maidment, 1985). In these and other countries, agencies have been set up to stimulate research and bring together findings to inform national policy (e.g., the U.S. National Center for Child Abuse and Neglect).

Estimates of the incidence of family violence have varied widely, partly because different assessment criteria and devices have been used, such as physical, sexual, and psychological (verbal) abuse, and neglect. The reporting agencies themselves are diverse and use different kinds of data, including social surveys, legislative investigatory committees, and medical and social welfare agency records. Additional variation in estimates is due to variations in reliability requirements, of whether a reported incident must be confirmed in order to be counted, and what authentication is required of its identifiable consequences.

In 1980 a sound estimate was arrived at, based on a nationwide Department of Justice survey. According to the survey, there were 1.2 million occurrences of family violence in that year, of which less than half were reported to the police. Seventy percent of these occurrences took place in the home, and 74,000, or over 6 percent, of these instances were committed by parents against children.

Saad Nagi (1977) estimated that the rate of child abuse is highest among children under the age of four (about 2 percent), declining with advancing age to under 1 percent for children in their teens. Mothers top the list of alleged abusers in about 50 percent of cases. Both parents are abusers in nearly 25 percent of reported cases, the father the main abuser in about 15 percent of cases, and an assortment of step-parents, grandparents, foster parents, babysitters, boyfriends, and others make up the balance. What the figures fail to capture are the processes involved: to what extent are the abusing mothers themselves abused, and to what extent are they lone parents, perhaps prematurely thrust into parenting responsibilities and living in poverty and isolation?

Nagi (1977) analyzed institutional responses and identified the agencies that come to know about these phenomena and those that are available to respond – the two are not identical. Among the approaches, he noted these:

> Advocating legislative measures to define and protect children's rights and parents' responsibilities
>
> Strengthening the powers of courts, police, doctors, and social workers to investigate and act on cases of child abuse or neglect
>
> Creating shelters and other protective agencies for abused individuals (e.g., foster homes, homemaker services, marriage guidance services)
>
> Strengthening informal (self-help) support associations such as Parents Anonymous
>
> Improving therapeutic interventions through research

The National Center for Child Abuse and Neglect was charged with the task of collecting and integrating information on these issues and stimulating local efforts to come to grips with them. Several voluntary bodies and advocacy groups have become active in the field, and the Children's Defense Fund has set up a citizen's monitoring network, "Childwatch," to increase public awareness and to stimulate preventive activities.

Research has indicated that there are contributory causes at various levels, with specific studies clustering around particular foci or disciplines. Henry Kempe and his colleagues have concentrated on clinical issues, identifying what they call the "battered child syndrome" and developing a therapeutic approach for affected families. They conceptualize the battering phenomenon as a symptom of family dysfunction and their interventions seek to restore the family to a healthy state of functioning, in contrast to the widespread tendency to concentrate on treating the symptoms or protecting the individual child (Kempe and Helfer, 1972; Helfer and Kempe, 1976). Straus, Gelles, and Steinmetz (1980) have charted the phenomenon sociologically and documented both the pervasiveness and the increase of family violence in all social classes of contemporary society.

Some sociologists (Dobash and Dobash, 1979) emphasize the causal force of power in the gender relationships in what they see as a persistence of patriarchal attitudes in our society. Some documentation of this viewpoint is seen in the research of Evan Stark and his colleagues (1981). Focusing on the mother-child relationship, they have shown that child battering does not occur primarily as a result of intergenerational transmission of the violent tendency. Most abusive mothers were *not* themselves battered children. Rather, they are victims of marital violence and themselves in need of protection. Finkelhor and his colleagues (1981) have provided an analysis of research in this field and have called for public support to improve methodologies for detection and intervention. Some legal authorities (Freeman, 1979) have emphasized the limitations of legal procedures in relieving the essential problems of family violence, and others (Katz, 1963) have outlined the importance of a multi-disciplinary approach.

The social intervention

Itself a social intervention of an earlier era, the Henry Street Settlement has developed an innovative program consonant with the last of Nagi's five approaches mentioned above. Within the Henry Street Settlement a number of special programs have evolved to meet new problems as they have arisen. Each is a social intervention. One of these, the Urban Families Center (UFC), is a shelter for homeless families in New York. The center was designed to meet a housing crisis for disrupted families in the early 1970s. A mayor's task force was set up in response to a public outcry in the press against the unsatisfactory "welfare hotels" where homeless families were housed at great public expense and were provided with little by way of rehabilitation.

The task force was not optimistic about the capacity of a family center based in a settlement house to deal with these housing problems. But the city was so overwhelmed by the problem of its homeless multiproblem families that it went along with the venture predicting, however, that the center would not last long. They reasoned that if the center concentrated on the hard-core multiproblem families, its staff would be overwhelmed, and if it provided all the supports it stated were necessary to help this heterogeneous group of families, it would subsequently find it difficult to move them out, as the shelter's housing unit would be more supportive than anything the families could find outside. Twelve years and more than 2,000 families later, the center has not only survived, but has been the source of a number of innovative ideas.

The overall approach of the UFC has been a "total push" method of helping families with whatever practical, social, or psychological problems they might have. The goal is *family self-sufficiency*. This is an example of a "social sanitation" intervention. Short-term sheltered housing was seen as a way of providing a temporary set of conditions for working with family problems. A case-work approach was taken which was task-oriented (Reid and Epstein, 1972). It was not intended to provide permanent solutions but to intervene while there was a sense of crisis and, through working together with families in dealing with the task confronting them, to increase family competence (Parad, 1965). The emphasis was on establishing with each family a set of realistic and realizable objectives, and on working together at this point of receptivity to attain their goals. The center can handle 90 families at a given time, and over a two-year period in which the early work was monitored 308 families came into residence.

The problems confronting these families and their case workers are diverse: economic, housing, drug abuse, police-related, juvenile, and marital. These are classic multiproblem families, living in high-stress environments, often with a history of having moved around from one agency to another without having developed an enduring solution. In terms of severity of their dysfunctions, the families are classified by social workers in categories such as apathetic-futile, impulse-ridden, psychotic, asocial, antisocial, and stress-overloaded.

The center is located in a public housing block made available by the city. It provides normal family environments for 90 multiproblem homeless families in its modestly furnished small apartments. A staff of social workers live on the premises. Staff members work with individuals and families to create a community atmosphere, described by one worker as a kind of "urban kibbutz." It could be called a type of therapeutic community, though the staff are not particularly oriented to this concept.

The center aims to keep families together, rather than dispersing them and placing children in foster homes. It provides a setting and professional support structure for families who need help in coping with their predicaments. The program includes

- Individual, family and group counseling
- Educational services for school-age children
- Referral to health care and legal services
- Separate, fully equipped apartments for each family unit
- On-site assistance from the City Housing Authority and the Department of Social Services to help families obtain more permanent housing

In 1977, five years after the UFC was formed, the Abused Women's Shelter program began operating within it. There was initial apprehension about how the local community would react to homeless families moving into the neighborhood. However, when a neighborhood school complained that some of the problem children of homeless families were disruptive, the center responded by helping the school to develop a remedial program, which was of broader use to the school and resulted in closer relations between the center and the school. The local community provided supportive activities (e.g., through local churches). Other links with the local community were forged to foster the feeling that the center was part of the local community, rather than another kind of welfare hotel fortuitously located there. Staff at all levels within the center were also involved. If a child acted out aggressively toward a nonprofessional staff member, the meaning of the child's behavior would be discussed so that the staff member's response could contribute to the child's understanding of its impact on others, rather than being seen as provocation and responded to in unhelpful ways.

The UFC staff were impressed by the degree to which multiproblem families, whether they had come as part of the homeless or battered women's program, used violence to cope with stress and thus set an example for their children. At the same time, they noted there was little guidance from their professional literature on how to interrupt the transmission of this maladaptive mode of coping from parents to children. As this was a *family* center, rather than a battered wives' shelter, the staff identified the issue as one on which they wished to concentrate. It grew out of problems raised by the multiproblem families themselves, as they were often preoccupied with the issues of what effect their problems would have on their children. Observation of the children in the center as well as from research reported elsewhere confirmed the tendency for children raised in violent families to show a number of characteristic developmental problems, and eventually to become prone to violence in their own subsequent family life.

Most shelters concentrated on the mothers exclusively, just as most hospitals that see battered children concentrate on the children (see Kempe, 1962). Phillips, in a report on the center's work observed that treatment means different things to people, but to the center's workers it meant "helping the families develop coping skills that will enable them to sustain themselves" (Phillips, 1981). However, the specific intervention in focus here – the special empathy development group – fits the strategy we have called "psychological inoculation."

The project's focus on the psychological level was in principle seen as part of a larger whole. From the point of view of the center, the focus on empathy was part of a set of questions arising in the work:

> What is the whole family picture where there had been serious battering?
> What impact does family violence have on children?
> Under what conditions do children incorporate their family's violence into their own patterns of behavior?

All of these questions were oriented to the issue of how best to intervene in the family's life to ameliorate the effects on children and to prevent the occurrence of a cycle of violence. Empathy, in this context, was a concept which presented itself as relevant to what Kronenfeld described as the effort to "tailor our program to be more effective in their short period of time at the Shelter . . . [and] to help us determine the best focus for this group."

From the point of view of practitioners, there are many possible intervention devices. The choice of a special "group within a group" was consistent with the overall approach of the shelter and of the Henry Street Settlement. Kronenfeld remarks:

[We wanted] to give these children an opportunity to discuss their feelings, reactions and concerns *re* violence in their lives . . . [and to] provide an opportunity for these children to problem-solve together while learning alternative ways of coping.

The center had had a history of a productive interplay between research and program development and, just prior to formulating this project, had received two grants which were complementary in character: a program development grant from the National Center for Child Abuse and Neglect, and a grant from the Ittleson Foundation to identify special needs of nursery-school-age children of battered women. Concern had been expressed about the intergenerational transmission of violence, but there was no plan to study it systematically. The extension flowed logically from these other grants, and from the interests and commitments of the associated personnel: Phillips's interest in discovering a key to halting intergenerational violence; Middleton-Jeter's commitment to providing services to children in such families; and staff members Aaron's and Peak's interest in developing special groups for these children. Previous research suggested a possible key concept and the agency accepted that research was necessary to determine whether a special group oriented to this plausible concept was, in fact, viable and valid in action.

The action-research project

The center's director, Daniel Kronenfeld, had had a long standing interest in social research, having studied sociology at the University of Wisconsin and earned a degree in social work. But prior researchers at the center had been confined to one resident participant-observer who had intended to write an ethnographic study of families in the style of Oscar Lewis's *La Vida*. When the center sought to develop a more ambitious project on the homeless multiproblem family and submitted a preliminary version to the Office of Health, Education, and Welfare, they were told that the research design needed strengthening. Michael Phillips was invited to help develop the project design further and to supervise its execution.

Phillips is professor of social work at Fordham University, but his research career has been closely intermingled with action. He had field experience working with street gangs, had studied violence for the Jewish Board of Family Services, and had worked as a social worker in a juvenile detention prison. Among his students at Fordham had been Donna Rich, UFC's project coordinator.

The interest in violence in families was, therefore, shared by the center staff and the researcher. They knew from available research and a voluminous literature that this was not only a serious and apparently increasing problem but also one which appeared to some extent at least to be intergenerationally transmitted (see Gayford, 1975; Gelles, 1974; Rosenbaum and O'Leary, 1981; and Sage, 1975).

Research design. The design of the research required the study and evaluation of a special group for increasing the empathy response; but as the special group had itself to be designed (rather like a piece of laboratory apparatus), the project as a whole had twin goals: to design and put into operation a special group for increasing empathy in the growing child, and to study the operation of this group in its total social services context to learn more about empathy development in children from violent families and the effectiveness of such a group in relating to it.

Taking these tasks serially, it is important to describe the underlying philosophy and concepts of the experimental team to understand their approach to developing the innovative experimental group. Of the principal theoretical orientations to aggression in the growing child, three were identified as relevant. The first was an emphasis on the biological basis for aggression (after Lorenz, 1966; Tinbergen, 1951) and the control of aggression as a function of normal maturation in the adolescent child (after Anna Freud and Burlingham, 1944). Maturation occurs when the child develops beyond the earlier stages of impulsiveness to an intermediary stage where the child recognizes aggression but enjoys the sense of power too much to appreciate that it may have a harmful impact on others. Finally, with maturity, the aggressive drives are "sublimated," after identification with loved role models who discourage the use of hurtful aggression. Empathy development is part of this process and crucial to reaching a mature stage of development. If empathy is poorly developed, aggressive behavior may erupt under stress or frustration. Ordinary defenses against its expression are easily overwhelmed in persons with an underdeveloped empathic response.

A second potential model was the social learning theory approach as expressed, for example, by Bandura (1975). The emphasis is less on taming aggressive drives which must be kept leashed, than on influencing the way the child incorporates aggressive behavior patterns learned in childhood. Research indicates that a child who witnesses aggressive behavior in parental figures is more likely to behave aggressively in adulthood (Kratcosci, 1984).

Phillips tended to favor a third model, which allowed the interaction of both sets of variables. This synthesis is illustrated in the research of the Feshbachs (1969), which indicated that faulty empathy development in youngsters may occur for a complex of reasons. When they come from violent homes, they may come to feel that development of power is necessary for survival. Violence seems to them to be an expression of power, particularly when they observe their parents using violence when under stress. They may have grown up in families and neighborhoods that lacked constructive alternatives for expressing aggressive drives. The Feshbachs demonstrated empirically the low levels of empathy in children living in such situations. Accordingly, empathy was conceptualized as a key control mechanism in the transmission of the uncontrolled violent tendency (Feshbach and Feshbach, 1969). The project built on this conceptualization.

The actual intervention for the study and treatment of children (presumably with empathy deficits) from violent homes had to be developed in the context of the center's service operations. As part of the routine procedures, parents were being taught about the developmental needs of children. The aim was to produce a better domestic environment. Suggestions were made about alternative ways of coping other than by physical aggression. If the family was socially isolated, ideas were provided about the importance of and techniques for social network construction.

The center's general service strategy was to begin by alleviating the high level of anxiety clients felt upon admission. This was done by dealing first with practical problems facing the family. It was only then that the interventions for psychological change might be applied. What form should the new intervention take?

Based on these ideas, a series of group sessions was proposed to provide elements hypothetically lacking in these children's empathy development. While the mothers were being given practical help in alleviating family stress, the children were presented with a set of remedial learning experiences, aimed at helping the child to identify, label, and communicate his or her feelings in frightening situations; to connect feelings to actions; to reach out to others and form relationships; and to develop coping strategies which might be constructive in future, including the capacity to come to terms with loss and eventually the termination of the agency's supportive relationship.

The ingredients with which the innovators worked came from the repertoire available to psychologists and social workers: individual psychotherapy, counseling, role playing, child-therapy techniques of drawing and play, group therapies, and so on (Schaefer et al., 1982). The immediate task was to devise a new set of procedures which could be specifically effective with empathy development in children from violent backgrounds. Previous efforts in this field have included the use of multiple therapists (e.g., cotherapists for parent and child), crisis intervention, and the alternation of activity therapies and discussion periods. The emphasis in such groups has been to develop social interaction skills and increased self-control. There had been some work using group therapy with delinquent youth in residential settings (Phelan, Slavson, Epstein, and Schwartz, 1960; Westman 1961, Schaefer et al., 1982, p. 314), but none of the reported approaches were located in institutions such as shelters, nor had any concentrated on altering empathy levels in children.

The actual experimental intervention contained a series of sessions designed to move stepwise toward the desired end—state of a higher level of empathy in the child. Each session was organized around a focal topic:

- Learning about relationships and how people seek to exert power over others
- Identifying and labeling the feelings of people engaged in different kinds of interpersonal relations (interpersonal sensitivity)
- Elucidating different ways of negotiating compromises in major conflicts
- Learning about one's own feelings in stressful situations, such as marital conflict and dissolution, and how to process one's feelings, for example, by verbalizing
- Understanding the implications of a pattern of behavior, and extrapolating chains of events and patterns of relationships from a given disturbed situation
- Assessing others' involvement in such situations, and identifying safe and dangerous patterns.

The program as a whole was designed to improve a child's empathic response, and this in turn was expected to inhibit subsequent maladaptive aggressiveness.

As for the research aspect of the project, instruments chosen to monitor and evaluate the new intervention were based partly on the schedules developed and used with families at UFC in the earlier project work:

> Intake interview and service contract
> Goal attainment assessments

> Child behavior assessments
> Exit interview
> Follow-up interview

These interviews, based on scales and formats developed by several experts in the family dynamics field, allowed for scoring and quantification of findings (cf. Holmes and Rahe, 1967; Zill, 1983).

Families were rated on the following characteristics:

> Degree of stress experienced
> Problems currently faced
> Incidence of aggressive behavior, the style of discipline used, the way in which violence is handled
> Degree of social isolation
> Degree to which changes occurred in the course of the stay at the center.

The measures of empathy in the children's short-term response were the following:

1. An interview/test instrument with the children to be used before the first group session (cf. Dymond, 1949)
2. The same measure to be used after the last group session
3. Videotape recordings of group sessions to identify specific behavior patterns and changes that occurred in them over time

Data on behavior changes in children who were in the same center but did not participate in the empathy training program were gathered from their mothers.

To test the long-term effect on empathy and its translation into new patterns of behavior was beyond the scope of the present project, but considerable attention was paid to measuring the short-term responses.

Throughout the study it was acknowledged that short-term changes did not guarantee long-term ones. The research-and-development character of the project made it more appropriate to emphasize the goal of understanding the processes at work, rather than assessing the long-term results of an experimental intervention. Thus, in contrast to an evaluation study of a developed and stabilized program, the aim was to use interim research observations in a *formative* way; that is, to discover in action how great an age span of children could be worked with in this way, how long the sessions might last, how many people would be involved, how many sessions there should be, what structure should be built into the sessions, and, of course, the measurable effects of the group experience on empathy development.

In summary, the design of the project had two interdependent goals being pursued simultaneously: an action one (to develop a remedial intervention program to increase empathy levels in children of violent families) and a scientific one (to assess the level of empathic response in children from such families, and the children's amenability to changing this response through participation in the innovative remedial program). The need for the intervention was perceived in the agency setting; the theory on which it was constructed, in the academic setting; the design for an action-research project was worked out collaboratively, with researchers and agency staff working together both on the development of the innovation and on its monitoring and evaluation.

Course of the project. In the preproject phase of their collaboration, the researcher had actively participated with the center staff to develop instruments for recording service delivery, codifying and disseminating information about the treatment methods, and developing viable goals toward which the treatment methods might evolve. This had established a trusting relationship and also a particular working arrangement out of which the high overlap model of action-research evolved.

Phillips, who had previously experienced various models of action-research (including his street work with fighting gangs), conceptualized the problem of developing constructive relations between researcher and action personnel as one requiring negotiation. It is, at heart, a trade-off relationship. He states that when it is turned into a hierarchical one, in his experience, it has negative consequences. Hierarchy may arise either by the researcher dominating the action personnel or vice versa. The researcher, in this instance, had high status and had raised the funds. However, the agency personnel "owned" the facility and controlled access to clients and regulation of their program. Phillips's thinking was in terms of What are they giving and what are they getting? and What am I giving and what am I getting? He has consistently sought a balance. On the basis of previous experience he felt that agency social workers are generally not interested enough in research to be satisfied with the idea that they are getting research results out of the collaboration. They are focused on doing, and want to "know" only insofar as it might affect what they do. Still, they do need information to do case work, and seen as an adjunct to collecting case data, the researchers provided something of value. Phillips observed that working on this particular research project produced the kind of situation he considered productive: "Within a week they know more about these cases than they would ordinarily know in a month. . . . We have really helped them [in a way they want help]." It worked well partly because the researchers gathered the kind of information that social agency personnel regarded as meaningful. Another reason for Phillips's interest in developing research instruments useful to agency personnel was for the future tasks of generalizing the work. "As we go through this process, we will identify what of the data we collect is vitally important [for agency personnel] to know. Once we know that, we can convince the workers in new settings to collect the information."

Initially the work commenced with a 7-to-12-year-old group. The core measurement of empathy was to be derived from videotapes of the sessions. One task was to observe the degree to which the children manifested an "unfreezing" of inhibitors to natural empathy development. Beyond this, the group leaders wanted to establish a sense in the children that they could cope, and that they could "make it" in the world by mechanisms other than the exercising of physical power over others. They saw this as a kind of rekindling of the Horatio Alger myth, applied to the ethnic minority predicament. An article by Leon Chestang, "Blacks Who Made It," was used for examples of positive role models. The real-life role model provided by the group leader was a visible and tangible specimen for children where such models were often missing or defective in their home environments.

In the first year of the project, several problems arose. One was how to introduce research instruments into the regular procedures, particularly the use of the videotape machine. Initially the staff felt that, though clients might comply with their request to videotape, there would be a feeling of duress. They might not feel they could refuse, being residents, but they might resent doing it. Also, with the agency personnel, though there was agreement that videotaping was going to be used and it had been incorporated into the application for funds, there were problems over the details of how and under what conditions. They were also concerned about how to protect the families and children from information being used in ways they might not want. What if the tapes were stolen? Who in the community had access to them? When families see and hear the reports of violence against their children on the tapes, how should their responses be handled?

These problems were resolved by taking cognizance of Phillips's standing as a certified social worker; as such, he was recognized as providing the same safeguards for patients as staff members themselves. This was an instance where the role overlap proved functional. The questions on physical location and protection of the tapes were resolved by keeping them in Phillips's Fordham University office rather than on the research site.

A second set of issues revolved around defining the researcher's role more precisely, that is, the part that was distinctive, not in the overlap zone. Previously the value of Phillips's authoritative competence as a researcher had been demonstrated in his help with developing a successful research procedure that was funded by a federal agency. The fact that he did so in a way that was comfortable for staff, whose orientation was more to learning about process rather than what Phillips calls "structural" (analyzing the roles and organizational patterns), was also a positive element. Out of this shared experience a firm basis for trust was established.

But there remained specific issues of how research goals could, in fact, be pursued in a way that was compatible with the agency's approach. Phillips had many ideas as an experienced professor of social work on how research could be used to help staff to explicate their treatment philosophy and also how to systematize their record-keeping and improve their relations with clients (e.g., though the introduction of a service contract), but he could not impose these ideas unless asked. He was not initially drawn into their staff training sessions because the treatment system was established and he was outside it. Only when the staff felt that they had to know more about a new set of problems and that they might have to alter what they were doing or add something did they turn to him. The problem that had occasioned their turning to him in this case was violence and its transmission within the family. Although this led to a second round of successful project applications, many detailed elements of the researcher's role definition remained unresolved. For example, there was the issue of how much videotaping could be done of the social workers at work. Videotaping was potentially threatening because it exposed the worker as well as the clients to public scrutiny. Also, there was the issue of how much written work the social workers could be expected to produce. Kronenfeld describes his staff as very "doing"-oriented in a "hectic setting" with little time to take on demanding report writing, unless it was required or seen to be useful in their work.

Kronenfeld describes the resolution of these issues from the staff perspective:

We attempted to handle [the written requirements] by involving staff in all aspects of the planning of the project [and] also having periodic meetings to give staff feedback. Some of the instruments designed for the research gave valuable information about the families which could be used in their clinical practice.

In relation to the videotaping, he notes:

There was no easy solution for this other than to try and set a non-critical tone. One of the more relaxed workers [who] was willing [got] some valuable clinical supervision based on the viewing of the tapes.

Research interviews were seen to have some elements in common with case-work interviews, but researchers did not use them for practical treatment purposes. They redirected treatment questions to the case workers and encouraged clients to contact their workers. It was understood, however, that the research data was confidential, particularly the ending interviews in which it was of crucial importance that clients give their candid evaluations. This was potentially threatening to case workers not only because of fantasies about what might be in the data but also because of the feeling that some therapeutically valuable material might be getting drained off into the research interviews. Also, research interviews with group leaders were felt to be potentially undermining to the relationship between the group leaders and their supervisors. However, Phillips's use of the action-research model allowed partial "formative" feedback, and feedback had elements in common with education and with consultation in social work practice. He also made appropriate research material available to staff. Thus, Phillips resolved the researcher's role dilemma by defining his own role as "partial consultant." He met with the service delivery personnel to discuss what was going on in the various sessions and fed back data relevant to the needs of those in treatment roles, while at the same time using the discussions to contribute to his understanding for the research requirements. By discussing the processes that had been observed, he worked simultaneously on giving the service personnel the quid pro quo they required to tolerate his presence and on obtaining the process data he required for research. At the heart of his evolving role was the idea that it was a *negotiated* rather than an imposed one. Ideally, both sides could see this way of operating as serving their eventual purposes. Understanding of the empathy concept was the shared vehicle around which they negotiated their distinctive project roles.

A further problem developed after the videotaping and role-definition problems were resolved. The families refused to leave the shelter. The center's housing, considered necessary to alleviate stress to enable staff to work with the families, was so comfortable that equivalent permanent housing became difficult to obtain. Certainly, it was impossible to reconstitute the community atmosphere easily and clients, with the improved awareness of their rights and an enhanced capacity to cope, turned these against the center and refused to budge. The immediate implication for the research was that the flow of families, necessary to fulfill the design's requirements, was halted. A serendipity, however, was found in the center's decision to double-up families in the apartments. While this did not add appreciably to the numbers in the experimental groups, it did provide a quasi-control group and enlarged the overall sample of children from violent homes. This improved the basis for constructing a profile of such children.

Results

The results of this project are equivocal in relation to the initial conceptualization and specific hypotheses but instructive in relation to the broader goals. Empathy levels were not found to be lower in children from violent families than in normal controls. However, these children responded to the special group intervention with greater increments in empathy levels than did controls.

To interpret the significance of these findings, the researchers provided a basic review of the data on hand and the assumptions surrounding their development (Phillips et al., 1984).

First, Phillips and his colleagues constructed a violent family profile or syndrome. It was this family syndrome which provided the context for the child's development and the application of empathic responses.

Based on data from 141 women and their children in the battered wives' shelter (about 60 percent black and 30 percent Hispanic, 48 percent between the ages of 26 and 35), the following profile emerges: for the overwhelming majority (84 percent) the batterer was the father of one or more of the children. Over half of the mothers (56 percent) were teenagers when their first child was born, and in most of the families (83 percent), all children under 17 live with the mother. Sixty-four percent of the mothers were not employed when they left the batterer. Those who were employed held mainly menial or service jobs. Only one had a semiprofessional position. A similar employment picture existed for the batterers, with 46 percent unemployed or in menial service occupations, 32 percent in unskilled or semiskilled occupations, and the remaining 22 percent in more skilled jobs.

In terms of health, 66 percent of the mothers indicated that they had at least one health problem which affected their functioning to some degree. Eight-two percent had had this problem for more than one year. Educationally, one-third of the mothers had finished high school and 16 percent had had at least some college. The families were not large, averaging two or three children per household.

In terms of the violence in the family, for most the experience of battering was chronic. For a third of the mothers the battering had continued for more than five years, and in only about 20 percent of the cases, it had gone on for less than one year. Table 2-1 summarizes the frequency of abuse reported. For nearly 60 percent of the mothers verbal abuse was a daily occurrence; for about 90 percent this kind of abuse occurred weekly. Physical abuse, too, was frequent, with about 75 percent experiencing it weekly. Forty-four percent indicated that they had experienced physical

Table 2-1. *Frequency of various types of abuse (%)*

Behavior	Daily	Twice a week	Weekly	Less frequently
Nonphysical criticism, hurt feelings, yelling, insulting	57	24	7	3
Moderate physical pushing, shoving, throwing objects	13	15	9	15
Violent physical kicking, biting, hitting, choking, beating up, threatening to kill	9	12	6	18

battering at least twice a week, and a further 31 percent, at least once a week. The usual form of physical abuse was being kicked, beaten, or hit with a fist (42 percent), though 27 percent described being hit with an object at least once a week and 49 percent had been attacked with a weapon on at least one occasion. Forty-five percent said they had been threatened with death at least once a week.

A variety of causes were cited for the maltreatment, with the batterer's drinking or drug abuse (29 percent) being the largest single category (though 53 percent indicated that drinking was not an issue and 73 percent stated that drugs were not involved).

As might be expected, an overwhelming majority of respondents were unhappy with their marital relationship, with only 15 percent indicating that they were happy with the *overall* quality of their relationship with the batterer prior to entering the shelter. The greatest number described the relationship as very unhappy (49 percent). An additional 36 percent rated the relationship as fairly happy or so-so. In explaining their response, 34 percent said their relationship had had *some* good aspects, though 16 percent said the relationship had had *no* positive aspects and 26 percent cited arguments and tension as problems in their relationship.

Another measure of the nature of the relationship between the man and woman is the mutuality of their sexual relationship. When questioned about frequency of unwanted sex with their partner, 24 percent of the women reported that this occurred frequently to constantly; 26 percent said occasionally. Of the group who responded to the question of why they had participated in unwanted sex, 28 percent said they had done so because of fear, and 48 percent said because they had been forced to. As for the continuation of sex after an incident of battering, 8 percent reported that it always occurred afterward; 20 percent said frequently or very frequently; 30 percent said occasionally, and 11 percent said seldom. Of the women who indicated that sex had occurred, the primary reasons offered were: out of fear and because they were forced. The data reflect a significant amount of lack of mutuality between the men and women in the sample.

When questioned regarding prior separations from the battering partner 29 percent said this had occurred at least once over a year ago and 34 percent said this had occurred at least once during the year prior to entering the shelter. Only about one-quarter of the women (30 percent) reported no prior separations. Of the group that had separated, 16 percent remained away for one to three years; 11 percent for at least six months, but less than a year; 32 percent for at least one month, but less than six months; and 41 percent for less than one month.

The women who had left their partners were asked both why they had separated and why they had returned. The explanations that were given for returning included promised change by partner (22 percent); lack of alternative resources (10 percent); pregnancy or other child-related issues (10 percent); and continued feelings for the husband (7 percent). With regard to why the women had separated from the batterer, 47 percent cited abuse.

Relevant to the child's experience is information about how the women reacted to abuse. A series of possible reactions was read to each woman who was asked to indicate whether she "often, sometimes, rarely, or never" had experienced each. Table 2-2 shows the women's reactions and the degree to which they were depressed and embarrassed by the abuse.

An overwhelming majority reported that they have often experienced psychological distress such as feelings of depression, fear, helplessness, and embarrassment. Actual physical damage is rare for severe injuries requiring medical attention, but quite frequent for minor bruising. Homicidal thoughts against the aggressor are very prevalent (69%), with suicidal thoughts being experienced "often" or "sometimes" an impressive 41 percent.

These reactions serve to explain to some degree why it is so difficult for women to escape from an abusive situation. The high level of feelings of helplessness, failure, and worthlessness contribute to their inaction.

Nevertheless, some abused women eventually do leave home. What makes them take this uncertain step? Their descriptions of why they came to UFC provide some possible explanations. Fear for their lives is a major factor (82 percent), as well as fear that their children might be hurt (70 percent). Fear of what the children would think or do was also a major concern to 83 percent of the women.

Another point worth highlighting is that 53 percent of the women indicated they often thought of killing their mate after an abuse incident,

Table 2-2. *Frequency of selected reactions to abuse (%)*

Reaction	Often	Sometimes	Rarely	Never
Pain but no physical damage	65	21	10	4
Crying	78	8	6	8
Depression lasting several hours	82	11	3	4
Bruises, black eye, bloody nose	38	34	18	10
Broken bones or broken teeth	19	33	16	32
Scratches, cuts, or punctures	16	14	36	34
Injury requiring medical attention	11	4	19	67
Thoughts of killing mate	53	16	12	20
Thoughts of killing self	26	15	16	43
Fear for life	60	22	10	9
Helplessness, hopelessness, or chronic depression	65	21	5	9
Fear children would be hurt	55	15	8	22
Fear of what the children would think	69	14	6	11
Fear of what others will think	45	16	9	30
Embarrassment	66	17	6	11
Feeling like a failure or feeling worthless	55	16	9	20

and 16 percent sometimes considered this action. When seen in the light of the 41 percent who often or sometimes considered killing themselves, the level of frustration these women felt and the degree to which they thought of violent actions as a solution to their problems becomes apparent. (Of note is the fact that a cross tabulation of these two items shows there is a tendency to think about *both* killing oneself and one's mate (48 percent).

The question of how these women and their spouses or mates disciplined their children is relevant to our focal interest of detecting key mechanisms through which violence as a life-style transfers from generation to generation. The respondents were asked to describe the usual form of punishment they used with their children. Thirty-eight percent indicated they used physical means to punish their children. Fifty-six percent described themselves as generally using nonphysical punishment, (e.g., walking away, ignoring the child, withdrawal of pleasure). Six percent said they do not punish their children. Although a high proportion were using physical punishment, the percentage was lower than anticipated. The same was true of the previous mates' discipline methods, with 21 percent not disciplining at all and another 31 percent using nonphysical means. Thirty percent of the mothers reported that the spouse used slapping as a usual mode of discipline; 18 percent hit the children with an object or physically abused them. Respondents were asked whether any child had ever been seriously injured by the partner. A little over three-quarters of

Table 2-3. *Perceived frequency of violence in families of origin (%)*

	Often	Sometimes	Rarely/never
Witnessed parental argument	26	13	61
Hit with a strap (belt) or whip	21	30	49
Felt self to be an "abused child"	17	9	74

the women (78 percent) said that this had not occurred; however, 20 percent said that such an injury had occurred and 2 percent indicated they were unsure if such an injury had occurred.

Respondents were asked several questions regarding aggressive behavior among their children. Of those responding, 60 percent described at least one child as having one or more aggressive behaviors (including fighting, temper tantrums, behavior problems at school, trouble with the law, and stealing). Of the total group, 31 percent described one of their children as having one of these behaviors, 20 percent as having two behaviors, and 9 percent as having three to five aggressive behaviors. A further analysis of aggression among the children involved asking the mother if she assessed any of her children as violent. Twenty-three percent said they did, and 15 percent of the mothers reported that at least one child had hit them. Examining intergenerational transmission of violence in the parental generation, Table 2-3 shows some of the data gathered by Phillips and his colleagues on the women's perception of their family of origin and how they were disciplined as children.

The high proportion of women who state that they rarely or never witnessed parental discord would suggest that actual *modeling* of violent behavior was not an overwhelming determinant of violence in the contemporary parental generation. But because there is a widespread impression that the incidence of family violence is growing, this does not rule out an increase in importance of this mechanism for the current generation of children. Though 45 percent said that they had never received a severe beating from their parents, 27 percent indicated that they considered themselves to have been abused children, with 24 percent indicating that they had been the victims of rape or incest prior to age 18. Both of these figures are compared with the population at large.

Direct data on the individuals who battered the women respondents is lacking. The women's impressions of the batterers' past history provided the only available information, and predictably there was a high number of "don't know" responses. However, according to these data, the battered

Table 2-4. *Perceived frequency of violence in spouse's family of origin (%)*

	Often	Sometimes	Rarely/never
In-law parental argument	66	8	26
Spouse's experience of receiving severe beatings	41	15	44
Spouse's self-image as an abused child	33	12	55

women perceived the families of origin of their spouses to be much more violent than their own (Table 2-4).

In general, the reported levels of violence experienced was higher among the batterers than among their battered wives, but both were higher than in the population at large. For neither was this an exclusive background factor, indicating diverse etiologies.

As for the behavioral characteristics of children in the current sample, data from parental interviews, child interviews, observations in groups, and analysis of videotapes yield the following picture of the 250 children of 90 families seen:

Demand a lot of attention	35%
Are easily frightened	29%
Hang onto parent	28%
Have temper tantrums	21%
Cry a lot	17%
Are often nervous	16%
Worry a lot	14%

The first two problems are characteristic of children of all age groups at the center. Difficulties with schoolwork emerge early after school entry (age six) and continue into adolescence. Being easily influenced and fighting with siblings are also problems that emerge in this period and become more prevalent among the adolescents.

The children describe themselves as having a variety of psychosomatic symptoms and fears, including anxiety when separated from their mothers, nightmares, and trouble sleeping. They also choose adjectives to describe themselves which are positive – loving, happy, smart, and nice – in addition to those associated with violence, such as angry, worried, and having difficulty concentrating. Phillips observes that the overall impression is a mixture of feelings and ideas. Their characteristic mental state, then, contains a sense of confusion.

Further evidence for their confusion is seen in their response to a face test in which they had to choose the emotion being expressed. This is a test which is standardized for normal populations. The UFC children scored low where they might have been expected to score high (e.g., 65 percent correctly picking the frightened face versus a 98 percent, norm; 75 percent, the worried face versus 96 percent; 76 percent, the ashamed face versus 94 percent; and 80 percent, the angry face versus 98 percent).

When asked about specific emotions, they expressed more worry, shame, and fear than their counterparts, although for somewhat different reasons. They also picked a sadder face when asked to choose a face that reflected their overall feelings about themselves. The denial is seen in the confusion of feelings reflected in the "personal adjectives" used to describe the self.

Phillips contributes some further insights into what he considers to be the confusion of these children through his analysis of their videotaped behavior in the treatment groups:

The children appeared to have difficulty in figuring out what part violence plays in a "so-called" loving relationship and how they should behave during a violent scene. They seem to feel guilty that they could not prevent the violence in the family. They were also at a loss to explain why the violence occurred, in some cases holding onto the belief that somehow their mother must be at fault or that their father had been driven to such behavior by external pressures, (i.e., drug use, alcohol use, or demonic possession).

As a group they appeared to feel powerless, trapped, endangered. Their dreams reflected a fear that they might lose their mother and be at the mercy of a capricious world. Even more clearly than the interviews the groups reflect the children's need for assistance in learning to cope with the world around them. (1985)

With relation to the empathy variable specifically, the children were assessed on observed (videotape) behavior and also on their responses to questions designed to assess their levels of empathy. Compared with data from the other major studies, they showed similar empathy responses. This was contrary to expectations and disconfirmed the initial hypothesis.

While research instruments to measure empathy were being developed and applied, the intervention program for empathy training and instruments for monitoring it proceeded in its own way. Progress was slow, due to the complications mentioned above of role relations between researchers and clinicians, and by the housing strike introduced by the client families, as well as technical difficulties in working out the new instruments. But, in the end, both goals were achieved. Findings in relation to the effects of the intervention were positive. There was a statistically significant increase in the children's level of empathy after their participation in the program, lending support to the hypothesis that the experimental group would increase empathy levels. (See Bryant 1982.)

Phillips notes several possible interpretations of the findings:

> The measure of empathy may be inaccurate.
>
> Children from violent homes may be more sensitized to others in their intimate environment and thus more responsive to empathy training than those from nonviolent homes.
>
> Empathy may not be the key control variable in the transmission of violence but may only be significant as an accompaniment to other changes going on for these children.

Examining the changes in children at UFC generally, in experimental and comparison groups, Phillips analyzed changes detected between the point of entry and the point of exit in seven personality dimensions that are considered potentially problematic for children of this type: he reports very significant changes in levels of aggression, depression, irritability, and anxiety ($p < .0001$). Lower, but still significant, degrees of change were found in learning problems ($p < .05$), psychosomatic complaints ($p < .01$), and miscellaneous other physical symptoms ($p < .001$).

The fact that the findings did not confirm empathy level as a key control mechanism in the transmission of the violent tendency did not signal the end of interest either by research or agency staff in the social intervention of a special group for increasing interpersonal sensitivity in these children. The demonstrated effectiveness of the intervention in raising empathy levels, and the feeling that it made a valuable contribution to the program, led to a continued interest in it. Conceptually it led to a reconsideration of the concept of empathy and its relation to interpersonal sensitivity. Staff were interested in how it could be improved on the basis of their experience and wanted to incorporate it into a treatment program for children and families of this type.

To sum up the results, the ingredients of an empathy-raising program were found to be these:

- Provision of a safe environment where children feel free to talk
- Help for children in identifying their feelings in a violent family situation
- Provision of labels for feelings
- Help in finding ways to reach out to one another to form mutually understanding and helping relationships
- Discussion of alternative coping strategies in stress situations
- A coming to terms with loss and termination

Each of these ingredients serves as a focus for a session, and together they form the empathy development program, but they need not be seen as linear (i.e., learning one does not depend on having gone through the others). Indeed, in groups like those formed in shelters it is impractical to hold to a regime based on a linear assumption. Movement of children in and out of the center makes it necessary to reiterate in each session reasons for being there and the general themes, and then to work at seeing that all members are exposed to each of the items at some point in their stay.

The techniques used to elicit the items are flexible and open to change; however, there are some sequences which have shown themselves to be more effective. It is helpful for a child to have gone through the identification and labeling of feelings (by whatever techniques of role playing, drawing of faces, and so on) prior to the attempt to develop constructive ways of channeling feelings or linking them to appropriate actions.

The conclusions jointly reached by Phillips and Middleton-Jeter and the center staff were that the relation between empathy raising and other elements in a total push program in shelters such as this is an interdependent one. Other elements in an effective program are

  • Individual counseling. This is based on the findings of confusion and ambivalence in the children and mothers. The child had both negative and positive feelings about the batterer and confused feelings about the victim. The victim not only frequently fails to communicate her feelings but is frequently seen to resume an intimate relationship with the batterer. Both child and victim are frequently confused about the meaning of violence in their lives and how they feel toward all of the parties concerned. The type of clarification that is required is facilitated in individual counseling sessions.
  • Family therapy. This is based on the findings of the child's reluctance to communicate about what has happened – the familiar "family secrets." This may give rise to problems and to the establishment of communication blocks which could hamper the family's efforts to cope with stress generally. Family therapists are trained to elicit and work with materials of this kind.
  • Parent education. This is based on the finding that parents do not recognize the distinctive characteristics of their children's problems. Their awareness is improved through an educational program under the guidance of someone well versed in developmental psychology, clinical issues of children, and family dynamics.

As for the research in relation to program development, the project experienced a movement from initial skepticism on the part of agency staff to a position of enthusiastic support for the idea of action-research. Verona Middleton-Jeter states that the initial ethos in the unit was one in which "research" was a dirty word. It was seen as demanding, not returning anything for a long time while results were analyzed (by which time it might not be needed); and probably oriented to academic concepts and concerns rather than clinical ones (possibly even using "cooked" data to make an impression on academic audiences). She noted that the key to winning her support, and that of her staff, was the promise of interim "formative" feedback, acknowledged by Phillips as part of the trade-offs for the demands he would be making on staff time. Later, she was impressed with Phillips's concern with similar goals and values, feeling that there was a role overlap between them. Finally, when his results were disappointing in relation to the empathy hypothesis, she and her staff were impressed that he did not try to sweep the findings under the carpet but discussed with them the various ways these results might be interpreted. His image of professional integrity grew and, in putting forward their own ideas about the findings, the staff became increasingly involved in the wish to pursue the problem, both at a practical and at a theoretical level.

Kronenfeld notes,

> [The] action research efforts had some lasting effects on our program. We have incorporated the violence group as an on-going part of our battered women's program and have [been considering] the notion of using it in our regular homeless program on a selected basis as we find many of our families also ridden with violence.

Thus the innovation not only became "institutionalized" but was extended to other groups.

There has been continuity in the researcher's relations with the center staff, as both have an interest in translating the findings into improved programs and procedures. Though the initial formulation on empathy was found to be oversimplified and to need reexamination, the other findings were convincing. This allowed interest in the development of the special group to continue. The identification of a distinctive "child in a violent family" syndrome also provided stimulation for further collaborative effort.

Discussion

In this project the need for a new intervention was experienced in the agency setting with what Rein called "service worries." The concepts on which it might be based came from theory and previous research. The researchers were interested in testing the basic theory in the action setting. The agency provided access to cases difficult to reach on a direct-approach basis. Data on violent families obtained in this setting were likely to be more valid than is usually possible using cases where the situation has grown "cold." Also, research in this situation allowed for the testing of promising ideas in action more rapidly, without all of the intervening steps required when action and research are located in different settings.

In this project the new group method served as a vehicle for collaborative interaction between action personnel and researchers. Each side had a specific interest in developing it, and successful negotiations and trade-offs were conducted around it. The role overlap between researcher and agency staff allowed mutual understanding and trust to develop.

When results were available, the conceptualization for the specific action program was not empirically supported. Nevertheless, the research and clinical team responded interactively, reconfirming the importance of the program, regardless of whether the original hypothesis about empathy levels was proven. The manifest positive results experienced in the program were convincing, and there were many reasons for possible false negatives in the research scores.

In relation to the larger theoretical or academic context, this study may be linked to work on self-understanding, what Markus and Nurius (1984) refer to as *self-regulation theories*. There are four types: ego control theories; social learning theories; cognitive-behavior modification theories; and composite models of self-regulation. The present project can be classified in the fourth group, though the program based on it includes elements from the other theories as well, particularly ego control theories. Because the links between self-knowledge, social knowledge, and self-management are multidimensional (perceptual, cognitive, behavioral, attitudinal, emotional, situational, and so on) and change through time, the evidence supports a perspective which integrates the various dimensional theories (Markus and Nurius, 1984, p. 166 ff.).

Researchers whose work has concentrated on the question of continuity of changes induced by interventions have emphasized two elements: the impact of the intervention on the personality, and the presence of the environmental supports operating after the intervention (see, for example, Karoly and Steffen, 1980). Markus and Nurius note (p. 175) that there has been much more attention given to the former than to the latter. There has been less systematic inclusion of social system variables in behavior research than on the stimulus itself and the individual's response to it. There is a need for better models of how social systems influence behavior and how they operate differently at different stages of the child's development.

This project potentially contributes to this gap in knowledge by demonstrating a link between a child's development of self-control mechanisms and his or her understanding of his or her social situation. The mothers' participation in the program, by also modifying their understanding, alters their role in the child's postintervention environment. To determine how various combinations of change in the child and change in the parental behavior affect longer term child development, we would require follow-up studies.

The equivocal findings on empathy levels do not negate the interest in this variable. On the contrary, the negative findings have stimulated possible explanations which might lead both to improved theoretical conceptualization and improved action. For example, in Phillips's speculation that children who experience domestic violence become sensitized to empathy issues; these children may be hypersensitive rather than deficient in empathy. If they cover this over with a "normal" facade in responding to test situations, their empathy scores resemble those of the population generally. The possibility that there may be a sensitized substratum is suggested by their tendency to show outbursts of aggression when their defenses are loosened in the therapy groups. It would also explain their responsiveness to the group program. These observations would require comparative studies not possible within the framework of the current project. Empathy test scores were compared with known normal populations, but no other populations had experienced the empathy training program.

If support eventually accumulates for this explanation – that covers hypersensitivity rather than represents an atrophy of empathy – then this project will have contributed to a theoretical breakthrough in knowledge about self-systems and about self-regulation strategies, with corresponding implications for therapeutic groups.

What difference did it make that this was an action-research project rather than a basic academic study? Members of this project are convinced that it would have been difficult to get equally valid data by methods that were detached from the agency setting, because of the sensitivity of the subject and the tendency for subjects to deny their feelings about it. Phillips states that, for valid conceptualization as well as for expediency in obtaining cases, the researcher should be closely engaged and not work from a remote office. The agency team feel that research helped them to develop and explicate their treatment methods. They are raising new questions which they feel should be formulated in terms of mutual interests and answered by a collaborative-interactive approach. Middleton-Jeter states that if they do any more research, she wants it to be action-research.

In developing this intervention the initial hypothesis was useful, but the more interesting results came from the fact that a wide net was cast around it. The development of the work beyond the initial project will require a progressive narrowing of focus, but the collaborative experience allows this to be negotiation, with recognition of trade-offs between the requirements of the research and the requirements of the program. Both parties formulate their goals, find in them a set of joint objectives, develop a clarification of the roles they each must take if they are to proceed toward these objectives, take agreed actions, and evaluate progress and outcomes. To do so requires flexibility in handling some of the canons of "normal" science. However, the participants in this project argue that it is erroneous to assume that departures from the experimental design model necessarily entail a sacrifice of scientific validity. They also argue in favor of feedback of interim results, a practice frowned upon by many classical evaluators because of the impact on the program being evaluated. A final point argued by this team following their experience is that innovation requires changing the program toward what it *might* be if it is to be developed toward greater efficacy. Concentrating on how well it works while it is still fluid would give erroneous results. Feedback contributes to strengthening relevant parts of the program. The summative form of evaluation is appropriate when a program is fully formed and stabilized.

References

Bandura, A. 1975. *Aggression: A Social Learning Analysis.* Englewood Cliffs, N.J.: Prentice-Hall.

Beck, B. 1979. The Lower East Side Family Union: A social invention. Paper published by The Foundation for Child Development.

Brim, O. G., and Kagan, J. (eds). 1980. *Constancy and Change in Human Development.* Cambridge, Mass.: Harvard University Press.

Bronfenbrenner, U., and Cochran, M. 1985. The ecology of human development. In *Children, Youth and Families: The Action-Research Relationship,* ed. by R. N. Rapoport. New York and London: Cambridge University Press.

Bryant, B. K. 1982. An index of empathy for children and adolescents. *Child Development* 53:413–425.

Caplan, G. 1964. *Principles of Preventive Psychiatry.* New York: Basic Books.

Citizen's Committee for Children of New York (CCC). 1960. *Babies Who Wait.* New York.

Citizen's Committee for Children of New York (CCC). 1962. *Protecting New York City's Children.* New York.

Citizen's Committee for Children of New York (CCC). 1971. *A Dream Deferred.* New York.

Dobash, R. F., and Dobash, R. 1979. *Violence Against Wives.* Glencoe, Ill.: Free Press.

Dymond, R. F. 1949. A scale for measurement of empathetic ability. *Journal of Consulting Psychology* 14:127–133.

Fanshel, D. 1985. Early findings from a study of families at risk known to the Lower East Side Family Union. Manuscript. Columbia University School of Social Work.

Feshbach, N., and Feshbach, S. 1969. The relationship between empathy and aggression in two age groups. *Developmental Psychology* 1:102–107.

Finch, S. J.; Marsters, P.; Fanshel, D.; and Thode, H. C. Allocation of reported time to tasks based on reports submitted in a management information system. Unpublished data.

Finkelhor, D.; Gelles, R. J.; Hotaling, G. T.; and Straus, M. A. (eds). 1981. *The Dark Side of Families: Current Family Violence Research.* Beverly Hills, Calif.: Sage.

Folberg, J., and Taylor, A. 1984. *Mediation.* San Francisco: Jossey-Bass.

Freeman, M. D. A., 1979. *Violence in the Home.* London: Saxon House.

Freud, A., and Burlingham, D. 1944. *Infants Without Families.* London: Hogarth Press.

Gayford, J. J. 1975. Battered wives. *Medicine, Science and Law* 15:237.

Gelles, R. J. 1974. *The Violent Home*. Beverly Hills, Calif.: Sage.

Gelles, R. J., and Straus, M. A. 1979. Determinants of violence in the family. In *Contemporary Theories about the Family,* ed. by W.R. Burr et al. New York: Free Press.

Gerschenson, C. 1983. Personal communication.

Helfer, R. E., and Kempe, H. C. (eds). 1976. *Child Abuse and Neglect: The Family and the Community.* Cambridge, Mass.: Ballinger.

Holmes, T. H., and Rahe, R. H. 1967. The social adjustment rating scale. *Journal of Psychosomatic Research* 2:219–225.

Jones, M. A.; Neuman, R.; and Shyme, A. W. 1976. *A Second Chance for Families: Evaluation of a Program to Reduce Foster Care.* New York: Child Welfare League of America.

Karoly, P., and Steffen, J. (eds). 1980. *Improving the Long Range Effects of Psychotherapy: Models and Durable Outcome.* New York: Gardner Press (Wiley).

Katz, R. L. 1963. *Empathy: Its Nature and Uses.* London: Free Press of Glencoe.

Kempe, C. H. 1962. The battered child syndrome. *Journal of the American Medical Association* (July 7) 181: 17–24.

Kempe, C. H., and Helfer, R. E. (eds). 1972. *Helping the Battered Child and His Family.* Blackwell/Lippincott.

Kratcosci, P. 1984. Perspectives on intrafamily violence. *Human Relations* (June) 37(6): 443–453.

Lorenz, K. 1966. *On Aggression.* New York: Harcourt, Brace & World.

Maidment, S. 1985. Domestic violence and the law. In *Marital Violence,* ed. by N. Johnson, pp. 4–25. London: Routledge and Kegan Paul.

Markus, H. J., and Nurius, P. S. 1984. Self-understanding and self-regulation in middle childhood. In *Development During Middle Childhood,* ed. by W. A. Collins. Washington, D.C.: National Academy Press.

Marsters, P. A.; Finch, S. J.; Fanshel, D.; and Alvelo, J. Rates of reported resolution of problems of clients in a preventive service organization. Unpublished data.

McCubbin, H., et al. 1980. Family stress, coping and social support: A decade in review. *Journal of Marriage and the Family* (November) 42:855–871.

McCubbin, H., et al. 1985. Family dynamics. In *Children, Youth and Families: The Action-Research Relationship,* ed. by R. N. Rapoport. New York: Cambridge University Press.

Minuchin, S. 1984. *Family Kaleidoscope.* Cambridge, Mass.: Harvard University Press.

Moynihan, D. P. 1985. Newsletter. National Council on Family Relations.

Nagi, S., 1977. *Child Maltreatment in the United States: A Challenge to Social Institutions.* New York: Columbia University Press.

Olson, D., et al. 1983. *Families: What Makes Them Work?* Beverly Hills, Calif.: Sage.

Parad, H. J. (ed). 1965. *Crisis Intervention.* New York: Family Service Association of America

Phelan, J. F.; Slavson, S. R.; Epstein, N.; and Schwartz, M. 1960. Studies in group psychotherapy in residential treatment of delinquent boys. *International Journal of Group Psychotherapy* 10:174–212.

Phillips, M., 1981. The research design and its findings. In *Homeless Welfare Families: A Search for Solutions,* ed. by R. Leavitt. Proceedings of workshop, Community Council of New York.

Phillips, M. 1985. The needs of children from families where violence occurs. Paper delivered to the American Orthopsychiatry Congress, New York.

Phillips, M.; Kronenfeld, D.; Middleton-Jeter, V.; et al. 1981. *The Forgotten Ones.* New York: Henry Street Settlement Urban Life Center.

Phillips, M.; Lukens, E.; Casriel, C.; and Potts, J. 1984. Addressing the needs of children from families in which women are battered. The Henry Street Settlement Urban Family Center Experience. Unpublished report.

Rapoport, R. N. 1985. *Children, Youth, and Families: The Action-Research Relationship.* New York: Cambridge University Press.

Rapoport, R. N., et al. 1977. *Mothers, Fathers and Society.* New York: Basic Books.

Reid, W. J., and Epstein, L. 1972. *Risk Centered Casework,* New York: Columbia University Press.

Rosenbaum, A., and O'Leary, D. 1981. Children: The unintended victims of marital violence. *American Journal of Orthopsychiatry* 51:662–669.

Rutter, M., and Garmezy, N. 1983. *Stress, Coping and Development in Children.* New York: McGraw-Hill.

Sage, W. 1975. Violence in children's rooms. *Human Behavior* 4:47.

Schaefer, C. E.; Johnson, L.; and Wherry, J. N. 1982. *Group Therapies for Children and Youth.* San Francisco: Jossey-Bass.

Schulberg, H. C., and Killilea, M. (eds). 1982. *The Modern Practice of Community Mental Health,* San Francisco: Jossey-Bass.

Skynner, R., and Cleese, R. 1983. *Families and How to Survive Them.* London: Methuen.

Sussman, M., and Steinmetz, S. 1986. *Handbook of the Family.* New York: Plenum.

Stark, E.; Flitcraft, A.; and Frazier, W. 1981. *Wife abuse in the medical setting.* Washington, D.C.: Monograph no. 7, Office of Domestic Violence.

Straus, M.; Gelles, R.; and Steinmetz, S. 1980. *Behind Closed Doors.* New York: Doubleday.

Tinbergen, N. 1951. *The Study of Instinct.* Oxford: Clarendon Press.

Weissman, H. 1978. *Integrating Services for Troubled Families.* San Francisco: Jossey-Bass.

Weitzman, L. 1985. *The Divorce Revolution: The Unexpected Social and Economic Consequences for Women and Children in America.* New York: Free Press.

Westman, J. C. 1961. *Family Violence: Intervention Strategies,* by E. R. Barnett, C. B. Pittman, C. K. Dagan, and M. K. Salus, DHSS Publication No. (OHDS)80–30258. Washington, D.C.: Governmental Printing Office.

Zill, N. 1983. *Happy, Healthy and Insecure.* New York: Doubleday.

3   Schools

Between the ages of five and fifteen, most children spend much of their time in schools. Schools are meant to ensure the basic competence for children to learn the skills required for adult roles. Literacy, numeracy, conceptual development, and a sense of history are among the core elements of school programs. While it is recognized that schools have other functions (e.g., training for moral development, citizenship, social competence, and the development of personal interests), these are often implicit and unsystematized (Epps and Smith, 1984). Schools vary in their social structure, pupil composition, and physical plant as well as in the quality of their teachers; all these things affect the child's schooling experience (Rutter et al., 1979).

Schools represent the only set of social institutions that is commensurate with families in the influence they can have over a child's development after infancy. There is an enormous body of research which seeks to identify and assess the role played by school factors, as compared with family factors, in a child's development. One issue has centered on the degree of influence a school can have on a child's development, and the extent to which education can or cannot compensate for deficiencies in a child's biological background or early socialization (Jensen, 1969; Jencks et al., 1972).

The relationship between home and school has also been a topic of considerable research interest (see Litwak and Meyer, 1967; Anderson, 1982; Entwisle and Hayduk, 1978). Evidence indicates that children from disadvantaged home environments are less well prepared to fit into the competitive environment of the school. If this is further compounded by a lack of communication between parents and teachers, there may be an escalation of social and psychological disadvantage in later life. This perception contributed to the formulation of the Head Start program, which originally used a relatively simplistic psychological inoculation strategy. Those with deficits in their home environments would receive compensatory educational inputs to bring them up to the level of others, creating more equality of opportunity at school. Subsequent experience and associated research has contributed both to an improved theoretical conception and improved educational practices (Maughan and Rutter, 1985; Zigler and Weiss, 1985). The Head Start program was in effect a loose-knit form of action-research in that the development, both of program and theory, emerged from an interaction between researchers and action agencies.

The style and content of social science research in schools has varied in its conceptualization according to the discipline of the researcher and the characteristics and problems of the school setting. Sociological perspectives on schooling have viewed it as a social system that produces certain effects (Barr and Dreeben, 1983). Rutter and his colleagues (1979) demonstrated that at least some of the effects of different schools cannot be attributed to obvious physical factors, such as buildings and resources. They suggest that the crucial differences may be in nontangible social-psychological elements, such as morale or atmosphere (p. 21). Attempts to identify and analyze critical social-psychological processes have focused on the study of interpersonal relationships in schools, for example, teacher-student interactions (Dunkin and Biddle, 1974).

Recent studies have taken a multivariate approach by including independent variables from different systems: school organization, teaching approaches, individual student characteristics, and so on (see Walberg, 1981). A wide range of background variables are seen to be potentially operative, including family, socioeconomic status, home environment, parental influence, ethnicity, and peer relations. Another element in the broadening of interdisciplinary perspectives has been the enlargement of outcome variables from the narrow range of IQ scores and quantifiable examination achievements to include variables like self-esteem and social and social-psychological competence, but more research is needed on the measurement of these nonacademic aspects of the schooling experience (Epps and Smith, 1984, p. 322). Argyris and colleagues (1985) have focused on schools as organizations and have advocated something very close to an action-research approach to developing needed alterations in school structures.

Substantively, the priorities vary with political exigencies and local needs. A good deal of research has focused and will continue to focus on achievement and mastery – the cultivation of excellence in education. Other research has focused on schooling problems: alienation, dropping out, underachievement. Urban schools in disadvantaged areas of New York, Chicago, Los Angeles, and London share certain problems that are less conspicuous and pressing in the schools of smaller, less volatile settings, such as the mid-western town given the pseudonym Middletown, (Caplow et al., 1982). The patterning and priority of concerns will vary in different school settings, but in a larger sense they share the requirement of more adequate theories of stress and coping.

As for the role of action-research, Maughan and Rutter, in their review of action-research in education, argue that the approach is particularly useful to improving practice through increasing understanding of innovatory practices (1985, p.26). Though educators' values are favorable to collaborating with social researchers, the actual experience of collaboration has a checkered history. Building both on the successes of past collaborations and the lessons to be learned from disappointments (e.g., the EPA and School Desegregation programs), we are at a point where we may be able to develop more productive links between researchers and action agencies. Maughan and Rutter suggest that the areas most amenable to the action-research approach today should have the following characteristics:

- Ability to allow a true collaborative relationship to develop, with tolerance of differences in work modes
- Flexibility to adapt to the requirements of the project.
- Recognition that various stages of the work, from planning and development through project evaluation, pose different issues and problems
- Long-term commitments and support for sustaining the effort through the various stages
- Settings in schools and classrooms, as recognition of the realities of the social context – the joining of a quasi-experimental with a naturalistic approach

The three action-research projects presented here have relevance for all children, but with different issues salient in the various settings. They are a curriculum for developing social problem-solving skills in an elementary school; a mentoring role to operate in conjunction with a formal high school teaching program; and an adventure/discovery program, adapted to an urban school from the Outward Bound type of programs.

Case study: Social problem-solving curriculum

The social intervention in this project was the creation of a curriculum for improving children's social problem-solving skills.

The action-research project was initiated and co-directed by John Clabby of the University of Medicine and Dentistry of New Jersey (UMDNJ) Community Mental Health Center, and Maurice Elias of the Rutgers University Department of Psychology. Together they collaborated with Thomas Schuyler, first in his role as principal of a Middlesex County New

Jersey elementary school, and later as a middle school principal. The project evolved over a six-year period, 1980–86, beginning with 9-year-old children and continuing with children in junior high school up to age 13.

Background

This intervention addresses a range of children's school problems that are not attributable to any deficiencies in their intellectual capacities. Many educators observe that deficiencies in scholastic performance often seem to stem from the personal problems that students experience in their social relationships, particularly outside the school environment. In to-day's turbulent world, youngsters increasingly find themselves in situations calling for social competence beyond their capacities: disturbances in family and neighborhood life, demands of new situations for which they are unprepared, and uncertainties and anxieties of many kinds with which they are unable to cope. Even "normal crises" such as the birth of a sibling or death of a family member, may disturb tenuous adaptations. When not well handled, they may leave troublesome emotional repercussions. Problems of prejudice, family disturbance, migration, and divorce present even greater threats to a child's functioning and development.

Social adjustment problems can interfere with a child's psychological state and personal development, but the most salient issue for educators is how they might affect school performance. Research findings show that if a child feels stuck, helpless, or incompetent to handle the stresses of everyday life problems, educational performance is likely to be affected (Putallaz and Gottman, 1982).

The basic awareness and skills needed to handle these situations are ordinarily developed in the home. However, many homes are not well equipped to teach these skills, and some home environments add further strains to children's normal developmental problems. Often the range of situations encountered by the child exceeds those in the parents' own experience. The schools are not generally well set up to deal with problems of this type. If a student is extremely disturbed or handicapped, professional help may be employed, and special classrooms or schools have been developed to address these problems. However, the recent trend – and legislation – has been in the direction of "mainstreaming" many of these children and developing ways to address their needs in the context of regular classroom teaching. It is true that not all teachers have a natural bent for inculcating social skills along with the three Rs; this is not generally part of the educator's regular armamentarium.

Existing modes of schooling are very patchy in regard to developing social skills and Dooley and Catalano (1980) and Bronfenbrenner (1979), among others, have cautioned parents and educators not to assume that their children are being provided at school with the competencies needed to help them with the stresses of modern life. Some educators feel that they need to develop ways of teaching effective coping strategies to young children and are seeking new inputs to the school curriculum.

Scientific literature on the development of children's competence focuses of course, much more broadly than the school context. However, in the educational setting, a developing field of research aims to be useful, not only in a practical sense for immediate school use, but also in a general way by adding to the understanding of social skills development (Cartledge and Milburn, 1980; Camp and Bash, 1981). It has a multidisciplinary basis with educators, pediatricians, and social scientists, and some of its principal innovators have been Elardo and Cooper (1977), Spivack and Shure and their colleagues, (1976, 1978), and Cowen, Gesten and Weissberg (1975). They have each concentrated on different age groups (preschool through elementary school) with varying degrees of emphasis on the various components of the learning process. Elardo and Cooper emphasized the need to recognize feelings, highlighting the child's relatively undeveloped awareness in its own affectional responses. This lack of awareness of affect in responses to a problematic situation is seen as a key factor impeding learning and development. Clinical research had identified certain social problem-solving deficits as pivotal in relation to school adaptation. Spivack and Shure gave greater emphasis to cognitive elements, focusing on thinking processes and problem solving. Cowen and his colleagues attempted a synthesis of the two approaches, retaining an emphasis on cognitive elements.

In this particular case study, the importance of developing the *social* dimension of problem-solving skills was apparent to Clabby and Elias, and they set their sights on the task of specifying this dimension and incorporating it with the others into a single conceptual framework by building on the work of these pioneers in the field.

The action-research project

The project to be discussed is a multidisciplinary action-research project involving the collaboration of researchers and educators who feel that the development of conceptual and practical aspects of this process should go hand in hand and who are prepared to work on developing a curriculum and have their experimental application monitored.

The idea of developing an action-research project to achieve certain goals evolved in the minds of the investigators with the help of discussions with the William T. Grant Foundation action-research program officer and through the influence in their own discipline of community psychologists like Julian Rappaport and James Kelly. Clabby and Elias proposed that a curriculum be developed by collaborating with the teachers who would have to apply it as they taught children social awareness and social problem solving skills at school. They proposed to build on the device that was being developed elsewhere by the researchers mentioned above. They used Elardo and Cooper's book (1977) as a tangible example to teachers of the project they had in mind.

In their pilot work they demonstrated the procedure using the following framework: children are seated in a circle and a story is read to them containing some kind of problem – for example, a child is left out of a group and wants to join, or a child has difficulty showing his or her feelings and becomes upset. The children are led through exemplary problem-solving steps, and each child develops a solution. Several then role-play the solution while the others act as observers and discussants, using these instructions as a basis:

1. Look for signs of upset ("not-so-good" feelings).
2. Know exactly what the problem is.
3. Decide on your goal.
4. Stop and think before you act.
5. Think of as many solutions as you can to solve your problem.
6. Think of different things that might happen next after each solution.
7. When you think you have a really good solution, try it.
8. If you find solution doesn't work, be sure to try again.

The existing literature and techniques provided a springboard for the further development of this social intervention. While there was much to support the relevance and efficacy of the existing procedure, there were gaps in knowledge about its application to different settings and to different age groups, and above all in the area of strengthening the *social relationship* dimensions. Some of the challenges in further developing the work were methodological, and Clabby and Elias were prepared to take on the challenges of evaluating efficacy.

The background ingredients for the development of the project were, therefore, these:

- A social intervention which had potential for further development
- A favorable field/laboratory setting. Local schools recognized the problem and there was legislative sanction for the schools doing something about it. The specific school principal, Tom Schuyler, was eager to build on the preliminary discussions with the researchers and was influential in his local area. The Middlesex Borough school system in New Jersey was

a multiethnic, predominantly blue-collar, community of about 15,000 people.

- A Community Mental Health Center to administer and encourage this development. Located at the University of Medicine and Dentistry of New Jersey, the center and its consultation staff were searching for more effective ways of meeting the mandates for providing preventive services. There was a general recognition that the research base for such services needed strengthening (Cowen, Gesten, and Weissberg, 1975; Rappaport, 1977; Klerman, 1985). At the UMDNJ & Community Mental Health Center, the specific staff psychologist, John Clabby, had begun forming a good working relationship with the local schools, thus providing a point of entry and potential for growth in this direction.
- Academic involvement to bolster the scientific component. The partnership with Maurice Elias of the Rutgers University Department of Psychology provided both a technical component and a formal link to the academic department. For his part, Elias was intrigued by the possibility of continuing problem-solving research he had begun while in graduate school. It provided an opportunity to study behavior using an action-research paradigm. This approach emphasizes the role of real-life influences, and he regarded it as an opportunity to increase the scientific validity of academic formulations, though he recognized that pursuing this approach exposed him to risks in relation to orthodoxies of his parent department, which favored the more controlled experimental research paradigm.
- A shared conviction among the three principal participants (Clabby, Elias, and Schuyler) that (1) an effective device could be developed to improve children's capacity to cope with social problems in their lives; (2) the device could be fed into a school program for application; (3) it could be evaluated using rigorous scientific methods; and (4) it could be continuously developed and disseminated for wider application.

Their goals were multiple: to conduct field trials and quasi-experimental evaluation of a new curriculum; to institutionalize it in the schools; to improve and disseminate it more widely in the educational system; and to contribute to scientific knowledge through encouraging research in association with the practical program.

Research design and methodology. The goal of the project was to develop and evaluate a device to teach children social problem-solving skills. The type of device wanted was something like that reported by Elardo and Cooper, only enlarged to cover a broader conception of social competence than their awareness of affect; it required both improvement to meet scientific aspirations and adaptation to meet educational requirements. Three tasks were envisaged: develop the device, incorporate it into a school curriculum, and evaluate it by applying it to one or more experimental groups and comparing the results with matched control groups. Pilot work, described above, had demonstrated feasibility. What was required now was final specification of the device as an innovative experimental intervention, and similar specification of instruments for measuring results.

Results were conceptualized in terms of a number of dependent variables which the intervention aimed to affect:

> The incidence of behavioral, emotional, and academic problems
> The development of general social and academic problem-solving skills, such as resourcefulness, competence, and self-confidence
> The child's application of the acquired skills to his or her own behavior in coping with transition into the middle school

A moderating variable was hypothesized to be the child's family environment.

Finally, the project aimed to disseminate the findings both to the local schools and beyond, and to the academic/scientific community.

The design of the project involved four phases:

1. A *pilot* stage to develop the intervention, train teachers, and conduct field trials
2. An *implementation* stage, to apply the innovating curriculum to experimental and control groups
3. An *evaluation* stage, to measure results
4. A *dissemination* stage

The first three stages each had an associated methodology as well as a goal. (See page 97.)

In this framework, it is notable that the research staff role varied with each phase. In the earlier phases, the staff's "formative" evaluation techniques allowed a close interactive participation with the school staff. In later stages, where the staff's evaluations were "summative," a more detached mode was adopted.

The phases covered a four-year period, and led into the final phase of dissemination, which took various forms: reports to the schools, papers presented at professional conferences, publications in the form of journal papers and books, and public presentations and discussions.

From the outset, the design of the project included an orientation that emphasized its shared character, that of researchers and teachers cooperating to develop an intervention that would benefit children and advance knowledge. Importance was attached to the idea of researchers working *with* teachers to develop the project, rather than, as many conventional university-based projects, of doing their research *on* teachers and children.

Course of the project. A pilot study was conducted in the spring of 1980 during which the Elardo and Cooper curriculum was tried out in the

Stage	Investigator involvement	Instrumentation
1. *Pilot* Develop the intervention Train the teachers Conduct field trials with comparison groups	Research staff to become informal part of the school, collaborating with teachers in trials (participant observation)	Social awareness/social problem-solving curriculum
2. *Implementation* Application of the stabilized form of curriculum to experimental and control groups, fourth- and fifth-classes	Reversion of researchers to specialist roles as external resources to the schools, available to train teachers in the use of the curriculum and to help children in need of therapy at the Community Mental Health Center	Extension of the application of the stabilized curriculum through creating a role of "master teacher," with original teachers training new staff in the new curriculum
3. *Evaluation* Administration of test instruments and questionnaires	Detached role of researchers emphasized	Social Problem Situation Analysis Measure (SPSAM) Group Social Problem Solving Assessment (GSPSA) Behavioral index (AML Rating Scale) Behavior pathways (questionnaire) Affectional development (interpersonal sensitivity indices in SPSAM and GSPSA) Social competence scores (peer nominations, school achievement scores, effort grades, etc.)

fourth-grade classes (one each in Hazelwood and Parker schools), while three other fourth-grade classes in those schools served as controls.

Working collaboratively with the teachers selected by Schuyler as being skillful in leading class groups and motivated to try a new approach, Clabby and Elias were able to establish a viable teaching curriculum and to develop data collection methods that ranged from codes for classroom observations to instruments for measuring change in the students.

From mid-January through May, there were two 40-minute lessons per week, per class, initially led by Clabby, who was educator/clinician at UMDNJ, and later led by classroom teachers trained by Clabby and Elias.

The children sat in a circle and each child gave his or her name and anything else he or she wished to tell the group. They were then read a problem story from the Elardo and Cooper procedure as already described.

Although data gathered during the first year was regarded as only exploratory because the procedures were not yet crystalized, there were indications that the effects on children were in the expected direction. The initial teachers remained enthusiastic; 95 percent reported improved coping, and 80 percent of the children were observed to try to help others with problems. Longer term effects and more controlled measures of effect would have to wait, but the tasks of revising and stabilizing the procedures and testing out their viability in the school context were accomplished.

An unexpected element arose at the end of the first year. Parents demanded that the social problem-solving (SPS) lessons be given to all four primary schools, not just the two experimental schools. This created the need for a larger cadre of trained and motivated teachers. As a solution, staff and teachers created a new role model: a master teacher, who would have the responsibility of modeling for the larger staff the skills that would be required. This was a truly collaborative act, because it could only be done through the school system with its carefully graded ranks and reward levels.

The enlargement of the sample had some positive consequences. From the point of view of the researchers it enhanced the analytic possibilities. As the two new schools were added only in February 1981, the students received only the instruction phase (i.e., that part of the program that emphasized teaching the eight-step problem-solving strategy). This created a quasi-experimental situation and prompted the question of whether the children receiving both instruction and application phases (the latter involving lessons that systematically applied problem solving to academic and interpersonal issues) would report fewer social problems of less magnitude than the children who received only the instruction phase, when both groups of children moved into the middle school. An invaluable component of the design was the availability of baseline data from students who entered middle school in September 1981 without having received SPS lessons. Their scores on a survey of middle school stressors served as an additional basis for comparison. From the point of view of the Community Mental Health Center, the expansion also had the advantage of providing a wider context for community liaison. The extra demands on funding were met by the schools and the Rutgers University Research Council.

In the second year, there was greater activity from the parents' side, with problematic and beneficial consequences. It had always been the intention of the researchers to take into account the parental variables involved, but the delicate issue of how to handle parental concerns with interventions into the social and affect domains – areas generally regarded as "family" concerns – became salient at this point. This potentially touchy issue was dealt with by arranging "family nights" at the school, in which family life/health issues, rather than purely school topics, were discussed. Parents were encouraged to take an interest in social problem-solving skills much in the same way as parents had been encouraged to take an interest in their children's cognitive development by reading to them. School newsletter articles describing the SPS activities were regularly written and distributed.

With the proliferation of classes, the introduction of parents meetings, and the progress of the children toward the transition into junior high school, attention had to be given to securing a larger financial base. The review by the foundation required the team to think more explicitly about action-research methodologies and theory. The concepts which they had developed, "role overlap" and "ownership," became more explicit and salient in this connection. The team wrote papers expounding the importance of these concepts in the development of a multifaceted action-research project such as this. The role overlap concept, which resembles the "co-learning" concept developed by Eric Trist and others, came to be seen as an important element in providing the continuing cohesion in the relationships: the educator's interest in psychology, the clinician's interest in research, and the academic's interest in applications. It is the team's attention to cultivating a sense of ownership of the project in the teachers and later the parents that has allowed the project to overcome some of the potential threats to its continuity and increase motivation to develop the teaching materials and train new staff. It also has increased the family's capacity to view what is being taught as constructive, despite its potential revelation of their deficits. This sense of ownership expands on such earlier concepts in the action-research literature as "stakeholders" and "constituents."

Also during the first two or three years it was the experience of teachers (and research staff) of being able to use the social problem-solving methods being taught in the curriculum to deal with their own problems. The principal found that they were useful to him in dealing with administrative problems and the majority of those who participated felt the program was genuinely useful and valuable.

As further results became available about the children's use of SPS methods and their effectiveness in helping them make the transition from primary school to middle school, the project itself began to move "upward." Teachers in the primary school became a self-sustaining group that could operate the curriculum without further significant developmental input from the researchers. However, initial work in the middle school made it clear that there could be no automatic and mechanical adaptation of the curriculum. Further exploratory research was called for to clarify the problems and identify the possible new intervention devices. The possibility of doing this as collaborative action-research was bolstered by Schuyler's movement upward into a principalship in the middle school.

Results

The results of the pilot study (January through June 1980) showed that the children made clear gains in their sensitivity to others and used more appropriate problem-solving strategies, especially when faced with interpersonal obstacles.

In a subsequent study, an attempt was made to measure the impact of training when children faced a stressful life event (i.e., entry into middle school) several months after completing the prevention program (Elias, Ubriaco, and Gray, 1987). Children receiving three levels of SPS training were compared. These levels included children receiving both instructional and application phases of the curriculum; children receiving the instructional phase only in the second half of the school year; and children entering middle school in the prior year without having received any SPS intervention.

First, the two schools receiving full training were compared with the two schools receiving partial training; children's responses were rated on a scale describing 28 middle school stressors. A significant difference was found between full-/and partial-training conditions. The children receiving only the instruction phase reported a more stressful reaction for 24 of the 28 stressors than did children receiving both instruction and application phases. Eleven of these differences were significant, in the areas of logistics of adjusting to middle school, adjusting to academic requirements, and coping with peer pressure.

Next, the researchers examined whether children who received at least *some* social problem-solving would report fewer or less severe difficulties than children with *no* training. Similarly, an analysis of individual stressor items showed that 14 items were significantly more stressful for the group receiving no SPS training. Overall, then, the results suggested that full training was superior to partial training and that both conditions were associated with a significant reduction in children's self-reported level of difficulty with commonly occurring stressors in middle school.

In a unique final step, the researchers sought to establish the specific role of social problem-solving skills in mediating children's responses to troublesome aspects of middle school. They used canonical correlation to compare stressor responses with children's SPS scores. The relationship was mainly between the problem-solving skill areas of "interpersonal sensitivity and problem analysis and action" and the two domains of stressors, concerned with "peer pressure" and "coping with authority-conflict." The greater the children's problem-solving skills, the less they reported difficulty with the two sets of stressors (Elias, Bruene, et al., 1985).

In summary, there was a positive association between the level of training and the children's reports of coping with stressors and adjusting to middle school, and that social problem-solving was an important aspect of this shared variance. These results could not be attributed to preexisting differences related to the children's elementary schools or to marked differences in the degree of stressors encountered by students from one year to the next. Empirical support was found to suggest that a consistent mediating factor in children's responses to stressors was indeed their social problem-solving skills, providing a strong linkage of the social intervention to a real-world, important outcome (Elias and Clabby, 1984).

Aside from the main pattern of results, which were reported in the team's publications, there were a number of ancillary results and seren-dipities which may feed into subsequent projects. One was in relation to gender differences. Boys, for example, tended to be more concerned with work overloads and homework problems, while girls tended to be more concerned with peer pressures, making new friends, being seen undressed in the locker rooms, or being teased. Another set of ancillary findings had to do with families.

An improved conceptualization of the action-research methodology was an important secondary finding. The concepts of "ownership" and "role overlap" were developed in the course of the project and have been discussed extensively and published.

The initial goal of the project – the development of the instrument itself – was achieved by the end of the first phase, and has been consistently applied in the various ways intended. The stabilized form of the curriculum, as it evolved through this formative period, took shape as a two-year program. Renamed the Improving Social Awareness–Social Problem Solving (ISA-SPS) curriculum, it is generally operated by a regular classroom teacher in the framework of a health or social studies course. The teacher leads two 40-minute classes per week in social problem solving. The curriculum is organized into three separate phases, which marks a departure from other available social problem-solving curricula.

The readiness phase: Unit I, developing self-control skills; unit II, developing group and social awareness. A 16-lesson set was developed in response to teachers' input stating that a number of the children were just not ready to sit down as a group to discuss problems. They felt that the students needed to develop such skills as listening, waiting for their turn to speak, and giving and receiving compliments. So during the first two months of both years of the curriculum the children are readied for group problem-solving.

The instructional phase: Unit III, understanding feelings, problems, goals; unit IV, decision-making thinking; unit V, planning, obstacles, action. The children learn the eight problem-solving steps, covering one step at a time, together with a review of those covered previously. In a typical lesson they arrange their chairs into a circle format, briefly share what they are currently experiencing, and review whichever social problem-solving steps have been learned thus far. There is emphasis on teaching the steps *explicitly*. All of the classes have large poster boards on which the steps that have been learned to date are listed. They are frequently referred to by teachers and the students.

   Following a review of the steps, the "new" social problem-solving step is introduced and discussed. On the fourth-grade level, a fourth-grade problem story is read to the children (in an animated, engaging manner), who then systematically apply the problem-solving steps to the situation. In the fifth grade, the problem stimulus is presented on videotape, using selected programs from the "Inside-Out" series produced by the agency for Instructional Television. Role-play is used to follow up class discussions and to teach children to put their skills to use.

The application phase: Unit VI, applications to academic and real-life situations. In this final portion of the fourth- and fifth-grade curriculum, the emphasis is on encouraging the children to generalize what they have learned and apply it to real-life and academic situations. The children are asked to collect examples of the opportunities they have had to use social problem-solving in their own lives. For example, they learn how problem-solving skills can be helpful to them in knowing how to use the library creatively for writing assignments.

Another ancillary finding was that referral rates to the Community Mental Health Center from Middlesex Borough (all schools) showed a meaningful decrease from original baseline rates, in contrast to adjacent comparable boroughs where no problem-solving programs were in place. Those Middlesex youngsters who were referred to showed a similar range of presenting problems, but they appeared to be functioning at a higher level overall and to identify earlier those problems requiring additional help than comparable youth from adjacent towns (Gara, 1984). The trend was replicated for two successive years, and the project leaders concluded that there was empirical support for the proposition that teaching the ISA-SPS curriculum had a positive impact on mental health (Elias, 1982; 1983; Elias and Maher, 1983).

There was also a marked positive impact on teachers' perceptions of their students' behavior and how they thought about handling problem situations. In relation to the teaching program, the use of the curriculum was considered an effective supplement. It provided a way of strengthening social problem-solving skills for children, teachers, and parents.

In assessing the outcome of the training in relation to adaptation in the middle school, a new range of issues emerged along with the findings on the problems of transition. Two points of application were suggested: that in the elementary schools' SPS curriculum, it was better to anticipate the coming stress patterns; and that in the middle school itself, it was better to provide a new phase-specific intervention for the different problems of early adolescence.

In the fourth year, a crisis developed during which one of the experimental schools was closed and the students redistributed among the other schools. While this presented problems with design and scheduling, it also presented an opportunity to observe the students' use of the problem-solving framework to adapt to the new schools. There were several other circumstances in which teachers' or students' coping capacities were tested in unexpected problem situations. The schools' commitment to their problem-solving framework was solidified through repeated small examples of its usefulness to both students and staff.

The strong demand for involvement by parents, and the research team's response to include them, subsequently led to additional unexpected results. Because academic and professional specialization has separated work in the educational and family-research fields, there have been few attempts to use similar instruments to assess family socialization practices and school socialization methods. There is very little written on the social and cognitive problem-solving skills taught in the family. Shure and Spivack (1978) established a correlation between mothers' and daughters' levels of social-cognitive problem-solving skills. They gave several possible reasons for it: mothers may use direct reinforcement of their daughters' competent performances, or they may teach informally by modeling the appropriate behavior for the child, or by verbal instruction, or by inducing or encouraging self-monitoring of reactions in performance situations. There are indications in current research that all of these mechanisms are operative, but little to indicate how they relate in specific cases to school behavior (Shure and Spivack, 1978; Siegel and Saunders, 1979; Baumrind, 1971; Hoffman, 1970; McGillicuddy-De Lisi, Sigel, and Johnson, 1979). Elias and his colleagues employed a case-study method to analyze data from participating families, systematically assessing several of the postulated mechanisms simultaneously (rather than one by one, as is common among specialist adherents to the various schools of psychology). Information about parental beliefs of how children learn and parents' teaching strategy is related to the child's social-cognitive problem-solving style and the child's school adjustment score. The analysis is suggestive for hypothesis generating and theory development and is not conclusive. It takes the form of formulating a set of postulates derived from the literature and exploring them with parents of the children in the study. The postulates are stated in the following list.

1. If parents believe that a child primarily learns through his or her own experiences, then parental teaching strategies should primarily involve asking and suggesting, and the result for the child should be positive social problem solving.

2. If parents believe that a child primarily learns through parents' logical explanations, then parental teaching strategies should primarily involve suggesting and telling, and the result for the child should be positive social problem solving and positive behavior.

3. If parents believe that a child primarily learns through adults' rewards and punishments, and parental teaching strategies involve telling, the result for the child should be negative social problem solving and positive behavior.

4. If parents believe that a child primarily learns through adults' rewards and punishments, and parental teaching strategies involve frequent use of positive and negative comments, then
   a. If positive comments are used almost exclusively, the results for the child should be positive social problem solving and negative behavior.
   b. If negative comments are used almost exclusively, the results for the child should be negative social problem solving (behavioral outcomes can be mixed).

c. If a balance of positive and negative comments are used, the results for the child should be positive behavior (social problem solving can be mixed).

In general, they found that the postulates "were useful guidelines for predicting school adjustments." In particular, the cases supported the first postulate. However, they found that the link between parental strategies and social-cognitive skills learning is not the same as that between parental strategies and school adjustment (the two are not intercorrelated in this sample). One of the advantages of the case-study method was that they were able to gain some insights into why this might be. Qualitative analysis indicated that where there was parental disagreement on beliefs and strategies, the conflictual interactions might not impair the social-cognitive skills development (indeed, might stimulate them), but they were likely to foster social maladjustment (cf. Rutter, 1980; Siegel et al., 1980). This kind of suggestive finding would not have been as likely to turn up if the study had taken only the child and the available parent, as in some earlier studies. In addition, a holistic approach to family studies allowed some insights into how different issues faced by families at different stages of the family cycle might generate different patterns of engagement with the child, and therefore result in different effects on the child's social competence in school.

In relation to the project's dissemination goals, the involvement with the families provided both the stimulus and the substance for a book *Teach Your Child Decision Making* (Clabby and Elias, 1986). For the Community Mental Health Center, a salient outcome was that the project promoted early detection of mental health problems in children and reduced the load of mental health problems in the target age group as compared with neighboring towns. This reinforced the impact of the direct research findings.

For the university, affirmation of the scientific validity of the project came with approval from the scientific review panels of funding sources, the acceptance of project-derived publications into the professional literature, the successful completion of a number of student projects and theses, and recognition of the project as an exceptional prevention program by the American Psychological Association's Task Force on Prevention, Promotion, and Intervention Alternatives in Psychology.

Discussion

Several elements of this project are relevant. First, as an action-research project, it illustrates the importance of a differentiated model of collaboration rather than the researcher-action agency pairing. As in technological fields, the importance of a team effort is seen, in this case with a tripartite input. The tripartite structure implies validation in three spheres: educational, clinical, and academic. The project provides sufficient yield to establish itself as valuable in all three spheres: academic papers and student theses have counted for something in the university department; teacher enthusiasm and the willingness to continue the curriculum beyond the experimental stage established the utility of the project in the educational setting; and, paradoxically, lower severity of problems (i.e., secondary prevention) validated the utility/efficacy of the project for the Community Mental Health Center. This is paradoxical because the clinic has two goals somewhat at odds with one another: to develop a new outreach preventive service in the community, and to provide therapeutic assistance for those in need. To the extent that the first is effective, the need for the second diminishes. And, despite the tendency in clinical settings to be facility oriented, the project demonstrated the value of using the center's staff to reach out and work with as many people as possible effectively to reduce stress in the community.

From the point of view of the educator, the project experience was instructive, both in terms of the complexities of developing a program of this kind (and disseminating it) and in the ways in which modifications were required for application to different settings. Schuyler does not see this as fundamentally different from other educational innovations, however. He writes in response to the question of what changes in the method occurred:

Our basic methods have not changed, however we have greatly improved upon them. This was done by adding and changing parts of the curriculum. It is like teaching any given subject. The basic vehicles remain, but they are tuned and polished for greater effectiveness. Methods were also improved and this was done through in-service training given to the staff. . . . The project has added additional vehicles at different grade levels to teach Social Problem Solving, but they all stay with the original concept and that is how to solve social problems by thinking things through and planning a step by step course of action.

Schuyler notes that in the course of developing this project, and with its growth and success, as well as its difficulties in establishing itself, the team encountered every conceivable type of problem that could be associated with a project such as this:

Apathy, disbelief, jealousy and fear. Parents and school personnel were not always ready to cooperate and often caused serious difficulty as we progressed. These problems were dealt with by using *every* strategy the leaders could employ to overcome obstacles that came before us.

In the end, the problem locally was to contain dissemination at a level that could be handled with available resources, rather than to get people to accept the program.

Serendipities, and the constructive use of opportunities arising, are seen in four events during the development of this project:

> The pressure to include additional schools
> Parental pressures for participation
> The early closure of one of the elementary schools
> Schuyler's move to another school

The request for larger participation strained the team's resources, but was responded to by the development of a more scripted curriculum that was less dependent on classroom consultation by project staff. This had the effect of enlarging the sample and the range of situations covered, making it possible to develop the quasi-experimental aspects of the project and to conduct multivariate analyses. The unexpected demand for parental involvement also enriched the project. By adding the parental participation there were not only gains from the point of view of facilitating the project by giving a *quid pro quo* to parents, but also a gain of knowledge through what was learned about parental knowledge and teaching strategies in the home. It became possible to learn more about how parents interact with teaching strategies being given to their children in the schools. A paper on this topic was published in the *Journal of Applied Development Psychology* by Elias, Ubriaco, and Gray (1987), and in a book addressed to parents (Clabby and Elias, 1986).

The third serendipity came from the closing of an experimental school. This detracted from the execution of the original design, but provided a valuable opportunity to observe how the students concerned coped with the "real" new challenges; in a conventionally designed project, they might simply have been dropped from the sample.

A fourth serendipity is in relation to Schuyler's moving up to the principalship in the local junior high school. The project would have had to face the issue of continuity at some point, but this precipitated the choice of one among the several logical possibilities. They chose to "move up" with Schuyler, rather than continuing to develop the instrument in the same setting, perfecting its form and execution, refining the associated family studies, and so on. In so doing, they concentrated on another element in the initial formulation, namely, the relevance of social problem-solving skills for the transition into junior high school. Initially in the background, this element became more prominent as the project proceeded. By focusing on the transition, the authors chose to develop the formulation of Felner and associates (1975). They identified five tasks to be accomplished in coping with the stresses of a school transition: (1) to shift role definitions and expectations; (2) to shift social networks and group membership; (3) to reorganize personal social support resources; (4) to make a cognitive self-reappraisal; and (5) to manage the stress resulting from uncertainty of expectations in the new situation (Elias, Bruene et al., 1985). The identification of tasks associated with the particular type of stressor brought the project's findings into the sphere of interest of the family life-cycle and life-span developmental researchers.

In following the students trained in the elementary school in their adjustments to the challenges of junior high school, Clabby and Elias were impressed by the fact that though the social problem-solving model worked for people of all ages in a wide range of situations, the way it was taught in elementary school did not work for a junior high school curriculum. Nor would there be the same reasons for staff collaboration. New formats would have to be devised geared to the new tasks the pupils faced, and a new rationale found for introducing it into the school. The previous rationale of outside stressors affecting school performance was still relevant, but not so salient. The researchers felt that something more in the area of discipline and relations with authority would be likely to offer relevance to both pupils and teaching staff. Accordingly, it was around this focus that the next phase of the work developed, with federal funds added to the Grant Foundation support.

Case study: The mentor role

This was a pilot project to clarify the concept of a mentoring role and to identify issues associated with its feasibility and effectiveness as a new intervention in the New York City schools. It was initiated by Frank Riessman of the Graduate Center of the City University of New York (CUNY) New Careers Training Laboratory. Andrew Humm of the university's Department of Education was project director. The pilot study took place between August 1982 and July 1984.

Background

At a very general level, there had been widespread dissatisfaction with the city schools' capacity to cope with their teaching responsibilities. Beset by high drop-out rates, a high incidence of truancy, violence, academic underperformance, classroom disturbance, and student alienation, staff had become increasingly dissatisfied, as indicated in various stress manifestations, such as high teacher turnover and low morale.

The Board of Education was trying to deal with the problems in various ways, ranging from alternative schools to remedial teaching and specialist consultations. The scope and vigor of the city's programs led to the impression that the city had been attempting an educational reform movement. For many within the educational establishment, this reform movement had as its principal focus the need to raise academic standards, generally associated with a tightening of discipline and recruitment of specialist experts both for teaching and nonteaching roles in the schools.

The idea of a mentoring role came to Riessman and to the school chancellor independently but with different emphases. Riessman's emphasis is perhaps best expressed in a letter he wrote to the editor of the *New York Times* after the project was well under way. He took issue with the view expressed in another article on the need to concentrate on standards of academic performance.

Praiseworthy as it is, the new consciousness about schools offers proposals that rest upon an extremely faulty assumption, namely that by demanding more of students – higher standards, more homework, more discipline – they will automatically comply.

This assumption completely overlooks the relevance of motivation and student involvement. Unless the students are self-motivated, little will happen, and they will continue to drop out. In fact, the students have been the initial critics of the schools as they tuned out, acted out and dropped out long before the new critics arrived on the scene. Unfortunately, their reactions went unnoticed and are in no way incorporated in the new reforms from above.

There is a strong need to redesign schools for real input from the students. Fortunately, we have many examples in alternative schools, demonstrating considerable success in reducing absenteeism and drop-outs when the students are involved. (Riessman, 1984)

The social intervention

Initially the intervention of the mentor role was at the conceptual level. As part of the long-term interest in broadening the structure of school teaching, Riessman and his colleagues saw peer counseling, peer tutoring, paraprofessional roles, and the like as part of a fundamental restructuring of the educational process (cf. Gartner, 1971; Gartner, Kohler, and Riessman, 1971).

Part of the body of academic knowledge and experience associated with this attempt to achieve structural changes in education was the interest in mental health and mental handicap. Recent studies at the CUNY laboratory had demonstrated the efficacy of the introduction of paraprofessional roles in the education of handicapped children (Caplan, 1974; Pickett and Humm, 1981). The mentoring role was conceived also as a kind of support role, now widely recognized as a potential buffer against stress (Schulberg and Killilea, 1982).

The mentor concept is traced to the Greeks. The term deriving from Mentor, friend of Odysseus, to whom he entrusted the care of his son, Telemachus, when he set out for Troy. From this, the term has come to mean a "wise and faithful friend and monitor" *(Webster's Third New International Dictionary)*. Use of the term in the social sciences has been mainly in relation to career development. For example, Daniel Levinson and coworkers (1978), in a study of men at midcareer, found that most of them recalled having benefited from a relationship of this type. Levinson used the term *mentor* for a more senior and experienced person who takes a special interest in a younger protégé. The concept of mentoring has also been used in relation to helping women who are breaking into new careers and find themselves confronted with challenges for which they have not been adequately prepared. Coaching from someone not directly involved in their immediate setting has proven valuable, and the concept has found its way into feminist career guidance and assertiveness training programs.

The mentor concept has also been used explicitly in educational contexts. Empire State College, for example, appoints community people – poets, playwrights, and others – as mentors for their students taking external degrees. Some university programs use the term to refer to the personal (as distinct from technical) help that a faculty member gives to a student or junior colleague. In some fellowship programs, one criterion for making an award is that the grantee have a designated mentor – that is, someone in a senior established position who will take an interest in seeing that the younger person is appropriately guided. At the heart of the mentoring concept are two elements: a more experienced person helping a less experienced one, and a one-on-one relationship that goes beyond the minimal obligations of a formal teaching or supervising role. A third element, its informal voluntary character, is more variable. There has been a mounting consensus that mentoring is important in various ways and at various stages in the educational and career development of most people (cf. Bolton, 1980; Bradley and Adamson, 1973; Collins and Scott, 1978; Roche, 1979).

The goal of the CUNY project was to define a mentor role that could be introduced and become viable in the school system. This constituted a "reinvention" of the concept itself (ie., defining it in terms meaningful to those involved in its use), and also the need for recruitment and training of prospective mentors and the preparation of the system into which the mentors were to function. Thus the concept was identified by the researcher as a useful idea (a type I invention) in relation to needed changes in schools. The researcher also took a lead in translating the concept into a viable role (transforming it into a type II invention) to be operated by the schools. In doing this the researcher acted in the type of role identified by Miles and Huberman (1985) as a "linker."

The action-research project

The project proposed was exploratory in character, and in the development stage there was a high degree of overlap between research and action. It proposed the use of community volunteers as mentors and that a suitable introductory point to demonstrate the viability and effectiveness of this role was with mentally handicapped children. Two schools were chosen on the Lower East Side of New York, P.S. 97 and J.H.S. 95. The schools' cooperation was obtained through the initiatives of Riessman and Andrew Humm, the project's field director. Success in obtaining this cooperation was a product of a long-term relationship between the CUNY researchers and the school system (particularly its then chancellor, Macchiarola), the school superintendent of that district, and the city's Education Department.

The complexity of the organizational involvement necessary to make this project work is indicated in the diagram in Figure 3-1 showing the key roles: CUNY staff, City Board of Education, school district personnel, and volunteers. The linking of researcher and action agency occurred at two levels: the senior level with City of New York education officials, including the chancellor, and the local school level. The CUNY staff visualized the mentor role growing out of their work with paraprofessional and social support roles as described above. The positive response they received, however, was due in part to the fact that the school officials, principals, and teachers were seeking new ways of dealing with their problems. So, while the initiative in this particular project came from the action-oriented researcher, it might equally have come from the educators because, embodied in the new concept, there was a clear overlap of interests.

The goal of the specific project was to develop and evaluate a mentor role. The two schools chosen as research/development sites were a junior high school and a high school. The aim was to learn from the experience of developing and introducing a mentor role and from its effective functioning so that, if successful, it could be disseminated on a much wider basis. The reason for concentrating on mentally handicapped students for the pilot study was because the teachers undoubtedly felt a great need for help

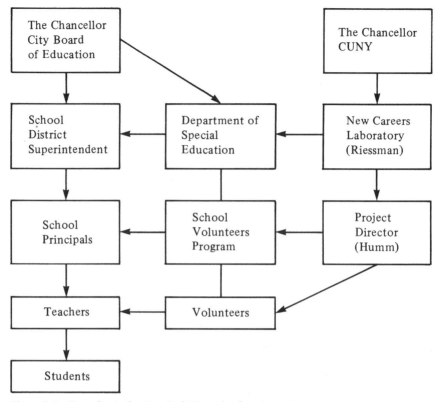

Figure 3–1. *Key roles in the New York City school senior project*

with this subgroup and would therefore be receptive to participating in an action-research collaboration. Volunteers were suggested because they were presumed to be readily available through the New York City Schools' Volunteer Program.

Project design. The project plan called for taking the necessary steps to design a mentor role, recruit and train volunteers for the role, liaise with principals and teachers in the schools for the appropriate way to introduce the role, put a working program into place, and evaluate its operation.

The principal investigator, Riessman, had a widely recognized capacity to innovate action roles, particularly in the field of social support structures, such as peer counselors. The model of action-research he espoused was based on an initial merging of action and research, with the scientist initiating the intervention and evaluating the outcome. Once the intervention was piloted, its operation would be taken over by field staff and the research role would become more disengaged.

In the initial conceptualization of the mentor role, it was recognized as multidimensional, having some elements of the teacher role (e.g., adult status and experience) and some of the peer role (e.g., informal, non-authoritative basis). In relation to role theory, it was an interesting new type of role. In relation to mental health theories, it was conceptualized as a potentially supportive role, buffering stress.

The methodology was eclectic, consisting of participant observation, psychological testing, interviews with teachers and students, and analysis of school records. Formal design features included control groups and test instruments, but, as the project was exploratory, it was recognized that these were provisional and that flexibility would be required initially.

Two measures of outcome were relevant: first, whether the new role could be made operative in the schools and was considered helpful by teachers; and second, whether it produced demonstrable improvements for students.

A pre- and postevaluation form was developed collaboratively with the Department of Special Education. Teachers rated experimental and control students on seven variables: promptness, responsibility for homework, attentiveness, class participation, relationships with classmates, responsiveness to adult staff, and overall attitude. California achievement test scores were also used.

Course of the project. Two problems became manifest early in the project. One was that appropriate volunteers did not materialize in sufficient numbers to fill the mentor role requirements in the project design. Second, teachers did not become as fully involved as had been expected. Both difficulties were understandable, but they impeded the execution of the research design.

Riessman describes the difficulties with potential mentors:

We started out in Lower East Side, District 1, in two schools, a junior high school and a public school, got wonderful cooperation from the teachers and the district superintendent on the Board of Education. Had no trouble having them accept that mentors could come in, found space for them to work with kids and developed a training program; drew up research instruments to evaluate the teachers' response to the kids who were being monitored, whether they were improving as well as the terms of the objective scores on their achievement test. The first big hitch that we had was in the recruitment of the mentors. We worked through the School Volunteer Program which was very cooperative and they had in the past recruited tutors, but they had never recruited mentors and they had never recruited them for a handicapped population, particularly one on the Lower East Side, which is slightly difficult to get to and a low income and "dangerous" neighborhood.

The project team spent a lot of time looking for other sources of recruits for this role, and finally worked out an arrangement with colleagues teaching social studies courses in city colleges. They succeeded in obtaining the participation of 20 students. Riessman found that motivating the appropriate volunteers to participate on the basis of several combined small reasons worked better than a single large one. Offering a small stipend played a part in students' willingness to participate, though this was not considered a universally applicable element. Also important for students was that they were given course credit in the social sciences. Additionally, there was the challenge of the problem and the excitement of the idea that this was an innovative project.

With the teachers there were different issues. They were, of course, overloaded – this was part of the reason for needing supplementary help. This limited their degree of participation in locating children, organizing the children's work to mesh with the experiment, filling out the required research forms, and so on. Nevertheless, their cooperation was obtained, though divergences among conceptual elements in the mentor role began to surface; many teachers automatically assimilated it to the teacher's aid model. Another problem had to do with differences of interpretation over how students were to be selected for the experimental and control groups. The design called for selection of pairs of individuals matched for specific research criteria, but teachers tended to select students for the experimental group whom they considered most in need of help. This was understandable in relation to the values of teachers as members of a helping profession. However, it tended to stack the cards against the possibility that the mentoring program would show a significant effect because the students were disproportionally "difficult" as compared with the control groups.

The issue in relation to the concept of the mentor role was instructive. The exploratory nature of the project made it acceptable to begin with a very wide and flexible general conception of mentoring, but it soon became imperative to define more precisely the relationship between the mentor and the teaching staff. Everyone concerned agreed that it was crucial that the mentor be outside the authority structure; on this depended the students' trust. However, the teachers were accustomed to exercising a degree of control over the activities of their teacher's aides, an orientation that was both understandable and necessary given the fact that teachers retained responsibility for the students' educational experiences.

Teachers tended to see the mentors as personnel who would help them with their over-extended workload and who were less highly trained than teachers, but working in the same direction. The crucial element was that they should be under the authority of the school, given directions by teachers and reporting back to them. But there were differences in the conceptualization of the mentor role vis-à-vis the teachers, not only among teachers, mentors, and students, but among researchers. On the one hand, Andrew Humm, in a preliminary report on the project, expressed the point of view of those wanting the mentors to be more under the guidance of the teachers:

During the progress of the mentoring relationships, the teachers, in the main, maintained a posture of not interfering with the mentor-mentee relationship. In retrospect, while there were valid reasons for this approach (e.g. they wanted the relationship to be untainted by any hint of collaboration with paid staff), it may be helpful in the future if the mentors and teachers work in closer collaboration in order to give the mentors a clearer sense of direction and to be of more help to the individual student.

Riessman, on the other hand, expressed the view that many of the students at risk because of their tenuous attitudes toward authority formed trusting relationships with mentors precisely because they expected them *not* to report back to teachers. Mentors for such students are somewhat outside the system, neutral, and therefore more approachable.

The mentor is there for the kid and is an advocate, coach, guide, close to the kid, and so forth. The model the school system likes better is the mentor is very close to the teacher and is involved very much in implementing what the teacher thinks should be done for and with the student. There are all kinds of issues here that might be looked at. To the extent that the mentor is way over on the teacher's side, the question of the closeness to the kid is potentially impaired, confidentiality is not as assured, and so on. From the institutional point of view, the school system wants the mentor to serve their purpose, and having a mentor provides another pair of hands working with the kid. To some extent the view that we are representing is that the mentor is an ally of the kid. But if they're too much of an ally of the kid you have the problem of conflict with the teacher or with the parents.

Riessman contended that the question of the appropriate model for the mentor should be answered by research, with choices between alternative models to be based on their empirically established capacity to produce the desired results.

Results

The project had three tangible products and a set of "intangible" experiences for potential broader application.

Product 1: A general information handbook. The *Questions and Answers About a Mentoring Program* handbook was developed as a general information document for teachers, administrators, and volunteers. It contained the following sections:

> What is a Mentor?
> How do Mentor relationships get started?
> What if the relationship does not work?
> What roles can a Mentor play in a student's life?
> How can Mentors be recruited for such a program?
> Why work in a special education program?
> What unique issues are there for a special education volunteer?
> What is the relationship between the Mentor and the student's teacher and other staff?
> How is a mentoring relationship developed with a student?
> How should a mentoring relationship be supervised?
> How can a Mentor program's effectiveness be evaluated?

The writing of this manual was accomplished with the collaboration of all concerned, including the students. It was pilot-tested in the schools during the 1982–1983 academic year. Designed to be more broadly applicable, it presents issues of the specific pilot population of volunteers and handicapped students in generic terms.

Product 2: A training handbook. A training manual was designed which concentrated particularly on the distinctive problems of working with handicapped students. Three exercises were incorporated into the handbook: a filmstrip (with associated discussion), an exercise simulating handicapping conditions of various kinds, and a role-playing exercise incorporating trials of situations encountered in the mentor-mentee relationship with a handicapped child.

Product 3: Findings from the evaluation study. Anecdotal reports of how much the program was appreciated by students, teachers, and mentors and of how it was helping the handicapped students were generally positive. But comparisons between the test and performance score of experimental and control groups showed neither significant improvement for the mentoring group, nor significant differences in changes recorded for the two groups. The findings of the evaluation study were therefore inconclusive, as summarized in Table 3-1. It was clear that there were no statistical differences between experimental and control groups in the numbers of those who improved and those who dropped in their ratings.

These inconclusive findings were interesting but, given the small numbers and lack of valid controls, lacked power to make a case for or against

Table 3-1. *Evaluation of performance and test scores*

Junior High School 25	Total rating			Attendance			CAT score		
	Up	Same	Down	Better	Same	Worse	Up	Mix	Down
Participants	4	1	4	4	0	5	4	0	0
Nonparticipants	3		4	1	0	4	1	0	0
Public School 97									
Participants	5	1	4	1	1	6	3	1	2
Nonparticipants	4	3	1	2	1	4	2	1	3

(Humm, A., 1983)

mentoring program. Most of those concerned had confirmed their conviction that mentoring was a "good thing." There was a growing conviction that the program was valuable and discussion of results centered on why the inconclusive findings appeared. Four reasons were produced in Humm's report:

1. Too little time was spent by mentors with students. Their program got started late in the academic year because of the logistical problems encountered, and though data was lacking on optimum numbers of contacts, there was consensus that there were too few.
2. An aim was to develop the mentoring role concept, but early unclarities blurred the focus of mentoring activity, detracting from possible effects.
3. A bias in the selection procedure resulted in a poor match between experimental and control groups, to the detriment of the experimental group.
4. Some of the necessary data to make balanced evaluations were lacking. Data were eroded to the point of blurring the statistical results.

In addition to these conclusions, suggestions were presented for correcting the conditions possibly contributing to false-negative findings.

- The program should start promptly at the beginning of the school year.
- Mentors should focus their work more closely to the teachers' programs by arranging regular consultations with teachers.
- Teachers should be more oriented to the importance of complying with research requirements for matched experimental and control groups if they wish a more reliable evaluation.
- Researchers should gather evaluation data independently, relying less on hard-pressed teachers to do the required assessments.

In considering issues associated with further development, a number of points are relevant. First, dissemination of results, ordinarily an essential step in program development, was not appropriate, not only because of the false-negative findings but also because this was an exploratory and not a definitive study. One option, as implied in the recommendations described above, was to move to the next stage of program development, toward making a more definite evaluation of mentoring next year. However, there was no assurance about continuities of support for this purpose, and furthermore, there were new developments in the larger environment of the Department of Education. While the original mentoring project had had the blessing of the then school chancellor, Macchiarola, it was not a focal part of his larger program. When Macchiarola resigned, the new chancellor, Anthony Alvarado, made the mentoring concept a major part of his program, because of his encounters with a number of psychologists, including Richard Gordon, who used the concept for graduate student training at Yale. Alvarado was quoted in the *New York Times:*

Wherever he goes these days, New York City's Schools Chancellor, Anthony Alvarado, has one special plea: "I need 275,000 people to give me an hour a week to do some mentoring with young people." He wants business and professional people to lay aside their attaché cases for that hour and deal personally with 275,000 high school students, giving them special help and inspiration.

The Carnegie Foundation recently recommended 1 guidance counselor for every 100 students, but in New York's high schools the ratio is 1 per 650. A third of the city's high school students are being raised by a single parent. The drop-out rate remains an appalling 45 percent.

It is thought that successful people, many of whom credit a mentor with inspiring them at crucial early moments, could help these youngsters deal with the pressures of life. Mr. Alvarado envisions his mentors and the students behaving at first "like two teen-agers at their first dance," but then developing a productive relationship. (Editorial, October 30, 1983)

Though this initiative was awkward for Riessman and his group, since they were associated with the former chancellor rather than the new team, Riessman wrote to the relevant city officials indicating the CUNY involvement in the field and offering to share their experience. Building on lessons learned in the pilot study with handicapped children, a proposal was produced that had several improvements over the original formulation. First, based on the experience of difficulties with recruiting volunteers, the use of college students as mentors was suggested. Working with the CUNY chancellor, a plan was developed for students who were taking courses allied to education, psychology, or the social sciences, to gain credit through the mentoring activity. Second, the goals of the new mentoring program were to be focused on reduction of absenteeism and drop-out rates; however, the specific means were less clear. The concept of mentoring is very broad; it is used with age-discrepant groups or peer relationships, permissively or directively, or with role models (setting an example through doing) or guides or tutors in relation to the student's schoolwork. The CUNY pilot study helped to clarify elements of the model itself.

And third, the process involved in successful mentoring was not addressed directly in the new mentoring program, but became a focal part of the city's own mentoring program, set up under Taraja Samuel with a special unit under the Board of Education.

Based on the pilot study, Riessman and Humm suggested that the specific goal of engagement of the student in the school/learning system could effectively be achieved by using the concept of *learning styles*. Riessman observed that the school's teaching timetable as well as its role structure was very closely geared to a particular standard learning style. The research of Kenneth and Rita Dunn (1978) on the diversity of learning styles indicated that altering the school's structure to fit variant learning styles (e.g., by changing the starting hour from 9 A.M. to 10 A.M.) could lead to a reduction in the truancy rate. The mentor could serve as an intermediary between students with discrepant learning styles and the teaching staff.

The approach would be to establish first whether students who are underperforming do indeed have discrepant learning styles. In such a situation, the effective mentoring role would be not to introduce a tutorial teacher's-aide model immediately (this would probably serve to drive the student further away), but to go along with the student's individual learning style while a friendly relationship was being developed. For example, if the student liked to work with noise, or by a window, or with a peer, or sitting on the floor, or at night, the mentor would initially work with them in the preferred way. As the relationship developed, the mentor would work with the mentee and the teachers to understand the nature of the misfit in learning styles and to develop strategies for working toward a reconciliation between the discrepant style and the dominant school one. The two strategic steps in the mentor relationship can be paraphrased as, I get friendly with you, and then you may do what you don't like doing.

The learning styles concept was suggested as useful in focusing the conceptualization of the mentoring role. Furthermore, any insights gained would provide a valuable experience for the student independent of the specific schooling situation. According to Riessman,

The potential dropouts who begin to understand the concept of learning styles will gain in indirect as well as direct ways. For example, they will begin to recognize that their difficulties in school may not be due to any personal inadequacy, but rather because the main learning styles fostered in the academic environment may not be entirely consonant with their own way of learning. In effect, [the mentor assists the student in] understanding the dimensions of their own style gives them the potentiality for developing a [new] learning strategy.

The mentor acts as a guide in constructing a new learning strategy for the individual and as an intermediary with the teachers in seeking ways the school might provide sufficient flexibility to allow this readaptation to occur (e.g., allowing the student to dictate lessons into a tape recorder, or to sit near a window, or on the floor while taking a test).

Essential in this approach is the idea that this is a *transitional* phenomenon. The student is helped first to discover that learning is possible for him or her under favorable learning conditions, and then to make the *extra* effort required to fit into other learning situations to achieve something important to him or her in the school or work situation. As Reissman said, "What is aimed for is long-range development of *learning power,* a very important aspect of empowerment."

The new initiative concentrated on obtaining mentors from among college students who might gain something from the experience. Initially it was expected that work-study students would be right for the program, because they required field experience and the mentoring program offered relevant practical experience. However, there proved to be insufficient numbers of work-study students available, particularly as the program could not pay competitively with alternative work placements.

Discussion

The model of action-research used in this case was that of the *merged* actor-researcher in the pilot phase, followed by a disengagement of research, training, and action elements for subsequent phases. In this model, the aim was to learn through doing. This seems to have had the advantage of bringing to bear the experience and creative capacities of the researcher at the grass-roots level. On the one hand, the lessons learned from the research experience fed into the tasks of reconceptualization of the action role. On the other hand, the project may have been less responsive to the teachers' requirements than had it been developed as a collaborative effort with teachers. Nevertheless, subsequent definitions of the mentoring role took into account both the project initiator's predisposition toward restructuring the schools, and the teachers' predisposition toward maintaining control.

The project demonstrated that a role could be put into place which had not been there previously. The schools indicated its value to them by continuing the program after the project moved on. Another practical benefit was that after its pilot stage the project was ready with a plan to feed into the new mentoring program when it emerged independently from the Department of Education with its new chancellor. This took the tangible form of the General Information Handbook, mentioned above.

Conceptually, the project developed an improved theoretical base. The mentor role was seen initially as a new social support role and would, like other support roles, be beneficial from a mental health point of view. There is relatively little conceptualization of how social support roles buffer stress, or of how they might facilitate growth. A wide range of psychosocial mechanisms may be involved: modeling, nurturing, bonding, counseling, and others. The idea of working with the modification of learning styles is a significant contribution to understanding the potentials of mentoring as an active stress-buffering role.

Sociologically, the mentor is interesting as a *linkage* role. It links teachers to pupils within the school system, and the school system to the adult world outside. In the CUNY student mentor program, a small part of the larger New York City schools mentoring program, the linkage has occurred between the public high school system and the university system. This linkage is of mutual interest because, from the schools' perspective, it focuses the student's attention on a possible continuity in educational development. From the university system's standpoint, the program helps to prepare prospective students for their transition into higher education, a transition which has been making increasing demands on special services because of the deficiencies of so many students in this regard.

Mentor and student in the CUNY program are closer in age than in other programs. They are in quasi-sibling relationships, each enmeshed in a contrasting subculture. The university culture has looser controls, a more flexible schedule of activities, and a more extended time span of discretion in completing assigned tasks than high school. The high-school regime not only is different but also is a regime from which the CUNY students have only recently emerged. Thus, while the college student is well-placed to give the high school student some perspective on the transition that is forthcoming, there are problems arising out of the degree of disjunction between the two systems. The college students may, for example, inadvertently initiate something acceptable in the CUNY system but not in the high school. This requries close supervision.

The expectations are that the mentoring relationship may have a number of beneficial outcomes: retention of the high school student in education, alteration of learning styles to achieve a better performance, raising of aspirations to continue into higher education, and, for the mentors, benefits to their personal and professional development.

The present project can be seen to have experienced a number of special difficulties in conducting field research. Recruitment of volunteers proved more difficult than the public-relations material led the researchers to believe. Working in schools with overloaded and stressed teachers proved more difficult than top administrators assumed. The need for trade-offs for the sake of feasibility in such a field situation meant some sacrifice of research design requirements. Compromises in the pilot project, however, were seen as acceptable because lessons were being learned and procedures field-tested. Though they felt under pressure to increase rigor – perhaps prematurely – at no point did the researchers feel that field work problems so undermined methodological requirements that they wanted to abandon the project. The equivocal summative evaluation was not taken to be negative, because subjective experience of the people concerned was positive and their sense of what they wanted and knew they might be able to have was reconfirmed.

Early experiments with action-research highlighted how positive findings and impeccable methodologies are sometimes rejected because they are incongruent with a larger field of forces. Here, the field of forces was favorable (the need for the social intervention was so great) so that inconclusive findings were overlooked.

The political forces in the project's environment also presented difficulties as well as favorable elements. Initially there was a favorable political environment which helped to get the project launched. When this was altered, the project survived because it was congruent with program elements in the new regime. The project leaders were thus able to transcend two unfavorable situations: inconclusive results in the pilot study and a change of regime.

As the mentoring concept expanded to meet the goals of the new regime for the high school system's problems, the CUNY student mentor program became a small part of a large-scale initiative that was less oriented to the basic mental health research issues.

Case study: Urban discovery

Project Discovery is a reinvention, aimed at adapting the Outward Bound principles to the urban high school curriculum. Initiated by Sister Maryann Hedaa, the Founder of Urban Adventures, this program was part of an effort to develop innovative approaches to the education of urban at-risk children. The project was initially proposed as an evaluation study of an innovative action program. It became an action-research project when a collaborative relationship was arranged with Barbara Falsey, of New York University's Center for Applied Social Science Research. The project was conducted over a two-year period, 1983–1985, at the South Bronx High School.

Background

The general problem addressed is that of underprivileged urban youth, whose disadvantages impede their own development and may add to their community's social problems. Blighted urban neighborhoods, such as the one in the South Bronx chosen for the project, are characterized by a cluster of high-stress environmental features: poverty, substandard housing, crime and delinquency, substance abuse, and unemployment. The local schools are characterized by high rates of absenteeism, dropping out, disciplinary problems, repeat years, and underperformance in academic work.

The at-risk children concerned show a characteristic pattern of low self-esteem, lack of self-confidence, poor academic performance, negative attitudes towards school, and inhibitions associated with being enmeshed in a poverty situation. Many programs have evolved to meet the educational problems of this type of population. They include the Boys Club and Girls Club, alternative schools (e.g., the street "Academy"), and a variety of urban outreach programs for youth who do not fit into the traditional educational system.

The Urban Adventures program is based on the Outward Bound movement and is not the first such program (see Miner and Boldt, 1981, for an account of the Action Bound program in Trenton). Rooted in European youth movements in the early twentieth century, the Outward Bound concept is best known in relation to the experimental school at Gordonstoun, based on the principles of its founder, Kurt Hahn. The motto of Hahn's school at Gordonstoun in Scotland is "Plus est en vous" (There is more in you than you think). In the British context, the concept has been associated with upper-class "public" schools. Hahn wrote:

In present day civilization five social diseases surround the young, even in childhood. There is the decline in fitness due to the modern methods of locomotion; the decline of initiative due to the widespread disease of spectatoritis; the decline in care and skill due to the weakened traditions of craftsmanship; the decline in self-discipline due to the ever-present availability of tranquilizers and stimulants; the decline of compassion, which is spiritual death. (cited by Miner and Boldt, 1981, p. 189)

The Gordonstoun concept and program attracted the attention of the British royal family and it became the school chosen for their sons. In the United States it was first introduced in Colorado with the opening of the

Colorado Outward Bound School in 1960, and it has also been associated with summer wilderness programs available mostly to affluent youth. A distinctive characteristic of the Outward Bound movement is its active approach to the environment. Emphasis is placed on mastering challenges such as mountain climbing, white-water rapids canoeing, and winter survival expeditions. The primary aim has been to develop character through enlivening curiosity and strengthening self-confidence. In a review of the American applications of the Outward Bound concept, Arnold Shore (1977) found that the *self* is a key concept, and that *enhanced self-esteem* is a frequently reported correlate of participation in Outward Bound programs. However, Shore noted some contradictory findings and identified a need to specify the conditions under which the desired effects are more likely to be found, and where less. Furthermore, the issue of the relationship between increased self-esteem and academic achievement is somewhat blurred among the more affluent clientele of Outward Bound programs who might have performed relatively well in school in any case. Hahn himself placed the greater value on the development of the whole person, relegating academic achievement to a lower priority. He has stated his beliefs in the saying "Character first, intelligence second, knowledge third."

Programs such as those described by Shore have not been used primarily to contribute systematically to the developmental problems of disadvantaged youth. There were a few pilot experiments, which tended, for a variety of reasons, not to persist; nor were they systematically researched. One, though it did not survive, has been vividly described. The Trenton Action Bound project is described by its then director, Gregory Farrell, in the following terms:

There are pitifully few channels in our society through which young men can move with dignity, success, and a sense of adventure from adolescence into manhood. Opportunities for positive, character-forming experiences are particularly limited for youngsters of low-income families. . . . They are the ones who most often sink finally into aimlessness and apathy, or who take out their frustrations on the institutions that have failed them in acts of violence and hostility. . . . They need experiences that will show them that they are not so limited as they think, experiences that will give them confidence and enthusiasm for the business of facing life, experiences that will assure them that they can make it. (Miner and Boldt, 1981, p. 188).

Project Discovery takes on the most daunting of challenges in the most turbulent of American urban environments, that of seeking to develop a program that could be incorporated into the school regimen, rather than constituting an alternative or a school vacation program, which, as Miner and Boldt note, can increase frustration as well as self-confidence when the difficulties of making the transfer of experiences into everyday life are confronted. A British counterpart is called City Challenge.

Previous programs systematically applying these concepts in urban settings have been rare and have had difficulties in relation to continuity. One reason seems to have been that such programs place heavy demands on staff. Staff undergo stress in simultaneously negotiating the city environment and managing the types of children most in need of such a program. Such projects have a high staff burnout rate. In addition, there have been problems of obtaining financial supports for a sufficiently long time span to allow the program to mature, to be understood, and to be appropriately incorporated into the schools. Gregory Farrell, formerly director of the Trenton programs, quotes a former colleague who, on becoming a superintendent of schools, attempted to introduce innovative programs and stated "he who would change schools must learn to grow trees." By this, Farrell says, he meant that it takes a long time to allow a program to mature and become established. Most of the programs operated on a shoestring with transient staff (cf. Miner and Boldt, 1981, p. 202).

The Urban Adventures program is run by youth workers who believe that experiential learning methods are particularly meaningful to children from urban, deprived, and minority backgrounds. Such methods are not primarily seen as an alternative to conventional education, but as an *ancillary* or *complementary* approach. This orientation emphasizes the potential of adventure programs to enliven the whole school experience, thereby making it more feasible for children who have difficulty with conventional schooling to engage the school system.

In the urban context, the necessary ingredients for incorporating a viable urban adventure program into the schools are a *charismatic leader with a dedicated team,* and a *receptive site.* Sister Hedaa and her Urban Adventures team provided the first ingredient, the South Bronx High School the second. The Edwin Gould Foundation provided financial support to do the pilot work necessary for initial development of the program and the William T. Grant Foundation provided support for a research component. The goal was eventually to develop the project to the point where it might be incorporated into the school curriculum. Previous experience (the Action Bound program) indicated that the communications disjunctions between the innovators and the educators could cause the loss of some of the most vital elements when and if an experimental program was mainstreamed. A coordinated research effort might help to minimize this kind of disjunction.

The South Bronx High School, which opened in 1979, is entirely composed of minority students (70 percent Hispanic, 30 percent black). It is located in an area of urban blight, poverty, substandard housing, unemployment, and overt street crime and drug trafficking. Over 80 percent of the students were achieving below their expected grade level, and daily absentee rates were 40 percent. In brief, it provided the kind of environment most in need of an innovative approach to engaging young people in a constructive pattern of development. Some of the staff of the school, particularly the coach who had a personal conviction that an environmental mastery program would have a generally more beneficial effect on school commitment and performance, had been interested in such an innovation for some time. Preliminary talks, however, had not produced anything very concrete, though the general school ethos may have been prepared somewhat to be receptive to Sister Maryann Hedaa's initiative when it came.

Sister Hedaa, a graduate of Outward Bound and a board member of the American Experiential Education Association, was a Connecticut school teacher who had been impressed with the impact on students of the field trips she led into the New York slums (the obverse of the usual Outward Bound pattern). Inspired by Outward Bound, she combined John Dewey's progressive education ideas with the Paolo Friere sense of mission to empower the poor through appropriate educational methods. Through her contacts through the Gould Foundation support, she heard about the interest of the South Bronx High School coach, made contact, and together with two other teachers put into motion an initiative which eventually produced plans for Project Discovery. The teachers took responsibility for the academic parts of the program to ensure that it met official course standards. Hedaa and her team organized the Outward Bound component, involving various challenges and mastery experiences and visits to diverse areas of the city.

For Project Discovery, research was added to the Urban Adventures program that had been underway for two years. The specific school's initiative was called Project Discovery because of its use of the discovery learning principle and also because of its emphasis on broadening the horizons of these highly provincial children. There were two parts to the school program, both applied initially to high school sophomores, juniors, and seniors: Discovery I and Discovery II. The first was a one-semester course offered to 30 students at a time; the second was a year-long course with similar components, all expanded and open only to students who had experienced Discovery I. Each course had both school and community components: adventure outings, service projects, academic skills development, counseling, and student (peer) advising groups. Project staff worked collaboratively with teachers and with service personnel from hospitals, women's shelters, and other community-based agencies. The new project caught the imagination of educators and media people. There were reports of adventure outings, weekend camping trips, urban activity days (rock climbing and canoeing in the park), cultural (museum) days, and a 24-hour urban experience. Newspaper pictures of students climbing the Brooklyn Bridge, for example, provided considerable excitement and public discussion.

In the early pilot work in developing the action program, staff were reassured about the potential importance of the *urban experience*, in relation to educational goals as well as to character building. Many of these children, unaware of the potential learning resources in their urban environment, brought back from outings a positive orientation to making use of them. The staff were impressed with the possibilities for self-perpetuation of these urban encounters, as compared with the camping and out-of-town trips, which were not easily incorporated into the experience of children of this type. The staff felt that they would have a particularly powerful learning potential if classroom activities could be coordinated with the urban experience activities. The impression was that maximum benefit could be achieved if the classroom reading and social studies could provide materials to enrich the adventure activities; and reciprocally, that adventure activities would whet the appetite for learning in the classroom.

In the initial stages of program development, students were referred by teachers on the basis of two criteria: those most in need and those amenable to participating. Most of these students had been identified as testing below their expected grade level and as having repeated at least one grade in high school.

Early experience with the program was reassuring, and many found it an exciting experiment. At the same time, there was a demand for evaluation, because applications for further financial support required objective evidence of the program's efficacy. The project action team thus became oriented to the desirability of adding a research component. Discussions were held with William T. Grant Foundation staff, and Hedaa affirmed her long-standing interest in research collaboration. There was some discussion of what kind of researcher would be compatible and a link was formed with the NYU Center for Applied Social Science Research. An introduction was arranged with Barbara Falsey through Barbara Heyns, the center's director. The center agreed to provide an institutional base and supervision. Conversations were conducted between the researcher and agency director toward testing compatibility and trust in the relationship and developing a viable project application.

The action-research project

The goals of the action-research project were formulated in terms of mutual interest to academic knowledge and to the development of the action program. Answers were sought to four questions:

1. To what extent is participation in Project Discovery associated with changes in self-esteem?
2. To what extent is participation in this program associated with improved school performance (in attendance, promotion, and academic achievement)?
3. To what extent do observed changes in self-esteem predict improved school performance?
4. What features of the program and what characteristics of the participants are associated with positive outcomes?

It was considered that answers to these questions might contribute both to the improvement of the action program and to social science.

Research design and methodology. The project had the following design elements:

Concentration on freshmen rather than the older students, allowing for the possibility of a longer follow-through study. Also, freshmen would have no previous knowledge of the program.

Provision for 60 experimental and 60 control students, enough for a multivariate statistical analysis

A set of structured instruments to assess objectively the development of self-esteem

A multidimensional evaluation of the experience, incorporating the perspective of teachers as well as students

Prior to assigning the students, it was decided to screen out those who required extensive remedial work. They were felt to offer a set of special difficulties that might disrupt the operation of the experiment, even though the program might be effective with them. This left two other subgroups to distribute at random between experimental and control groups: those performing below expectations (testing below their expected grade level or repeating a grade, or with poor attendance) and those performing at par for their grade level and with satisfactory record of attendance.

The research formulation was based on self-concept, which has been heavily researched by psychologists. Markus and Nurius (1984), Mussen et al. (1969), and Elkind (1975) have emphasized the dilemmas of adolescents with the changes they experience and the intense preoccupation with acquiring a positive self-image in the identity-forming process at this stage. Young people from deprived and disturbed social environments are particularly at risk in this regard. Rosenberg's (1965) analysis of self-esteem in urban high school juniors demonstrated a correlation between socioeconomic position and self-esteem. Students from lower social class groups and from underprivileged minorities show a generally lower level of self-esteem, which in turn is associated with a wide range of delinquent, socially maladjusted and personally disturbed behavior. Psychotherapy and counseling have been important devices for helping individuals, but they can help only a relatively small number and are inefficient in relation to the need. The challenge is to invent a device which can facilitate the development of a satisfactory level of self-esteem in larger numbers of children at risk.

Falsey was concerned with social institutional factors associated with deficits in performance. She noted that though the earlier research on Outward Bound-type experiences used the self-esteem concept, they failed to give sufficient attention to the social dimensions of the experience, treating it more or less as a "black box." A simple pre- and postexperience measurement of modal responses in relation to the experience was not good enough. If the experience was to be understood and developed to be more effective, its workings would have to be better understood.

The following hypotheses were formulated initially:

- As time is a developmental factor working equally for experimental and control groups, both groups should show some increase in self-esteem after one year of schooling. However,
- The experimental group should show a significantly greater increase in self-esteem than the controls, due to the effects of the following factors:
  Pleasurable engagement in the most challenging events (e.g., rock climbing)
  Formation of close friendships within the group
  A congruence of goals between student and staff
  Success in a wide range of components of the program (rather than a single element)
  Age of the participant (with older students doing better)
  Length of participation (those who do the year-long program will do better than those only in the brief program)
  Parental and peer support for the program
- Increased self-esteem should show itself in the school setting in behavior, achievement, and aspirations. Behavior changes would include lowered truancy and drop-out rates. Achievement indicators would be improved school grades (recognizing the limitations as well as the strengths of this measure). Aspirations would be indicated by the student's expressed

wish to go on to higher education (modified by such intervening variables as expectations about whether this is realistic and knowledge of available options).

The research methodology was a mix of relatively structured and relatively unstructured methods. The basic structured instrument lending itself to quantitative analysis was a student questionnaire administered at three points: at the beginning and end of the program and after a lapse of six months. Semi-structured instruments were interviews with key personnel, including students, program staff, and teachers. Relatively unstructured methods were participant observation on the outings and in the classrooms and staff meetings.

The questionnaire elicited data at the beginning and end of the Project Discovery classes. The first questionnaire elicited information on each student's background, psychological and attitudinal variables (self-esteem, education aspirations, educational expectations, occupational aspirations, occupational expectations, attitudes toward school, attitudes toward the program, attitudes toward the staff). The second questionnaire included items concerning the experience with the program, reactions to it, and friendships formed.

Interviews were designed to gather data on attitudes and motivation about the program, and its place in the individual's development and information about family and parental supports. Observations included the actual behavior of the staff and students in relation to the urban adventure program, and in the school situation as well. Additional information was gathered where available from school records. The original design also called for the creation of a control group as well as the experimental ninth-grade group.

Course of the project. The project was an "arranged" collaboration. When Urban Adventures sought funds from the William T. Grant Foundation and learned of the foundation's emphasis on research, Hēdaa indicated a strong interest in adding a research component as a logical development of the work. The pilot stages of work had demonstrated that there was a viable program; the school authorities considered it potentially useful and were prepared to include it in the curriculum for a further experimental period, and the project team sustained their enthusiasm for what they were doing.

In early discussions with the foundation staff, emphasis was placed on the importance of the researcher having an independent academic base in the interests of objectivity. Hedaa was asked what her reaction and her staff's would be if this kind of research produced results which did not match the idealized, public relations image of the project. The difficulties that this might present in sustaining the collaboration and in maintaining staff morale were discussed. Hedaa indicated that she and her staff were aware of these issues and were keen to learn from the experience, not simply to have their ideology "rubber-stamped."

When the project had been underway for several months, Falsey expressed a number of anxieties:

- How much reassurance should be given? On the one hand it was important to maintain detachment and objectivity; on the other, to be sympathetic in order to sustain working relationships and to participate in order to achieve a better understanding of process. The people who staffed the program had to believe in it, or they would not put themselves into the arduous and often frustrating situations they did. What if they were sensitive to criticism, even though they had verbally accepted that this could be a constructive contribution of the research?
- How much attention should be given to making relationships with teachers in the school in addition to staff members of the discovery program? Experience with some earlier action research programs (e.g., the British Educational Priority Area Program) had indicated that failure to relate to teachers could jeopardize the research project. Yet, time and energy were limited, and this was not a focal element in the research.

  From the beginning, the project was structured as an action-research venture, with importance attached to working out a collaboration between the researcher and members of the action program. The model had not provided guidance as to how much of the researcher's time and energies should go into extending the collaboration to teachers (vs. leaving that to the action staff). Falsey felt the need to allocate time to consolidate a sense of collaboration with teaching staff as well as with program staff, but was uncertain about how to balance the diverse demands this would entail.
- How should the program handle research design and methodology compromises that had to be made as a result of changes in the field situation?

Some of the difficulties that the researcher initially experienced were those commonly found in field situations. For example, there were problems in getting teachers to assign students according to research design criteria rather than other criteria (Rutter et al., 1979). Return rates for questionnaire forms were unsatisfactory and students had to be reminded. The researcher encountered remarks by students about watching what they said when she was around, and she had to redouble her efforts to ensure validity of the data. However, by the end of the first semester, she was a familiar figure in the schools and was getting very rich data, particularly as a result of her participant observation.

However, some more serious compromises had to be made as a result of changes in the school setting. Paradoxically, some of these resulted from the success of the program. During the first year of the project, a new

Chancellor of Education was appointed, and he began a search for innovative programs, especially programs that could come to grips with the
problems of at-risk youth. The South Bronx High School had already been
oriented to these problems (dropping out, poorer academic performance,
vulnerability to unemployment, and the lure of the streets). When the
chancellor directed all high schools to develop "prep" programs (i.e.,
programs to prepare students for higher education), Project Discovery was
available on the scene at South Bronx High School and it was a logical
development for the school to use it for its prep program. The Urban
Adventures director observes,

At South Bronx High School they have always looked for something to justify their
existence as a good educational institution. And, we're finding more as we work
with them that they begin to use Project Discovery on many levels that we weren't
even aware of before. Like the minute the Chancellor wanted a high school prep
program, he issued a directive last Fall that schools should have a prep program for
incoming Freshmen who are reading more than two years below their grade level.
So they could shift a gear and change the ninth grade project that we wanted to do,
so that all of a sudden it became their high school prep program.

This meant the collapse of the experimental/control group design, though
it also led to a decrease in resistance to the program in the school because
it became in their interest to support it.

These changes were experienced as dilemmas, as movement in one
direction meant losses in the other. The issue at this point was how to
achieve the right balance between relations with the school and con-
formity to the original research design.

On the action-team side, a problem was developing between the field
director and the overall agency director, which had to be handled diplo-
matically by the researcher, as she had working relationships with both.
Essentially the problem related to the rapid growth of the organization
through its success in attracting funds and generating new projects. As
with many innovative programs that attract attention, a growth spurt was
experienced as it "took off." Hedaa observed,

In 1979, when I founded it . . . there were two of us and a budget of $25,000 a year.
Two years later we found that tripled, and then three years later we found it almost
twenty times that size.
    You find that most non-profits start with one or two people with a good idea, and
if they are successful it will grow very, very rapidly and managing that growth is a
very difficult thing. There was an article in the *Harvard Business Review* on the
management of nonprofit organizations, and it mentions this phenomenon – and
the various stages of growth.

Hedaa went on to say that this growth, which she sees as generic to
nonprofit organizations that catch on, is also associated with a change in

leadership style. When the structure gets to a certain size with large fiscal responsibilities, staff continuity, and other large-scale organizational management issues, then having the charismatic creatvity of a mission-oriented founder is often not enough to sustain the large structure. "All of a sudden you are at a stage where you need some type of rational structure as well as the charisma, the vision, and the mission."

As the program grew, the start-up of several other action projects, including a new building at their urban farm project, took Hedaa's attention away from the South Bronx project. There had to be a good deal of discussion about new project issues and of initiatives with grant-giving bodies. In the earlier stages, the field director of the Discovery project had been included in all of the organization's discussions about project development. As the organization grew and became involved in activities that had little to do with the Discovery project and would only have diverted the field director's energies, the latter felt left out, criticized, and increasingly dissatisfied. Hedaa describes the process thus:

One thing becomes clear. When you start out it is a mom and pop shop type of operation. Then as it grows, decisions can't all be made jointly – some have to be made independently, and you have to be able to accept that direction without knowing all of the facts.

She recalls that when she read the *Harvard Business Review* article about this phenomenon "It was like a light went off in my head. For a minute I thought they were sitting on my shoulder, it sounded so much like what I was going through. It really gave me consolation to know that others had gone through this same nonsense."

According to one article on the problems of developing data systems in nonprofit organizations states:

Obviously many factors inhibiting improved information handling are beyond the control of a non-profit organization. Yet the one factor accounting for most failures of information systems lies directly within the control of the organization: the characteristics and attitudes of top management.

Rarely does one hear the executives of a non-profit organization described as being "good with numbers". More frequently, the accolades are "creative", "innovative", "caring", or "great scholars". Being good with numbers may actually do the managerial image a disservice, for it implies the absence of such qualitative skills as creativity, courage and humanitarianism. Indeed, some managers at nonprofits view their lack of quantitative skills as a rather endearing imperfection – like having freckles. (Herzlinger, 1977, p. 47)

Other contributors to the *Harvard Business Review* series on nonprofit organizations note that nonprofits are judged by how much money they spend, not how much they earn, and that what they have produced and marketed is often intangible and therefore difficult to evaluate.

Hedaa recalls that the real challenge came with the conflict between wanting to discuss everything and sort out various feelings and problems versus getting on with the job and doing a quality piece of work, which is very demanding: "It amazes me how some people are really content to sit around and talk about everything instead of getting up and doing something."

Eventually the situation came to crisis point. Hedaa made a move, first to concentrate on developing an urban farm project, and eventually to leave the agency to return to teaching. She arranged for her replacement as president, John Flanagan, a board member of Urban Adventures. He had been executive director of Bronx Frontier Development Corporation, a community development agency in the South Bronx which he had founded. After running the agency for 15 years he was looking for a change, though he wanted to stay in the area and continue his relations with the organization. Hedaa was, he said, "a good friend, and we talked about this." She said, "Well, why don't you come down and outline your area of interest." He did and won the approval of the program's sponsors and board and was hired for the job. Indeed, being more senior and experienced with running a much larger organization (40 employees instead of 7, and a budget of a million dollars), he was able to take on a larger share of the direction of the whole organization.

The need for someone with these leadership abilities to head the overall organization had been recognized prior to the crisis with the field director. Hedaa had been feeling the need to improve her own professional knowledge and competence and had been taking a course of studies at Columbia's Graduate School of Business Administration. However, the crisis in relation to the field director could not be averted at this point, and she resigned at the beginning of the school year. It was not until the spring semester that the new field director was appointed.

One of the first things Flanagan noted when he took on the job was that there was a research project associated with it. "I knew that when I came on I'd wind up inheriting Barbara." There had been no formal research component in his previous organization, and though they made numerous small studies, student papers, and journalist articles about their work, "It was all street stuff – not [any] pure empirical research or anyone with Barbara's credentials." He says, however, that he had always found research interesting, so long as it did not interfere with the operations. He noted that Falsey had a very unobtrusive manner and

she doesn't get in the way. . . . I always enjoy an outside opinion on what we are doing, because we are always evolving. Everything we were attempting was for the first time, so I always encourage feed-back.

Researchers bring in information about a wider experience with the issues being confronted. Subsequently, he stated that the research had been particularly useful to him as a "management tool," in learning about the work of the organization.

In the second semester, the researcher succeeded in improving the rates of questionnaire forms completed, though she had to accept the collapse of the original research design. She attributed her success to more support from the teachers, who had come to accept her, and better acquaintance with the children themselves. The new Urban Adventures director and program staff had also deepened their commitment to the research, and the morale of the staff was raised by feeling part of an important research study connected with a prestigious university. They found that it was intellectually stimulating to talk about their work. The teachers and administrators at the school were "flattered to be part of a study," and the students who "adore tape recorders," came to feel special, too, as part of a research study.

The implications for the original design requirements were twofold: first, a true control group was not feasible, for it required either random selection from a pool of students who had applied or random assignment from the school as a whole. Two sections of a ninth-grade global history class did participate in a modified version of a Project Discovery program. While the global history lists provided a norm for comparison in overall patterns of attendance and school performance, there was no way to ascertain what specific selective factors may have differentiated those who volunteered for Project Discovery from the others.

Second, the number of students involved in the program was smaller than expected. While the fact that the classes studied were small had value, permitting greater student involvement and visibility, it restricted the possibilities for analysis of variations in student outcomes within the program.

Results

Falsey's findings are grouped in four categories:

1. Attendance
2. School performance
3. Self-esteem
4. A set of affectional variables described as enthusiasm

Attendance. Overall, enrollment in the Project Discovery classes appeared to be positively associated with school attendance. This outcome variable, though mundane, is crucial because previous research has shown that nonattendance signals a dramatic shift toward negative outcomes, for the school and society. Two kinds of analyses were performed comparing the number of recorded days absent and late of Project Discovery students and a sample of students not enrolled in the program. First, the mean number of absences and lates for the two groups of students for three school semesters were compared. In each semester the Project Discovery students had fewer recorded absences and lates than nonprogram students. The greatest differences were in days absent, with the Project Discovery students absent on the average four to seven fewer days than nonprogram students.

Another analysis used a multiple-regression procedure, which yielded further confirmation of the pattern. The Project Discovery I and II program students were pooled and their prior attendance records were used as an estimate of expected absences and lates in a given semester. Project Discovery enrollment was coded 0 for students not enrolled and 1 for students enrolled in the program, and an estimate of the attendance effect of Project Discovery enrollment was calculated in relation to prior attendance patterns. While differences in prior patterns between enrolled and nonenrolled students was small, there was a negative effect following enrollment (i.e., being enrolled was associated with a *decrease* in number of days late).

School performance. A similar set of analyses were performed using two indicators of academic performance: the percentage of classes students pass, their grade-point averages (GPA), and their subsequent progress in the educational system. The overall results suggested that enrollment in Project Discovery was somewhat associated with better school performance. First the average number of classes passed and the average GPA of Project Discovery I and II students were compared with those of nonprogram students for the two semesters of the school year 1983–1984. In each semester the Project Discovery students had both higher GPAs and a higher percentage of courses passed than nonprogram students. All differences were statistically significant at the .01 level.

In order to determine the effect of program participation on subsequent educational development, Falsey examined the 1985 records of students enrolled in Project Discovery during the 1983–1984 school year, and compared them with a sample of the 1983–1984 global history students, stratified by grade level to match the grade levels of the Project Discovery students. While the sample of students was small (58 Project Discovery students and 46 nonprogram students), and while, as described above, the nonprogram students were not a true control group, the data indicated that enrollment in Project Discovery was associated with positive school outcomes nearly a year after the period of enrollment. The two groups of students were compared according to percent currently enrolled and attending school; percent enrolled but truant (i.e., on the long-term absence lists); percent graduated; and percent discharged, transferred to other schools, or with no known status. On the basis of these comparisons the Project Discovery students were more likely than the nonprogram students to be currently enrolled or to have successfully graduated from the school (79 percent compared to 50 percent). Conversely, they were currently less likely to be truant or to have transferred or been discharged from school.

Student self-esteem. While the behavioral variables of attendance and academic performance are crucial from the school's vantage point, a key variable from the point of view of the child's long-term coping capacity is self-esteem. This variable is central to the ideology and sense of mission of the Discovery program, reflecting that of the Outward Bound movement. It is also consistent with a considerable body of psychological theory that treats it as a pivotal variable. The growth of self-esteem has been a central concern also for the more socially oriented social psychologists, along the lines of George Herbert Mead and Charles Cooley. There is a considerable body of research tying the different observable degrees of self-esteem to social background variables such as social class, race, peer-group experience, and family background. For children from the more socially deprived backgrounds, the link between self-esteem and school performance has tended to be weak, presumably because of countervailing influences outside the school and the relatively weak commitment to schooling itself.

Using Hare's (1980) standardized self-esteem scales, which allow for a differentiation between self-esteem in different zones of life – home, peer-group, and school – Falsey obtained equivocal findings. While self-esteem scores of all students in this group tended to rise as the academic year proceeded, the Discovery program students' scores rose less than those of the nonprogram students. In fact, when the subscores were calculated, the Discovery program students' school self-esteem scores actually dropped, while the nonprogram students rose. The rise in overall scores of the Discovery students was brought about by a relatively greater rise in their home self-esteem scores. Both groups showed a slight drop in peer self-esteem scores, but the nonprogram students' scores dropped more. Falsey indicates that these findings are surprising given the perceptions of staff that the program students increased in their self-esteem. A multifactorial analysis produced some indications that the aggregate scores were masking individual and subgroup differences in responsiveness to the program.

Even granting that the time period was too brief to expect dramatic changes in such a fundamental character variable, some interesting contrasts emerged. Those who participated in all of the program activities and formed close relationships with others in the program were more likely to have increased in not only their peer self-esteem but in school self-esteem as well. This suggests that Project Discovery served to generate peer group energies which were consonant with, rather than dissonant with, those of the school.

Age is another relevant variable. The youngest group, ages 13 and 14, showed the greatest tendency to gain in self-esteem and the lowest losses. This is apparently due to their not yet having had a chance to experience the phenomenon of a drop in self-esteem, which minority students are reported to have as they progress through school and are increasingly aware that they do not match up to performance standards. The 15- and 16-year-old group showed this, with low proportions reporting gains and high proportions reporting losses in school self-esteem, despite participation in the program. The 17-plus age group showed a steep rise in school self-esteem. This is a group that has been exposed longest to schooling, and for them the participation in the program may have added a new increment to their self-esteem. In relation to peer self-esteem, the Hispanic and male students were found to be more likely to gain in peer self-esteem than were black and female students.

While the measured outcomes in the self-esteem areas were not impressive and were to some extent counter-intuitive, there was a widespread conviction among the participants that this was an important outcome area. As far as measurement was concerned, a more sensitive indicator of the kind of outcome being observed was found to be enthusiasm.

Enthusiasm. The variable enthusiasm really stands for a complex of affective orientations toward the program. This dimension has often been neglected in educational research that emphasizes cognitive variables; however, in other fields, such as occupational research, variables like job satisfaction have been shown to play an important role in determining behavior. On the negative side, alienation and disaffection have received considerable attention, but little concern has been given to variables associated with commitment, or as Falsey calls it, enthusiasm.

Assessing the enthusiasm of students participating in the program against a background of overall levels of enthusiasm among students in this school, Falsey used a number of indicators to show that the majority of students in the program (84 percent) responded enthusiastically to it. They indicated that they would like to sign up again and that they would recommend the program to other students. Reasons given were that it was "fun" and that they felt affection toward it (74 percent), that it gave them "exciting experiences" (58 percent). Coding open discussion data, program students were found to use a high frequency of adjectives about the program such as "new experience," "trust," "courage," and "family." These epithets reflect the staff ideology about the program, but students were found to have been socialized into Project Discovery culture by acquiring and using this language. As the language involved peers and teachers as well as program staff, this effect apparently reflects affectional bonds forged in the course of the shared experience. Examples are seen in student journal reports:

Project Discovery is a very special class. . . . It puts you on challenges you will never experience just in the city. You make very close friends who you will always cherish. You will not like it at times, but you would expect that in any thing and any place. You will see beautiful scenery you will never see in the city. At times you will cry from the agony of carrying a backpack or canoe, but all in all Project Discovery will change your attitude. It will show you love and a whole new experience.

Another student, who began the semester with no enthusiasm for the program wrote:

This is the last trip. . . . I thought Project Discovery was boring when I first heard about it but I was wrong. . . . [Of the staff the student writes] I never had brothers so that's why I say they been like brothers to me. [— A teacher and a staff member] are so kind it seems like they cared for everybody. [They] showed me lots of things, for example rock climbing, canoeing etc. Today we are leaving home [referring to the camp site] Good bye, nice having a notebook to write my thoughts in.

Falsey also examines the variant cases, or those who indicated that they did not enjoy the experience, would not reenroll, and did not get anything special out of it. Reasons given included practical ones (conflict with other commitments at weekends, moving away), interpersonal (not getting along with the others) and personal (did not like the food, the rugged conditions). Correlated with an enthusiastic orientation to the program were three variables: degree of attendance, number of friendships on the program, and popularity. Hispanics were more enthusiastic than blacks by a large margin, and males more than females. The older students were more enthusiastic than the younger ones.

The importance of this analysis is less in relation to enthusiasm as an independent variable than as a moderating variable. Enthusiasm correlates with improvement in academic performance, but the high level of enthusiasm for the program makes it too broadly applicable a variable to be useful on its own. Rather, it helps to explain variation in the patterning of other relevant variables such as attendance and self-esteem. The enthusiastic student is more likely to have high attendance and is more likely to show improvements in self-esteem in the course of program participation. Cumulatively, the impact on academic performance is greater than taking each variable individually.

Discussion

The findings of the study were equivocal in relation to the initial design and associated hypotheses. Changes in the field situation as well as in the program itself made it impossible to produce the desired data from experimental and control groups. In any case there would have been questions about whether the program effects were truly measurable in the time span available and under the prevailing conditions.

However, a considerable amount of information was gathered which confirmed the overall impression that the program was having the kinds of effects its enthusiasts were proclaiming, and allowed for the pinpointing of variant, less-responsive groups, notably blacks and females. In addition, the research brought out the importance of a dimension which was not so much unknown as unhighlighted – enthusiasm.

The fact that this was an action-research project rather than an orthodox field study brought the researcher into a more interactive dialogue, both with program personnel and with school staff. This led to the discussion of a number of issues that might have been less prominent in a straight evaluation study or a conventional field study. To her analysis of empirical materials on the program and how it functioned, Falsey added insights into how it could function more effectively. For example, concerning the issue of the relationship between Project Discovery and the school curriculum, Falsey argued that greater integration was possible, and that this might be expected to lead to increased correlation between program participation and academic performance.

When students are rock climbing, for example, they can talk about the kind of rock they are climbing, how it got there, etc. An awareness of students' classroom behaviors might help both staff and teachers informally to address student problems that are most visible in school. For example, a student who is reluctant to speak up in class may be given extra attention on a trip, or a student who is regularly disruptive in the classrom may be engaged in informal discussion about the reasons for his or her classroom behavior.

Falsey also pointed out *indirect* consequences of participation in the program, which might be beneficial both to students and to others. Students in the program were notably active in extra-curricular student activities following their participation. And many teachers involved in the program volunteered the information that participation in the program was "an exciting and memorable experience in their teaching careers." This reaction was interesting in light of the fact that teachers and Project Discovery staff experience a number of stresses and show high turnover (if not burnout). Falsey was able to make some recommendations about the management of the program from this point of view. Recruitment and training issues, rotation, role clarification, and program goal-clarification were discussed based on project data rather than random impressions.

As a generic issue, the idealism (if not grandiosity) of many innovative programs provide a sense of guilt and shortcoming as well as an inspiration. Goal clarification and prioritization are called for, both within the program and between program and school curriculum. And, in relation to the role of evaluation and research in developing this and other information, Falsey writes:

Project Discovery began in a climate of intense public interest in and support for programs targeted for poverty areas like the South Bronx. While not specifically remedial, the program also drew on a firm ideology of "compensatory education" for poor and minority children. While concern for these issues persists at both the local and national levels, the overall emphasis within education has shifted from remediation to "excellence" and the spotlight of publicity concerning the South Bronx has dimmed considerably. With these changes in climate the pressure to point to "results" has increased. One administrator worried that, to the extent that the organization could not claim to be dramatically addressing critical needs and reaching "students not already doing ok, Project Discovery looks like simply an adjunct to the school, a nice program for kids who don't really need it anyway, and not worth the money." At a conference concerning the outcomes of this and other innovative programs for youth, the President of Urban Adventures stated, "We're hitting singles out here, but everybody wants to hear about home runs."

The perceived pressure from external sources to "hit home runs" intensifies on a daily basis the uncertainty felt by all of the staff within the organization. The staff themselves want dramatic results and small incremental base hits are in general less satisfying than a ball hit out of the park.

Falsey concludes that the high and comprehensive expectations should be accepted, but equally it should be accepted that there will be different degrees of realization of these goals, particularly in an elective program within a public school such as the South Bronx High School. There are also significant differences that need to be recognized, between the situation in which Outward Bound arose and flourished and those of contemporary New York City. All of the differences in motivation, selection, participation, and program execution are relevant, requiring reinvention or re-formulation of the intervention. One of the program directors is quoted as saying, "The students don't automatically buy the idea that having a hard time rock climbing or being scared scaling a high wall is good for them. We can't shove it down their throats. They have to be seduced into it."

Falsey adds that the seduction occurs through creating an experience which is fun; but there are doubtless children who are unseducible, and others for whom seduction does not ensure the desired consequences.

Another issue in articulating the different parts of this program to make it work optimally has to do with differences between the teachers' perceptions and Project Discovery staff's perceptions. Of course, these are subject to personal differences, but there are also differences that seem to arise out of behavior-setting contrasts. One illustration may be the child who was described by the teacher as "off the wall" (and a class problem) versus the perception by staff that this same child was a "high energy kid," with "real leadership potential." The need to reconcile differences in the way learning styles are perceived and responded to – a task which emerged as central in the mentoring role study – was a serendipitous observation in this study.

The success of the program – taking it, in the words of one staff member, "a long way from Mom and Pop," – makes a prima facie case for its effectiveness. However, with changes in the directorship of the program, together with staff turnover based on stress and other factors already indicated, there are problems of continuity. The eventual niche for the program in the curriculum will take time to be determined and will depend in part on unresolved issues about the source and degree of economic support for the work. Innovative programs can be incubated through the help of a foundation like the Gould Foundation, and developmental issues clarified by research efforts such as the one described here. However, longer term mainstreaming of the program depends on larger political and economic forces.

Finally, though this was an action-research project, with more than the usual attempts to coordinate the requirements of research and action, the classical problem of differences in time scale between completing an action episode and completing a research analysis was apparent. This was amplified by career issues, as Falsey had to move on to a university teaching position when project funds ran out. Her move meant delay for the program, but not defection from the writing-up. The disarticulations caused by delay were somewhat ameliorated by the interactive relationship that Falsey sustained with the urban Adventures directorate. Falsey notes:

I continue to be struck by the differences in time scale involved in action episodes and research analysis. My sense is that the research was useful to the agency nonetheless, because I was able to give feedback during the analysis and to write brief memos to them as results were coming in.

With two changes of agency director during the span of the project, these research feedback sessions contributed to agency continuity as well as to the specific program development. Discontinuities of the type described, along with those created by the larger school and program changes, are "facts of life" in such projects.

By analyzing the issues raised in generic terms, Falsey has contributed to the possibility that they may be handled in such a way as to minimize their negative repercussions and maximize their benefits. In her final report, Falsey observes that there are several kinds of partnership involved, each linking partners with distinctive inputs. The partnership between Project Discovery and the school is one in which two contrasting types of educational organizations shared an involvement with a group of students. The school is large, involving dozens of faculty members and a thousand students, and it is part of a much larger, impersonal bureaucracy, the city school system. Project Discovery is part of a small face-to-face organization which is highly personal in its commitments, relationships, and styles of work. Whereas the operation of the school requires a high degree of organized routines and codified procedures, the project emphasizes flexibility, freedom to adapt to varied and changing challenges, and to experiment with innovatory practices.

Another partnership is between staff (both school and project) and students. As in families where there can be tension between parents, splits between the two kinds of authority figures may be disturbing. Falsey indicates that points of tension can occur between project and school staff, and how repercussions on the students may blur the benefits they might otherwise be deriving from participation in the program. As Project Discovery has grown, its emphasis on administrative orderliness and planning has produced internal tensions between newer administrative-minded staff and older, more charismatic, innovatory staff. In adapting to the requirements of the larger systems in which the program must function, there has been a move toward greater congruence with the school program. The partnership with research has contributed to this development in documenting its value in objective terms.

However, Falsey in her analysis notes that the distinctive quality of the new intervention is to some extent blunted in this adaptive process. She cautions that in a system that "wants it all" (Goodland, 1984) there are distinctive risks and pitfalls (Sarason, 1983). It would be a loss to abandon the distinctive contributions of Project Discovery, and blunting the idealistic drive that brought the program into being could sap it of its capacity to generate enthusiasm in students, which is, as the research indicates, a key to the program's effectiveness.

Against this, on the up side, Falsey notes that while a favorable balance of inputs remains, there will be positive though modest effects:

Students who call themselves "The PD Family," field staff who feel "burned out in a good cause" and teachers and administrators at the high school who describe themselves as "energized," if occasionally exhausted, by the infusion of new blood and contrasting ideologies in the busy and bureaucratic world of a (large urban) public school.

References

Anderson, C. S. 1982. The search for school climate: A review of research. *Review of Educational Research* 52:368–420.

Argyris, C.; Putnam, R.; and Smith, D. McC. 1985. *Action Science*. San Francisco: Jossey-Bass.

Barr, R., and Dreeben, R. 1983. *How Schools Work*. Chicago: University of Chicago Press.

Baumrind, D. 1971. Current patterns of parental authority. *Developmental Psychology Monographs* 4(1): part 2.

Bolton, B. 1980. A conceptual analysis of the mentor relationship in the career development of women. *Adult Education* 30(4): 195–207.

Bradley, A., and Adamson, J. 1973. About empire state college mentors. *Research and Review*, no. 7, p. 5.

Bronfenbrenner, U. 1979. Contexts of child-rearing: Problems and prospects. *American Psychologist* 34:844–850.

Camp, B., and Bash, M. 1981. *Think Aloud: Increasing Social and Cognitive Skills*. Champaign, Ill.: Research Press.

Caplan, G. 1974. *Support Systems and Community Mental Health*. New York: Behavioral.

Caplow, T., et al. 1982. *Middletown Families*. Minneapolis: University of Minnesota Press.

Cartledge, G., and Milburn, J. (eds). 1980. *Teaching Social Skills to Children: Innovative Approaches*. New York: Pergamon.

Clabby, J., and Elias, M. J. 1986. Project Aware: A community partnership model for school-based consultation and education programming. In *Creativity and Innovation* ed. by H. Fishman. Davis, Calif.: Pyramid Systems.

Clabby J., and Elias, M. J. 1986. *Teach Your Child Decision Making*. New York: Doubleday.

Collins, E., and Scott, P. 1978. Everyone who makes it has a mentor. *Harvard Business Review* 56(4):89–101.

Cowen, E.; Gesten, E.; and Weissberg, R. 1975. *New Ways in School Mental Health*. New York: Human Sciences Press.

Dooley, D., and Catalano, R. 1980. Economic change as a cause of behavioral disorder. *Psychological Bulletin* 87:450–468.

Dunkin, M. J., and Biddle, B. J. 1974. *The Study of Teaching*. New York: Holt, Rinehart and Winston.

Dunn, K., and Dunn, R. 1978. *Teaching Students Through Their Individual Learning Styles*. Reston, Va.: Reston Publishing Company.

Elardo, P., and Cooper, M. 1977. *Aware – Activities for Social Development*. Reading, Mass.: Addison-Wesley.

Elias, M. 1982. Using programs for emotionally disturbed children in mainstreamed or special class settings. In *The Mainstreamed Library: Issues, Ideas, Innovations*, ed. by B. H. Baskin and K. H. Harris, pp. 178–186. Chicago: American Library Association.

Elias, M. 1983. Improving coping skills of emotionally disturbed boys through television based social problem solving. *American Journal of Orthopsychiatry* 53: 61–72.

Elias, M.; Bruene, L.; et al. 1985. A multidisciplinary social problem solving intervention for middle school students with behavior and learning disorders. In *Advances in Learning and Behavioral Disabilities*, vol. 14, ed. by K. Gadow, pp. 49–75. Greenwich, Conn.: Jai Press.

Elias, M., and Clabby, J. G. 1984. Integrating social and affective education into public school curriculum and instruction. In *Organizational Psychology in the Schools: A Handbook for Professionals*, ed. by C. A. Maher, R. J. Illback, and J. E. Zins. Springfield, Ill.: Charles C. Thomas.

Elias, M.; Gara, M.; and Ubriaco, M. Sources of stress and coping in children's transition to middle school: An empirical analysis. *Journal of Clinical Child Psychology* (in press).

Elias, M., and Maher, C. A. 1983. Social and affective development of children: A programmatic perspective. *Exceptional Children* 49:339–48.

Elias, M.; Ubriaco, M.; and Gray, J. 1987. A cognitive-behavioral analysis of parental facilitation of children's social-cognitive problem solving. *Journal of Applied Developmental Psychology* 6: 57–72.

Elkind, D. 1975. Recent research on cognitive development in adolescence. In *Adolescence in the Life Cycle*, ed. by S. Dragastan and G. Elder. New York: Wiley.

Entwisle, D. R., and Hayduk, L. 1978. *Too Great Expectations*. Baltimore: Johns Hopkins Press.

Epps, E. G., and Smith, S. F. 1984. School and children: The middle childhood years. In *Development During Middle Childhood*, ed. by W. A. Collins. Washington, D.C.: National Academy Press.

Falsey, B. 1986. *Project Discovery* Final Report. New York University Center for Applied Social Science Research.

Falsey, B. 1987. *Barriers to Change*. Ph.D. dissertation, New York University.

Felner, et al. 1975. Crisis events and school mental health referral patterns of young children. *Journal of Consulting Clinical Psychology* 43:305–310.

Gara, M. 1984. The impact of the ISA (improving social awareness) project on CMHC-RMS admissions. UMDNJ-CMHC of Rutgers Medical School Program Planning and Evaluation Unit, Piscataway, N.J.

Gartner, A. 1971. *Paraprofessionals and Their Performance*. New York: Praeger.

Gartner, A.; Kohler, M.; and Riessman, F. 1971. *Children Teach Children*. New York: Harper and Row.

Goodlad, J. 1984. *A Place Called School*. New York: McGraw-Hill.

Hare, B. 1980. Self-perception and academic achievement: Variations in a de-segregated setting. *American Journal of Psychiatry* 37:683–689.

Herzlinger, R. 1977. Why data systems in non-profit organizations fail. *Harvard Business Review* (Jan.) 55:81–86.

Hoffman, M. L. 1970. Moral development. In *Carmichael's Manual of Child Psychology*, vol. 2, ed. by P. H. Mussen. New York: J Wiley.

Humm, A. 1983. One-on-one: The mentoring project. New Careers Training Laboratory, Graduate Center/CUNY, unpublished report.

Jencks, C., et al. 1972. *Inequality: A Reassessment of the Effects of Family and Schooling in America*. New York: Basic Books.

Jensen, A. R. 1969. How much can we boost IQ and scholastic achievement? *Harvard Educational Review* 39:1–123.

Klerman, G. L. 1985. Community mental health: Developments in the US. In *Children, Youth and Families*, ed. by R. N. Rapoport. New York: Cambridge University Press.

Levinson, D., et al. 1978. *The Seasons of a Man's Life*. New York: Knopf.

Litwak, E., and Meyer, M. J. 1967. *School, Family and Neighborhood*. New York: Columbia University Press.

Markus, H. J., and Nurius, P. S. 1984. Self-understanding and self-regulation in middle childhood. In *Development During Middle Childhood*, ed. by W. A. Collins. Washington, D.C.: National Academy Press.

Maughan, B., and Rutter, M. 1985. Education: Improving practice through increasing understanding. In *Children, Youth and Families*, ed. by R. Rapoport. New York: Cambridge University Press.

McGillicuddy-De Lisi, A. V.; Sigel, I.; and Johnson, J. 1979. The family as a system of mutual influences. In *The Child and Its Family*, ed. by M. Lewis and L. Rosenblum. New York: Plenum.

Miles, M., and Huberman, A. M. 1985. *Qualitative Data Analysis*. Beverly Hills, Calif.: Sage.

Miner, J., and Boldt, J. 1981. *Outward Bound USA: Learning Through Experience in Adventure-Based Education*. New York: Morrow.

Mussen, P. H.; Conger, J. J.; and Kagan, J. 1969. *Child Development and Personality*. New York: Harper and Row.

Pickett, A., and Humm, A. 1981. *Paraprofessional bibliography*, New Careers Training Laboratory, City University of New York, case 15–81.

Putallaz, M., and Gottman, J. 1982. Conceptualizing social competence in children. In *Advances in Child Behavior Analyses and Therapy*, vol. 2, ed. by P. Karoy and J. Steffen, p. 133. New York: Gardner.

Rappaport, J. 1977. *Community Psychology: Values and Research*. New York: Holt, Reinhart and Winston.

Riessman, F. 1984. A student design for education. *New York Times*, Nov. 29. Letters.

Riessman, F., and Humm, A. 1984. Training outline for the student mentor program of the City University of New York and the New York City Board of Education. Unpublished manuscript.

Roche, G. 1979. Much ado about mentors. *Harvard Business Review* 57(1): 10, 14–28.

Rosenberg, M. 1965. *Society and the Adolescent Self Image*. Princeton, N.J.: Princeton University Press.

Rutter, M. 1980. *Changing Youth in a Changing Society*. Cambridge, Mass.: Harvard University Press.

Rutter, M., et al. 1979. *Fifteen Thousand Hours: Secondary Schools and Their Effects on Children*. Cambridge, Mass.: Harvard University Press.

Sarason, S. B. 1983. *Schooling in America: Scapegoat and Salvation*. New York: Free Press.

Schulberg, H. C., and Killilea, M. (eds). 1982. *The Modern Practice of Community Mental Health*. San Francisco: Jossey-Bass.

Shore, A. 1977. *Outward Bound: A Reference Volume*. Greenwich, Conn.: Outward Bound.

Shure, M., and Spivack, G. 1978. *Problem Solving Techniques in Child Rearing*. San Francisco: Jossey-Bass.

Siegel, E., et al. 1980. Hospital and home support during infancy: Impact on maternal attachment, child abuse and neglect, and health care utilization. *Pediatrics* 66(2): 183–190.

Sigel, I., and Saunders, R. 1979. An inquiry into inquiry: Question-asking as an instructional model. In L. Katz, ed., *Current Topics in Early Childhood Education*, vol. 2. Norwood, N.J.: Ablex.

Spivack, G.; Platt, J. J.; and Shure, M. B. 1976. *The Problem Solving Approach to Adjustment*. San Francisco: Jossey-Bass.

Walberg, H. J. 1981. A psychological theory of educational productivity. In *Psychology and Education: The State of the Union*, ed. by F. Farley and N. Gordon. Berkeley, Calif.: McCutchan.

Zigler, E., and Weiss, H. 1985. Family support systems: An ecological approach to child development. In *Children, Youth and Families*, ed. by R. N. Rapoport. New York: Cambridge University Press.

4   Courts

Children generally come into contact with law courts either as offenders or as victims. In whichever case, it is recognized that they are different from adults. As minors they are not, in the legal sense, fully competent. Various kinds of competency are recognized in law: to have committed a crime, to be able to stand trial, and to be responsive to dispositions of one kind or another, among others (Weithorn, 1984). Defining children as not yet fully competent affects both judgment and disposition.

As immature "dependents," children are vulnerable not only to the circumstances bringing them before the courts but to the impact of the various legal proceedings. Legal reforms have produced a variety of experiments aimed at maximizing the protective elements in the court experience and minimizing the traumatic ones.

An appreciation of these issues was behind the historical development of special institutions and procedures for juveniles. Earlier social interventions included reformatories and houses of refuge. Juvenile courts evolved with an increased recognition of the needs of the child and an emphasis on children's rights. Emerging at the turn of the century, the juvenile courts expressed this emphasis in what Parsloe (1978) calls the "welfare approach." Based on the medical model, the court was seen as a "friend of the juvenile" (whether an offender or a person in need of care), a confederate of his family, and a place where expert help could be mobilized as a matter of human rights for individualized assessment and treatment of the problems confronted.

While this "rights" strand of evolution is a strong one in the juvenile justice field, underlying many of the reforms which have taken place, it has not always been the dominant one. In contrast there is the "criminal justice" approach, which emphasizes the eradication of crime. Within the juvenile justice strand there are individuals who are to some degree welfare-oriented, but the primary concern is with the protection of society rather than with bettering the child's mental health, which they would consider to be the primary concern of other professionals. It is a "figure-

148

ground" issue; both types of orientation – welfare and criminal justice – are discernible, but sometimes one, sometimes the other, is more salient.

Leslie Wilkins (1985), in a review of the criminal justice part of the juvenile justice field, noted that various conceptual orientations to the child have prevailed at different periods. Viewing the child in a psychodynamic framework, within which criminality was more or less equated with psychopathology, led to efforts to reduce juvenile delinquency by administering psychotherapeutically oriented interventions to young people at risk. This has been found to be unfeasible logistically on any very large scale and, in some cases, counterproductive. Where the child has already been convicted of an offense, the psychotherapeutic approach has sometimes been applied individually or in groups. This, too, has proven arduous and controversial. Larger scale programs have been developed using a variety of approaches based on a succession of Juvenile Delinquency Prevention and Control Acts (Youth Policy Institute, 1981). These include efforts to improve custody arrangements for children and a national initiative to develop innovative techniques for diverting youth away from the traditional juvenile justice system through the development of alternative programs aimed at prevention. Among the innovative programs is one emphasizing restitution, that is, requiring that juvenile offenders repay crime victims through some form of financial remuneration or through community service.

Notwithstanding these ingenious and well-intentioned innovations, there has been a strong countercurrent toward strengthening traditional procedures in the face of a rising number of juvenile problems. One emphasis that has emerged in the 1980s is the "just desserts" approach. According to this, the child is dealt with in relation to actual behavior, rather than according to potential for behaving differently under hypothetical circumstances (Wilkins, 1985).

The need for experimentation with new approaches has been apparent, whether arising out of theory or practical experience. The important thing, it is widely agreed, is that new programs be properly studied and evaluated so that the ineffective ones are discarded in favor of more promising ones. Johnson, Bird, and Little (1979) of the Center for Action Research, reviewed a number of recent theories and strategies in delinquency prevention and noted, as did Wilkins, that theories of delinquency prevention can be divided into those which emphasize individual characteristics, those which emphasize social interaction patterns, and those which emphasize social structure and subcultural factors. They concluded that empirical evidence to support programs based on specific causal elements in conceptualizing delinquency prevention are inadequate (particularly those based on individual personality factors). Some, though they incur substantial costs, have limited evidence of benefits, while others incur moderate costs and indicate some promise. In this last category are programs associated with modifying existing organizational practices in schools, justice institutions, and the work place.

Approaching the issue of preventive intervention from a welfare perspective, the emphasis has been on the dangerous potential that legal involvements pose for the developing child; the child is subject to stigmatization, labeling, criminalization, and distress in becoming a focus of parental strife in a public advocacy context. At one extreme are those who argue that the welfare concept of the child is incompatible with that of crime and punishment. From this position, procedures have been set up to avoid the need to expose children to courts, lawyers, and judges. Diversionary programs, neighborhood dispute resolution programs, the Scottish Children's Hearings Panels, and so on, represent this approach and broadly reflect a "delegalization movement." Goldstein, Freud, and Solnit (1973) entitled their book *Before the Best Interests of the Child* (1980) to emphasize their view that every effort should be made to avoid getting the child into the litigation situation, because the child is best served by dealing with the issues *before* they have to go to court.

When the child must go to court, or *should* go to court, to ensure the observation of due process in obtaining his or her rights, the issue becomes one of how to achieve a blend of justice and welfare in what Landsman and Minow (1978) call "lawyering for the child." This might be through providing a lawyer for the child, or through the cultivation of alternatives to litigation so that lawyers need not be involved. In the two cases presented in this chapter, two kinds of resolution of the justice/welfare dilemma are presented: the first, the law guardian, is a social intervention which provides a way of giving every child coming to court a lawyer (whether for criminal or welfare proceedings). The lawyer, as the designation implies, has guardian as well as advocate functions. The availability of such a role aims to ensure that justice is done and is seen to be done not least by the child. The second case study is of a court-connected mediation project. It lies somewhere between those programs that are provided outside the courts, either privately or by what Parsloe terms the "community approach" (Schlossman, 1977) and those that are mandated by the courts. The mediation panels described here are provided through the court services, but are not currently part of mandated court procedure.

There are many issues associated with the relations between social research and legal interventions–in the courts and elsewhere in the legal system (Stapleton and Teitlbaum, 1972; Lipson and Wheeler, 1987). The case studies presented allow only fragmentary insights, but they do serve to highlight some of the issues and problems together with some approaches to developing solutions through action-research.

Case study: Children's lawyer (law guardian)

The social intervention here is the *law guardian,* a lawyer for a child appearing in court.

The action-research project, to assess The Law Guardian Program, was conducted over a two-year period (1982–1983) and was sponsored by the New York State Bar Association with the joint financial support of the State Division of Criminal Justice Services, the Foundation for Child Development (FCD), and the William T. Grant Foundation. A technical advisory committee made up of representatives of the bar association's Special Committee on Juvenile Justice and other interested parties and chaired by State Supreme Court Judge Howard Levine selected the social scientist who was to conduct the research. The committee's task was to formulate recommendations based on research results. The state legislature would then act on the future of the law guardian role.

Jane Knitzer, then director of the Institute for Child and Youth Policy Studies in Rochester, New York, was principal researcher, forming a team with legal consultant Merril Sobie, professor of law at Pace University.

Background

The occasions when children are required to appear in court are of great importance both to the child and to society. Ideally, a balanced consideration is given to protecting children's interests as individuals and to safeguarding social values. For the child, such an event has a potentially powerful impact. Whether a case of delinquency, custody, or care, the outcome of such proceedings may radically affect the child's whole subsequent life.

The right of a child to have legal defense in courtroom proceedings is now widely recognized. However, there is no single, universally acceptable formula as to how this should be equitably arranged, taking into account the diversity of circumstances. Within a single state like New York (which was a pioneer in the introduction of the law guardian role), various arrangements are practiced in relation to services linked to courts.

There has by no means been unanimity on court-related services for children. Some argue, for example, that the services may contravene others' rights, particularly the decision-making powers of parents. And there is no consensus about which arrangements best serve children's needs. Nevertheless, there are powerful grounds in our cultural values to support the idea that a child in court has a right to be heard through counsel (Knitzer, 1982; Wald, 1979).

The history of provision of special procedures for children in court can be traced back to the late nineteenth century when the juvenile court system was created. Setting up special procedures was not, at that point, a matter of providing children with lawyers. The predominant model was a medical one, of diagnosis and treatment, rather than the traditional legal one of determination of guilt and punishment. This tended initially to be done behind closed doors by judges in consultation with the involved parties. The emphasis was on the *needs* of children and on finding a way to help them other than simply punishing the guilty.

In the intervening years there have been many relevant developments. The growing use of probation was important in the evolution of an emphasis on rights as well as needs, and it was part of a movement toward individualization in the provision of justice for juveniles. The juvenile justice movement has also been helped by the development of research by the Children's Bureau and others on children's rights and on standards of operation of courts dealing with children. The need to take steps to ensure that the juvenile courts operated in the best interests of the child was established by the historic Supreme Court decision (*In re* Gault, 387 US [1967], which condemned a juvenile court incident in Arizona in which a child had been given a severe punishment for a misdemeanor through an arbitrary judicial action. The Supreme Court made the assignment of counsel mandatory for all minors facing deprivation of liberty as a possible outcome of judicial proceedings.

New York state had already recognized children's rights to legal representation under the Family Court Act of 1962. This was the first such provision in the country and called for discretionary representation to be provided for delinquency or status offenses, child neglect or abuse proceedings, and guardianship proceedings. It implied a conviction that the best interests of the child may, under some circumstances, be served neither by parents *nor* by judges in closed session. Fair procedure in the family courts required that the child have a legal representative or advocate in court, not only in delinquency proceedings but more generally in cases of neglect, abuse, guardianship, and all proceedings under the Family Court Act.

The social intervention

The Law Guardian Program was created to meet the requirement that the child have a legal representative in court. The Family Court Act sought to bring together the specialist perspectives of lawyers and other professionals concerned with families. In so doing it had the effect of marrying the lawyers' conception of due process and the social workers' conception of child welfare. The former perspective placed emphasis on "children's rights" to due process under the law; the latter on the needs and "best interests of the child."

Putting such a role into place seemed appropriate at the time, but in the longer run its built-in dilemmas have entailed some problems. After 20 years of operation and with various criticisms being voiced, there was widespread feeling that there should be a review of the operation of the system. The law guardian was a key role in the family court system and, according to a study, it was seen as contributing both to the improvement of procedures in defending children and to the broader review of the Family Court Act being undertaken by a special commission for the recodification of the act.

Thus, the law guardian role was not a new intervention but one in need of overhaul; nor was it a unique intervention. Though New York was in the vanguard of the movement to improve legal representation for children, having instituted the role five years before national legislation, it was not the only place to use law guardians. Similar roles with similar titles were instituted elsewhere, and in all cases the new role expressed the social movement to improve children's rights under the law.

In New York, the act designated three methods of assigning a law guardian: the Office of Court Administration could contact the legal aid association to provide a lawyer from their roster; the Apellate Division could retain a lawyer or group of lawyers; or a panel of attorneys recommended by the local bar association could serve as court appointees. The first and third methods have been the principal ones used, each having specific advantages.

In the two decades since it was started, the Law Guardian Program mushroomed from a $200,000 statewide budget (50 percent for New York City) to a program in which New York City alone allocated over $4 million in 1978, with lesser amounts allocated in the various counties around the state. Disparities in expenditure began to stimulate queries about whether the allocations represented genuine differences of need or other considerations. For example, in 1978, New York City, with its 17,650 petitions and $4,218,286 in allocated funds, managed an average case load of 327 per fulltime law guardian. This compared, for example, with Erie County, with its 3,668 petitions and allocation of $136,765, where the average case load per law guardian was 917. These differences could have been due to differences in population, court procedures, type of representation, or a number of other possible variables.

At that time, several studies by local bar associations and meetings among administrators had led to a mounting feeling that there was a need to examine the issue of quality of representation. There were questions about the implications of differences in the way the role was defined and administered in different judicial departments. There were questions about whether law guardians were being responsive to the complex legal and psychological issues associated with the increasing number of child abuse and neglect cases, and whether they were alert to the issues – fiscal and psychological – of various aftermaths of their involvement, such as placing the children in foster care. A need was felt for a systematic assessment in order to recommend the most equitable methods of recruitment, training, and monitoring of the law guardian system. As judicial departments have considerable latitude in adopting their own rules and procedures, it was not expected that there would necessarily be a high degree of standardization. However, those concerned with child welfare and children's rights, both within the legal profession and among other concerned groups, were expressing dissatisfaction with the way the system was working.

A book by journalist Peter Prescott (1981), who sat and watched the courts in action, caused considerable stir because it highlighted the unevenness in the application of justice, even within a single court. The poor, the black, and the ethnically disadvantaged fared poorly. Prescott's book was a sympathetic account of the family courts system, recognizing the overloads and turbulent conditions under which it had to operate, but it also noted that the courts were falling short of their own goals in relation to children's rights. And it was this issue that was drawing public concern.

A research report sponsored by the New York Community Services Agency suggested that too lenient or cursory dealings with juvenile delinquents might deprive the public of the protection that was also the court's responsibility (Fabricant, 1983). Another report supported by the FCD argued that too harsh handling of juvenile offenders under the Juvenile Offenders Act of 1978 had set back progress toward rehabilitating juvenile delinquents through special family court procedures. The act had the unintended effect of undermining the status, and therefore the effectiveness, of the family courts (Sobie, 1984).

The Prescott and Fabricant studies, though considered to have methodological problems, nevertheless had the effect of potentially weakening public confidence in the court system. Sobie's report, more analytic in character, represented a move to bolster the family courts through indicating the consequences for children of the alternative.

History of the project. The project arose out of the concern of the New York State Bar Association that the rapid but uneven growth of demand for due process protections for children had led to a situation where there were wide disparities in the quality of legal representation. A major study was necessary to assess the situation and propose remedies based on factual findings.

The state bar association acted as the sponsor for the study and sought funds from the New York State Criminal Justice Services Department. Due to the size of the budget, additional support was sought and gained from the William T. Grant Foundation and the FCD. The FCD had a number of involvements in the juvenile justice field in which this project was seen to fit; and the Grant Foundation was developing an action-research program for which this project was seen as suitable. The characteristics of the project which made it action-research (as distinct from a routine program evaluation) were the high degree of collaboration between sponsors and researchers and the intention to follow through from the results of the study to a collaborative formulation on recommended implementation. Classically, a program evaluator assesses the program, writes a report, and moves on. In this case, the intention of the researchers and sponsoring agency was to work together to make recommendations, disseminate the findings, and to follow through on shaping a course of action.

The project was intended to cover the state of New York, excluding New York City, as the city was a special case being handled by the Legal Aid Society and had recently been described in reports of various kinds. The mechanism used to develop the research component of this project was a Request for Proposals by the State Division of Criminal Justice Services (with Howard Schwartz, chief of the Juvenile Justice Unit acting as coordinator). A technical advisory committee was appointed by the bar association's special committee and functioned throughout the project, eventually assisting the bar association committee to draw up its report and recommendations. After the researcher was recruited, a collaborative partnership was formed between the bar association (through its special committee) and the researcher. The technical advisory committee did not govern the detailed conduct of the study, but its recommendations guided the bar association committee in decisions at each stage of the project, from hiring the research director to shaping the conclusions and recommendations.

Research design. The Request for Proposals (RFP) issued by the Juvenile Justice Unit of the Division of Criminal Justice Services was for a project" to examine the adequacy and quality of legal representation provided to children in the family courts throughout New York State." Submissions were reviewed by a technical advisory committee chaired by State Supreme Court Judge Howard Levine (chairperson of the state bar association's Special Committee on Juvenile Justice). Members included representatives of the funding bodies, the Legal Aid Society, the family courts, the Office of Court Administration, the State Council on Children and Families, and the attorney general's office. These people represented agencies concerned with children's rights, with issues of equity and child welfare, and with effective political and professional devices to make a public service system work.

The proposal selected was that submitted by Jane Knitzer, of Statewide Youth Advocacy. Knitzer's proposal stated the questions in researchable terms and provided excellent legal participation (in the person of Merril Sobie, professor of law at Pace University and a former clerk of the family court). Both Knitzer and Sobie had records of competent research and productive work in the children's rights area. Because Knitzer's position was with an advocacy group, there was some concern both about image and about possible pressures on the researcher that might bias the eventual report and how it was received. Knitzer argued that the advocacy group did not have a preconceived position on the topic of the project, and that its advocacy role would help to ensure that whatever findings emerged would be vigorously pressed for application. Accepting this, but retaining a concern for the risks associated with advocacy groups, the committee suggested that a semi-autonomous research institute of child and youth policy studies be set up, with Knitzer as director. This was done under the administrative aegis of the advocacy organization, but with a high degree of autonomy. The arrangement proved acceptable to all concerned. The research institute was given four linked goals:

1. To develop and test out working criteria for effective representation of minors in specific procedures
2. To assess, using the criteria, the quality of individual representation accorded to juveniles throughout the state
3. To assess and compare the effectiveness of the two types of delivery systems used in New York state, the panel system and legal aid societies
4. To develop feasible recommendations to improve the quality of representation and the efficiency in providing such representation to juveniles in New York state.

The project was alert to the possibility of finding conflicts within the profession relative to the law guardian role, but this was not a primary objective. Another "implicit" but subordinate element of the research goals was the impact of the court experience on the child. The impact on the child is a topic of concern in relation to administration of court procedure and to how the legal role is exercised (in court and in the actual interpersonal relationship with the child) (Landsman and Minow, 1978). But though these issues were of interest, it was not considered to be feasible in the framework of the project to do more than gather qualitative information as available. The assumption was provisionally accepted that high quality legal aid was, by and large, better for the child than lack of such aid in the troubled circumstances leading to court action.

The project was relatively atheoretical as far as the action-oriented participants were concerned. The basic merit of the law guardian role was accepted in relation to the constitutional rights of children to enjoy due process, and attention was focused on obtaining a high-calibre evaluation of how well the law guardian role worked. The project was seen as an instrument for generating data on which new legislation could be based.

The researcher's use of theory was somewhat eclectic. Initially, the focus was on role theory, within an implicit, social-ecological framework. Eventually the ecological model became the dominant one, with emphasis on the multiplicity of perspectives on representation for children.

Course of the project. The initial research task was to develop criteria for assessing the role. Law guardians function under multiple mandates: to seek dismissal or reduced sanction for the client, to see that due process is observed, to contribute to the child's development, and to consider the protection of the community, among others. While none of these is the exclusive responsibility of the law guardian, they are mandates of the court system in which the law guardian performs his or her role, and it is not always clear which criteria should be salient if they conflict. Law guardians themselves vary in relation to how much they see these issues as their concern at all.

In order to develop systematic criteria and apply them to the analysis of the role, four methods were used: a review of documentary indications of existing criteria of national standards for lawyers and of legislation pertaining to juvenile justice in the state; a statewide survey of law guardians to obtain their conceptions of the role; on-site observations and interviews in the courts of 15 representative counties; and interviews with key officials with statewide perspectives and responsibilities.

The *survey* was conducted to establish what lawyers themselves considered to be the criteria for good representation of children. It was sent to all law guardians in the state, seeking information on their experience with juvenile law, their pattern of activity in the law guardian role, problems encountered, and their own assessment of criteria for fulfilling the role requirements. In addition, in order to compare legal aid specialists in children's situations with the general panelists, questions were included about the attorneys' specialist knowledge of the laws pertaining to juveniles, and where they saw themselves in relation to specific procedures.

On-site observation was conducted in the courts of 15 counties, selected to represent a range of populations, geographic distribution, appellate departments, and so on. All four counties (excluding New York City) where legal aid societies represented juveniles were included to enable the study to obtain maximum information on critical differences between full-time and part-time law guardians. In the on-site visits, interviews were conducted with judges, local bar association members, and others who work with law guardians (e.g., probation officers and child welfare workers). In each county visited, at least 10 percent of the practicing law guardians were interviewed, and observations were conducted on law guardians in action in the family court.

The *interviews* with the law guardians focused on two concrete, recently closed cases, as well as covered general issues of the role, the system, and the philosophy of legal work with minors.

In the county studies three distinct perspectives served as bases for assessing the quality of practice: the law guardians themselves, those who worked with them in the courts, and the researcher as observer. This allowed composite profiles to be constructed of the 15 counties.

A *statewide system analysis* of the way the law guardian system is organized, financed, and administered was accomplished through the study of official documents and interviews with public officials in relevant agencies such as the Office of Court Administration and the Appellate Department.

All of the above methods addressed the primary objectives of the project which were evaluative. The secondary objectives were analytic and descriptive, encompassing the various interfaces in which the law guardian functions, including the relationship with the child. To preserve the primary focus, the secondary objectives were pursued only after completion of the county profile studies. Low-key interviews with juveniles, for example, were conducted with the cooperation of the Division for Youth in two contrasting youth facilities and two residential facilities. This substudy was designed to provide proxy descriptive information on attitudes and experiences of juveniles similar to those who are the subjects of the law guardians' work.

The primary objective reflected the concern of the legal sponsors who were interested in an analysis of the law guardian role in the courts. The secondary objective reflected the interests of the sponsors who were concerned with child development research and the possible impact of the experience on the child. Different component bodies in the advisory committee were interested in different types of cases, for example, delinquency cases and cases of children needing care. It was decided to retain the focus of the legal sponsors for the formal report, but to gather *ad hoc* data for the secondary interests as possible.

A problem arose in the course of developing the statewide survey and the court studies. Initially this was to have been subcontracted to an outside organization that had national experience with related topics and the technical resources to do the specialized aspects of social survey research. After pilot survey material was gathered and reviewed, the researcher felt that, although the national perspective was important, a more state-specific form of knowledge and involvement would be required for the subsequent stage of local courtroom studies. However, some areas in the state held a negative image of researchers because of insensitive intrusions in the past. And while responsibility for conducting the survey was reabsorbed by the main project team, the team was only partly able to overcome some judges' unwillingness to give researchers access to the courts. One of the originally intended 15 counties totally declined to participate.

On completion of the draft report, a decision had to be made about the main recommendations that the committee would make on the basis of the report, together with the development of a strategy for implementing it. The question was not so much whether or not the findings were acceptable, but what policy recommendations might be effectively pushed in relation to them. There was resistance to any interference with local autonomy in some areas of the state and there were fiscal limitations produced by cutbacks in state funding generally.

The relations between the researcher and the component bodies in the project were harmonious throughout. Though the project was a dispersed one and the links between the research team and the various stakeholders was loosely knit, communication remained excellent and a high degree of involvement was maintained by all parties throughout the project. The research director was able to incorporate technical aspects of the project outside her own discipline and worked well with her legal consultant. The advocacy link did not interfere with the conduction of the project, and the fact that the researcher was based in an institute dedicated to this project's work ensured that draft materials were promptly produced and circulated. Major decisions were worked through both with the advisory panel and the funding bodies.

When the project was terminated, continuities were maintained through the continued functioning of the bar association's Special Committee on Juvenile Justice. The principal investigators, continuing to work in related fields (Knitzer on child policy, Sobie on the history of juvenile justice in New York state) were able to retain a continuing interest in the aftermath of the project.

Results

Research findings are published in a book-sized monograph by the bar association (New York Bar Association, 1984). The monograph describes the multipronged design of the study, with reports on interviews with the law guardians as well as views and observations of others about the functioning of the law guardian role. The 14 counties forming the sampled sites are described, together with the methods used for selection. Reports are presented on the views of 785 attorneys who had served as law guardians on 335 cases and on 119 courtroom episodes. Interviews with public officials concerned with the program are summarized and, finally, descriptions of the attitudes of the 24 children in placement are provided.

The first data source – the survey of law guardians – yielded the following profile:

- Most law guardians do not represent many children a year, nor do they see themselves as specialists in children's law. (The typical law guardian represents less than 20 children a year. This is less than one-fifth of his or her total practice.)
- As a group, the law guardians have few experiences to prepare them specifically for law guardian work. (Almost 70% of the law guardians reported they did not have any special screening, orientation, or co-counsel experience prior to joining the panel.)
- The lack of prior experience is compounded by a scarcity of training after appointment to the panel. (Forty-two percent of the law guardians have had no relevant law guardian training within the last two years.)
- Overall, the panel law guardians in New York state viewed their role as representing what they perceive to be the child's best interest. Even in juvenile delinquency and Persons in Need of Service (PINS) proceedings, under 15% viewed representation of youth as analogous to that of a defense lawyer. A still smaller percentage said they would consistently represent their client's wishes in the face of personal disagreement.

  These views were greatly affected by region; downstate law guardians were twice as likely to take a rights-oriented view and want to represent the child's wishes. However, within both upstate and downstate counties, the full range of views about representation was visible, including reports from a substantial number of law guardians who were simply uncertain about their role.

- Although individual levels of frustration with the Law Guardian Program were rarely seriously problematic, as a group law guardians were surprisingly critical of the system. (Most individual panel law guardians, despite widespread frustration related to reimbursement levels and court delays, anticipated serving as law guardians indefinitely.)
- From the panel law guardians' perspective, their greatest training need was for updates on current case law and legislation. Further, 87 percent reported they would like to have access to independent social workers and mental health professionals. Half of them would also like access to a brief bank and paralegal assistance. This was particularly true of law guardians living downstate.

These findings have significant implications for the Law Guardian Program. In the first place, the majority of law guardians see only a limited number of children a year, making it difficult to develop great expertise in juvenile proceedings. Further, the fact that over half the panel attorneys are in solo practice means they have limited opportunities to draw on special skills from others. Also apparent is that for a good many attorneys, exactly what a law guardian is expected to do is not clear. And finally, the lack of training available to the law guardians is conspicuous, particularly since the substantive laws in New York state governing many key proceedings for children are complex and detailed. Also a significant proportion of representation involves nondelinquency cases and child protective and child welfare cases (e.g., foster care approvals, reviews, and termination of parental rights), which require knowledge of the complex and changing pattern of welfare provision.

In relation to the courtroom observations and interviews, serious and widespread problems were evident. There was very uneven performance of the most basic requirements of effectiveness: to meet the client, be minimally prepared, have some knowledge of the law and of possible dispositions, and be active on behalf of the client. The project findings revealed these shortcomings:

- Overall, 45 percent of the courtroom observations reflected either seriously inadequate or marginally adequate representation; 27 percent reflected acceptable representation; 4 percent effective representation; and 24 percent of the observations lacked sufficient information to be coded. Similar patterns were visible in the transcripts.
- In 47 percent of the observations it appeared that the law guardian had done no or minimal preparation. In 5 percent it was clear that the law guardian had not met with the client. In 37 percent of the cases it was not clear whether the law guardian had met with the client before the court proceeding. In 35 percent of the cases, the law guardians did not talk to,

or made only minimal contact with, their clients during the court proceedings.

- As to observed instances of effective representation, in 5 percent of the cases the law guardians gave evidence of interviewing their clients carefully; in 17 percent they argued in an informed way about the facts, the child's best interest, or the child's rights; and in 5 percent they seemed especially responsive to their clients during the proceeding.
- Evidence from case-specific interviews with law guardians confirmed that discontinuity of representation is a problem. In only 35 percent of the cases in which the child had prior court contact did the same law guardian provide representation in subsequent proceedings. Particularly troubling was the evidence of missed opportunities in foster care review proceedings when the law guardian representing the child at the initial removal proceedings was not reassigned at subsequent reviews of the placement. (Since data suggested that over 40% of the children in placement were likely to have at least two, and often more, periodic court reviews, the pattern of changing law guardians was likely to affect large numbers of children.)
- *Ineffective* law guardians exhibited two widely visible patterns. The first involved a lack of preparation or investigation, even when there were clear questions of fact, as in serious abuse cases; the second involved the law guardian who was physically present, but otherwise inactive, unprepared, and unresponsive to the client. As an indication of the importance of this from the point of view of due process rights, an analysis of transcripts showed that almost 50 percent included appealable errors made either by law guardians or made by judges and left unchallenged by the law guardians. Violations were especially visible in delinquency and PINS cases, particularly when detention was involved.
- Conversely, *effective* law guardians were observed to use legal strategies actively to protect the rights of their clients, to be knowledgeable about the laws, and to be vigorous and creative at the dispositional stage. They also tended to become important sources of psychological support and information to their clients.

Three additional findings also have significant implications for the quality of representation: the comparative effectiveness of panel and legal-aid law guardians, the level of appellate activity, and the law guardians' view of their role.

- Legal-aid attorneys were more likely to give acceptable or at least perfunctory representation, while panel attorneys' representation tended to be polarized, either very poor or very effective. Forty-five percent of both the legal-aid law guardians and the panel attorneys were identified in the overall coding of the observations as seriously inadequate or marginally adequate. Further, while a higher percentage of panel law guardians were coded as seriously inadequate, compared to legal-aid attorneys (19 percent as compared to 8 percent), more panel attorneys were also judged to be effective as compared to legal-aid attorneys (6% as compared to 1 percent). A somewhat higher proportion of legal aid attorneys (37 percent as compared to 21 percent) were found to be providing acceptable representation.

The researcher concluded that the data did not give sufficient support to arguments for either delivery approach (panels or legal aid) to warrant an endorsement, but rather that both approaches could operate effectively if strengthened in different ways to improve the level of representation for children.

- Appellate actions, brought by either panel or legal-aid law guardians, were virtually nonexistent outside of New York City, and this absence constituted a conspicuous deficiency in current practice. This deficiency was problematic not only for individual juveniles, but for the general quality of representation. The absence of appeals meant there was virtually no check on judicial or law guardian errors, and statutory issues requiring interpretation or clarification went unresolved.
- Children generally wanted to view the law guardian as on their side, whether or not they liked the outcome. Their comments tended to be critical not of the role, but of specific experiences with how it was exercised. The significance to the child of having the same law guardian at different proceedings was another frequently noted theme.

The report questioned whether these were isolated lapses or whether the system itself was inadequate. The delivery system for the Law Guardian Program involves law guardian panels, legal aid offices, the Appellate Division and the Office of Court Administration, all of which have roles in the delivery of representation to children in New York. The quality of representation is affected by the character of the system as well as by individual lawyer capacities. Essentially, the findings were interpreted by the research team as suggesting that the current bifurcated, and essentially *ad hoc,* administrative structure worked against the delivery of a uniformly high level of representation.

- Within the counties there were no written or informal guidelines governing recruitment, appointment, and recertification of panel law guardians. Assignment practices were variable; of the ten panel study counties, four made assignments based solely on the judge's decision, one on a perceived match between the law guardian and the child, and two based on a modified rotation system. The remaining study counties used a combination of methods.
- Policies with respect to the four legal-aid societies studied also reflect local decisions. Annual case load size varied considerably from 300 to 800, as did expenditure per case. In both the largest and smallest legal-aid office studied, each law guardian handled approximately 800 cases per year; in the other two legal-aid offices case loads were between 300 to 400 for each law guardian. The largest legal-aid office studied had no back-up

panel and so routinely represented co-defendants in conflict or potential conflict situations.

Only the smallest office had access to a social worker; the largest office had no nonlegal support staff at all. No legal-aid office studied had any formal policies regarding continuity of law guardians either within proceedings or from one proceeding to another. In two offices, assignment policies virtually precluded continuity. Formal ongoing training was not provided.

State-level involvement with the Law Guardian Program is fragmented and focuses primarily on fiscal, rather than programmatic, issues. There is now no one place where all the issues pertaining to a coherent and effective system can be addressed. The report found that neither the Office of Court Administration, which has responsibility primarily for budget issues, nor the Appellate Division, which oversees the panel system, gave law guardian matters high priority.

The report outlined nine essential functions for operating the law guardian role effectively on a statewide basis. In abbreviated form they were as follows:

1. Develop consistent administrative guidelines.
2. Strengthen the quality, accessibility, and scope of training.
3. Review and clarify fiscal policies.
4. Review appellate and special litigation capacity.
5. Stimulate efforts to improve quality of representation.
6. Provide mechanisms for evaluating and changing methods of selecting a law guardian.
7. Monitor programs.
8. Ensure collection of data.
9. Ensure overall planning, decision-making, and leadership capacity within the law guardian programs.

In discussing alternative policy recommendations potentially based on these data, the advisory committee considered four alternatives:

1. Leave the system alone, hoping that once the problems were diagnosed and publicized, self-corrective measures would come into play.
2. Use existing agencies, but get them to coordinate better and give more attention to strengthening the law guardian role.
3. Create an agency within one of the existing agencies with its sole responsibility to be the operation of the law guardian role.
4. Form an independent law guardian agency with statewide responsibility for the role.

In the advisory committee, the discussion centered on whether to support the fourth, far-reaching recommendation or one of the more moderate ones calling for the strengthening of existing mechanisms. An anomalous situation developed in which the researcher, together with her legal consultant, led the argument for the more activist recommendation. She based her recommendation on these findings:

> Preparation of law guardians for their role was minimal.
> Backup, training, and remuneration were widely considered unsatisfactory.
> Overall administrative responsibility was lacking.
> There was no mechanism for establishing and maintaining standards.

Arguments against the more far-reaching recommendation were:

> It would be costly, and this was a time of retrenchment.
> It would require strong support from lawyers and politicians for passage in the legislature.
> It would be resisted and strong defenses would have to be available to deal with attacks on, for example, the analysis of effectiveness of the law guardians.
> There would be arguments for operating with existing machinery (e.g., the Office of Court Administration) rather than introducing a new agency.
> Where would a new agency be located and who could lead it with sufficient status and lack of conflict of interests?

Arguments in favor (in support of the researcher's recommendation) were the following:

> Justice based on geography is recognized as wrong, and there is a need for a statewide agency to insure equal standards.
> Defense services for indigent juveniles are vitally important and their quality must be assured.
> The New York Bar Association, in its Special Committee on Juvenile Justice, is dedicated to improving services, though they themselves are not in a position to run the program. The participating lawyers also want a program like this one.
> Existing machinery is not satisfactory, nor is it likely to become so because of structural, historically built-in inadequacies.
> The experience of other bodies (e.g., the Council on Children and Families) has indicated that it is possible to work with existing agencies to create an executive body to oversee, coordinate, and monitor, rather than usurping functions for an entirely new body.

In summary, there was consensus that the field of responsibility for operating the law guardian system was divided and confused. There were many gaps in responsibility: no group or individual responsible for overall program effectiveness, no long-range planning, no devices for monitoring or improving services. Existing departmental advisory committees had not been sufficiently active or uniformly effective, as witnessed by the lack of change in the way the system had operated since its inception, despite various expressions of dissatisfaction. It was accordingly recommended that an agency be established to centralize and coordinate the Law Guardian Program in the state; that the state bar association draw up new guidelines for the role; and that each county set up review procedures involving the local bar associations, the family court judges, and others working with law guardians.

The report was disseminated in several ways. The main report was published by the state bar association (1984). Press releases were disseminated that summarized the principal findings prior to the publication of the full report. In addition, the project experience fed into academic papers and monographs (Sobie, 1987a, 1987b).

To pursue the idea of establishing a new agency, legislation had to be drafted. Sobie, in collaboration with the bar association's special committee, worked on this during 1984–1985. Accepted in principle was that the bar association would draw up a set of guidelines for law guardians, with commentaries on responsibilities, and that counties would set up review procedures for the functioning of the law guardians within their jurisdiction.

As of mid-1986, little more had happened systematically, though there was a widespread feeling of a job well done, useful information for thought and application, and so on. In the recent aftermath, the reservations expressed by some members of the committee regarding contemporary political and economic constraints on action seemed justified.

Discussion

As an action-research case, this project has several elements of interest. First, there is the close link between the researcher and an advocacy organization, about which there was initial hesitation. This link did not yield trouble in the way it was potentially envisioned, but trouble surfaced in another way. Knitzer fought for her conclusions against many arguments that would have cowed most conventional academic researchers, who tend to take a neutral position on the political elements in formulating recommendations and leave the assessment of feasibility to the action members. Although there was a clear-cut conceptual division of roles and responsibilities, a different situation occurred in practice. Many of the action people expressed views on the methodology and on substantive issues of the research, while the researcher showed a highly goal-oriented dedication to pushing through a vigorous course of action.

Another interesting point is in relation to theoretical stance. The researcher was eclectic initially, and found role theory most useful in discussing conceptual issues with a secondary implicit interest in the social-ecological conceptualization in the data on value dilemmas of the law guardian (e.g., the familiar "justice" vs. "best interests" goals). In the end it was the implicit rather than the explicit conceptual orientation which informed her analysis and recommendations. The ecological orientation made apparent the gaps or *deficits* in the functioning of the law guardian role in relation to its social context. Knitzer's analysis was replete with the identification of areas (e.g., the courts, the state legal system) in which the lack of environmental supports undermined the role, where there was a "lack of coordination," "lack of preparation," "lack of continuity and follow-through on case disposition," "lack of appropriate rewards," and so on.

Knitzer's report gives a great deal of information about the identification of problems or malfunctions and provides analysis of how they arise and can be dealt with. If the report seemed critical of the law guardian role, it may partly be because the Law Guardian Program was conceived idealistically. The report makes explicit precisely how the program falls short of its goals and how more progress might be made toward reaching them.

Though this project does not provide direct information on the impact of the court experience on the child, there are indirect implications for child development theory. The law guardian and the system in which the role is embedded are elements in the environmental set of forces acting on the child. A courtroom appearance is a critical event in a child's development. Much child-development research has concentrated on the family or the school. This study highlights the importance of other roles and other organizations. While the study gives more to our understanding of the legal organization's handling of the child than of the child's perceptions of the organization, it alerts us to issues in this relationship. Events leading up to the child's appearance at court engage persons who may be in roles new to the child, such as social workers and lawyers. In expanding beyond the family and school, a number of ambiguities arise for the child, and how they are resolved affects the child's experience and ultimate development (cf. Minuchin, 1984).

From the point of view of research methodology, this project reveals the importance of competence in a range of skills not generally taught in academic settings. The action-researcher, in addition to needing the technical expertise of her discipline, had to cultivate skills necessary to work with people in very different settings from those of the university classroom or laboratory. This also involved the capacity to develop new techniques which are not taught in standard psychological methodology courses. It required the kind of capacity to understand how these people think and what their sensitivities are. While these considerations are sometimes taught in field-work courses in anthropology and sociology, they are less present in academic psychology. Yet a capacity to develop this understanding can play a crucial role in helping or hindering the research enterprise, particularly in an action-research framework.

Also, there is the need to understand issues associated with the implementation of results. Academic researchers entering policy or applied areas are often accused of failing to understand the play of political and organizational forces affecting the application of the findings. In this case, the researcher's experience with advocacy groups had given her a realistic understanding of what *could* happen; but it remains to be seen whether it *will* happen in this situation, and when.

The researcher's capacity to collaborate with the committee was important. In practical terms it opened doors, through the sponsorship of the state bar association and the good relations that Judge Levine had with family courts. In the committee meetings and discussions, it provided a perspective to anticipate issues that might arise and to support the researcher in dealing with them. For example, when the shape of the findings and conclusions were emerging, some predicted a blood bath in response to the report, and then if the program survived that, a period of positive reconstruction. Something like this did occur, and being prepared for it helped.

From a dissemination and advocacy perspective, Knitzer indicated an awareness of the possibility that a backlash could be harmful to children if the report's conclusions were too critical of the law guardian role ("If they were doing such a poor job, why support the system?"). Such a reaction would not help those who were working for due process for children. The task was seen as getting the right balance. Here, too, the guidance of the advisory committee was useful.

After the project was completed and the report submitted, some money was promptly appropriated by the state legislature to strengthen the law guardian role. But though presiding justices were in agreement with the findings of the study and the need to take action, they opposed the idea of creating a new office to monitor the Law Guardian Program. Furthermore, a fundamental impact could be achieved only through legislation and this was a matter beyond the powers of the action-research group. Thus there was only a modicum of immediate action and considerable uncertainty about longer term results.

The same may be said for scientific impact. Though this project was not directly oriented to academic conceptual issues, it does provide an interesting case that might be relevant to social science concerns.

On the applied side more generally, the case highlights the problem that

Landsman and Minow (1978) call "lawyering for children." The law guardian is a role designed to steer a course between what Freeman (1984) calls the Scylla of paternalism and the Charybdis of state power. The lawyer has to be a "friend of the juvenile offender and a confederate of his family," while representing the law and exercising the law's power to provide representation. Lawyers in the role, however, do not have a clear conception of what this should mean. The deficiency in the role reflects a problem in the way the role is conceived and operated.

One solution, represented in the "delegalization" movement, seeks to disengage the child from this kind of role altogether, on the grounds that it is too insensitive to the needs of the child. But this solution risks "throwing out the baby with the bath water," if the protection of the child's rights to due process is jeopardized. The issue is how best to combine both agenda–the child's rights and the child's best interests–in the context of an institution designed to enforce social values. The law guardian role was invented for this purpose, but the need to reconceptualize the role is apparent today.

Case study: Mediation as an alternative to litigation in divorce proceedings

The intervention in this case is the *mediator* appointed by the court as an alternative to litigation in divorce custody disputes. The project was initiated by Robert Emery, of the University of Virginia Department of Psychology, where there has been an outstanding program of research on the impact of divorce on child development (See Hetherington, 1980; Emery, Hetherington, and Dilalla, 1985). Judge Ralph Zehler of the Charlottesville Albemarle District Court sponsored the project on the action side, where collaboration was arranged with Ms. N. H. Scott, director of the Court Service Unit. Joanne Jackson has been principal mediator, housed at the court and serving as liaison person between the court, the university, and the community. The project began in 1983 and is continuing.

Background

The problem to which mediation is addressed in this case is the psychological harm that children can suffer when divorce negotiations between their parents become problematic and conflictful. Where there is continuing disagreement about such issues as support, custody, and access–even when there is consensus that the marriage has broken down–the child is often caught in a "tug of love" and may be emotionally bruised by the conflicts between the parents. The adversarial system of legal dispute settlement, while having positive elements in bringing matters to a decision and forcing a decisive break between the couple, is considered by many to be stressful for the child. Though the concept of the "best interests of the child" has provided some guidance in custody disputes, the disputes themselves are often costly and acrimonious, with unsatisfactory social-psychological residues. In fact, it has been argued that the "best interests" standard has made things worse. Unlike the "tender years" presumption it replaced, the doctrine is quite vague and thereby encourages potentially bitter litigation. While many questions can be raised about the tender years presumption, it had the advantage of locating a child's special vulnerability in an identifiable age band, making the likely outcome of litigation clear, thereby discouraging litigation.

Relevant background literature has two principal strands: mediation, which is a social movement, and psychological impact of family dissolution. Mediation as a formal field has grown exponentially in the United States over the past decade. This is, of course, in response to the vast increase in divorce rates. The current generation of young parents are as likely to divorce as they are to remain married (Glick, 1984), and the projection that one-third of all children born in the 1970s will experience parental divorce by the time they are 18 may be an underestimate (Furstenberg et al., 1983).

Historically, mediation has been used in conflict resolution back as far as ancient China and Greece and has been known in the United States since the seventeenth century (Burger, 1982; Folberg and Taylor, 1984). Its principal use in the twentieth century has been associated with industrial disputes. The concept of negotiating solutions between disputants has accumulated a voluminous literature (see bibliographies on alternative methods of dispute resolution by the American Bar Association, 1979; and of the Family Mediation Association, 1982). There now exists a full complement of elements associated with a major social movement: training centers (see American Bar Association, 1982), journals (e.g., *Mediation Quarterly; Conciliation Courts Review*) academic positions (e.g. Frank Sander of Harvard Law School), research projects (e.g., The Denver Custody Mediation Project; the Toronto Conciliation Project), professional associations (e.g., the Family Mediation Association; The Association of Family Conciliation Courts), and a wide variety of activities such as training programs, conferences, and workshops.

Family mediation is one subfield within which there have been a number of specialized activities directed toward the resolution of specific conflict situations. Rowan Wakefield, in a special issue on family mediation of

American Family (1981), notes a number of points along the family life cycle which give rise to conflicts to which mediation has been addressed. Some are "normative crisis" points:

> Premarital mediation
> Teenager and parent relationships
> Pregnancy (with teenage pregnancy being a special case)
> Relocation
> Retirement
> Wills and estate planning

The more problem-oriented foci include:

> Management issues with disabled and handicapped family members
> Domestic violence
> Runaways
> Homosexuals in the family
> Unmarried cohabitants
> Separation and divorce
>> Property settlements and support payments in divorce
>> Child custody and visitation issues
> Special problems of the elderly

The generic processes and issues are widely applicable, but in a field that has grown so rapidly there is a certain amount of relabeling and repackaging of the activity to suit specific situations. Emery (1982) has collected various definitions of the process at the heart of mediation:

A process of power equalization. (John Haynes, social welfare professor, Stony Brook, New York)

A process which posits a neutral third person who will guide the parties toward a resolution of their disputes. . . . (Linda Silberman, law professor, New York University)

A presence to be shaped by the parties and the issues for use in negotiating. (Thomas Colosi, American Arbitration Association)

Different from therapy (in that) it focuses on the product (not the process). . . . Mediation gives people back the responsibility for making their own decisions about their own lives. . . . (Ann Milne, practitioner, Family Counseling and Mediation)

Perhaps the clearest statement of the relationship of mediation to court procedures was generated in the Massachusetts Conference on Children, Youth, and Parents in 1981. Based on a report of the advisory committee appointed by the governor, a special commission on court procedures was appointed and published a report on probate and family court procedures. Its specific recommendations were that probate court procedures in the areas of divorce, family violence, and child custody should be standardized, that there should be a program of public education on how the probate and family courts work, and that there should be developed (and researched) nonadversarial options in the settlement of family disputes. Summarizing five arguments in favor of mediation as a valuable addition to existing court procedures, the commission concluded that while mediation is not a panacea for all disputed divorce and custody cases, "some forum of nonadversarial dispute resolution should be available in every probate and family court as an option for the many families that can benefit from such an alternative process." Various models were indicated: independent mediation paid for privately, mediation offered as a service by specially trained members of the bar, and mediation provided as a service through the courts.

Two general features of mediation that distinguish it from other methods of conflict resolution in the divorce field, such as litigation, negotiation between attorneys, or arbitration, are that there is a single mediator with whom communication between the parties takes place, and that the mode of communication sought is cooperative (rather than competitive, or combative). The parties themselves make the decisions, rather than a judge or arbitrator. Mediation differs from psychotherapy (though the process may be therapeutic) in that it focuses on solving an interpersonal problem and requires a professional mediator who is knowledgeable in legal and economic issues rather than the social and psychological issues generally concentrated on by therapists. A closely related concept, still used in Britain but common historically in both countries, is conciliation. The goal for both conciliation and mediation is to bring the disputants to an agreement, though not necessarily an agreement to reunite. The latter is encompassed in the concept of "reconciliation," which is often a latent goal in conciliation proceedings, but is conceptually distinct (Murch, 1980).

The idea of mediation has been embraced enthusiastically by some judges and politicians and is mandated in several states. Lawyers are mixed in their responses, as are the disputants themselves. While the concept of mediation is a welcome contribution in a situation where there are few legal doctrines to guide the decision-making process, there are many competing ideas about what the most appropriate, effective and cost-efficient method of structuring the role would be. Different models have been suggested, based on experimental attempts to introduce the role into various settings and on the professional backgrounds of particular theorists (cf. Bienenfield, 1983; Coogler, 1978; Haynes, 1981; Saposnek, 1983).

Within the law, there is a trend toward less public involvement in divorce and more simplified divorce proceedings and "no-fault" grounds. Mediation has been encouraged as a device for what Mnookin (1975) calls more "private ordering," or coming to agreement without the sometimes harsh public confrontations in courtrooms, with adversaries vying with one another to establish fault. However, whatever the problems may have been with the concept of fault, it at least offered a ready basis for decision-making on custody. As with other historic doctrines which have eroded with social change, custody decisions have suffered from the growing complexity of family dynamics. Prior to and through most of the nineteenth century, fathers were given preference on the basis of paternalistic property assumptions. This policy was replaced by the tender years doctrine and the recognition of mothering as crucial in early personality formation (Derdeyn, 1976). With the judiciary acting as parens patriae, most custody decisions in the mid-twentieth century were made in favor of the mother and were not disputed; and there were many fewer divorces involving young children. In the 1960s and 1970s, with a rise both in divorce rates and in ideas on gender equality, there was a wider range of interpretation of what was in the child's best interests and a greater amount of disputation (Mnookin, 1975; Weitzman, 1981).

Given the erosion of traditional prescriptions and the uncertainties in the new fields of force, from the purely legal point of view litigation is necessary so that due process may be observed. However, litigation increases acrimony, is costly, limits appellate review by vague judicial guidelines, and involves economic factors which introduce bias.

Where court-based mediation programs have been tried, indications are that in between half and three-quarters of the cases, agreements were reached. In addition, evidence suggests that there is greater satisfaction and less relitigation when mediation is used (Emery and Wyer, 1987b).

Psychological grounds for considering alternatives to litigation are also compelling, though here the issues are more complex and difficult methodologically. However, the evidence of stress on children caught up in parental conflicts over custody is so robust that it comes through strongly whether from unselected case studies, quasi-experimental studies, or court-based, family-based, clinic-based, or community-based research. The research shows that children suffer adverse social and psychological distress when their parents divorce. This is mitigated, of course, by the age of the child, the social and economic supports which intervene, the nature of the difficulties from which divorce is a release, whether or not the custodial parent remarries, and whether or not there are therapeutic interventions. In this array of intervening variables, the variable of litigation looms large as a potentially negative factor, exacerbating the stresses. Among the short-term effects identified in recent research are sadness, fears, anxiety, and unrealistic expectations; whereas among the longer-term effects are behavior problems, academic performance problems, difficulties in relations to the opposite sex, and, in some cases, more extreme social and psychological disorders (Emery, 1982; Emery et al., 1985; Hetherington, 1980; Kurdek, 1981; Wallerstein and Kelly, 1980). Social stigmatization exists, though it may be less than previously and is certainly different in different social niches. Diminished contact with the noncustodial parent is a tendency, though there are exceptions. There is also a diminished economic standard of living, particularly if the custodial parent is the mother (Weitzman, 1981). There are a number of other factors which tend to increase the stress, including residential relocation.

An inevitable conclusion from reviewing this literature is that much depends on how things are handled in the immediate situation, in the short-term aftermath, and in the longer term. Furthermore, it is clear that deep-rooted family conflicts may have existed for a long time prior to the actual dissolution of the family household, and that they often continue beyond the divorce. In considering preventive interventions, there are considerable difficulties in identifying appropriate families and in making interventions unless voluntarily requested by the troubled couple. Frequently these precipitative family conflicts are concealed from friends, relatives, and neighbors, and occasionally it comes as a surprise even to a spouse, who may be precipitously abandoned; variation is rife. Nevertheless, current interest is in preventive intervention through educational and media devices, as well as through the courts and the human services professions.

Emery points out that there is a "striking irony in the current legal structure for settling child custody pursuits. In an attempt to reach an *ends* in the 'best interests of the child,' the judiciary is limited to engaging in a *means*–the adversarial custody hearing–that would appear to be in opposition to the ends." The potential is great for such procedures to increase acrimony, undermine the couple's future cooperation in regard to co-parenting, and perhaps discourage the loser (the noncustodial parent) from maintaining future contact. Goldstein, Freud, and Solnit (1980) advocate, on combined psychiatric, legal, and child-development grounds, that interventions should be considered before the child is enmeshed in a system that preaches the best interests of the child while functioning to its detriment.

A number of questions also emerge: Does mediation work? For whom is it appropriate? What is the constellation of factors that goes into establishing a program that will make mediation work?

The action-research project

Emery, who initiated the project in the context of the university's Department of Psychology, rooted his interest in two sides of his professional experience: the clinical side that bore witness to the psychological toll taken in the divorce experience, and the academic research side that showed that much of the published discussion on mediation took the form of a polemic with little in the way of solid data to support the various assertions and counterassertions from diverse case experience. He noted that though the reasons for the growth of mediation are apparent, out of the frustration of the judiciary and the negative responses of those experiencing litigation, little systematic research has been done on the workings of mediation. The paucity is due to various reasons, including the recency of interest in the topic, and the issues of territoriality. However, the need is apparent and there is a consensus that mediation must be studied, evaluated, and improved collaboratively by those employing it, if it is to develop effectively as a constructive intervention for children.

Research to date on the effectiveness of mediation in several settings where it has been introduced as part of the court procedures (e.g., California, Connecticut, and Toronto) has uncovered numerous methodological problems in the specification of variables, instruments, selective procedures, and so on, all of which affect the findings and their interpretation. Nevertheless, the general impression is that mediation works in settling disputes among half to three-quarters of cases coming to court. (Only about 10 percent of cases come to court, with about 90 percent being negotiated outside.) This is impressive given the fact that these are probably the most difficult cases.

Two situations made the Virginia setting a favorable one to further develop the mediation intervention: the link with a psychology department particularly strong in the field of the impact of divorce on children; and the link with a district court particularly interested in developing this intervention. In this small-town setting the chances of forming a constructive collaboration for action-research were favorable. In previous studies, suggestive correlations had been found between successful mediation and such factors as socioeconomic class, degree of conflict, and number of disagreements. However, these findings were used primarily for targeting the application of the procedure, rather than for developing the instrument and its workings. To do that, the action-research approach seemed suitable.

On the court side, the judge of the Charlottesville-Albemarle Juvenile and Domestic Relations Court was interested for the same reasons as were his forward-looking colleagues in other parts of the country: he wanted the introduction of a device that could deal with problems lacking in judicial guidelines. In addition he sought the reduction of public as well as private costs and the reduction of persistent conflicts often calling for relitigation. The judge himself was a leading thinker in this field and had published on it. From the point of view of the court services activity, the project offered a chance to develop and monitor a new form of service. The director of Court Services had studied social sciences at university and was responsive to the intrinsic interest that the project held.

What, then, might be distinctive in the Virginia project? The emphasis on the impact of mediation on children is an element scarcely touched upon in the other mediation projects, which have concentrated mainly on other criteria of success (avoidance of litigation and relitigation, reduction of public and private costs, and continuation of subsequent communications between the parts of the sundered family). Prior research had demonstrated that there were problems to be dealt with and undesirable effects to be avoided. The task in the Virginia project was how a role might be structured to cope with the former and forestall the latter.

Of course a role could be defined in theory, and a process prescribed. But one goal of action-research is to consider the relationship between the conceptual orientation and its translation into practical action. The issues involved in the Virginia project included legal and ethical concerns, as well as the practical tasks of recruitment and training, obtaining space, scheduling times, and so on. One of the issues was deciding from which profession the mediator should be drawn. Mental health professionals are likely to be strong on psychological and interpersonal issues and less strong on legal and fiscal issues, whereas lawyers may have the obverse skills. Other issues included the question of which of the various areas of dispute were most amenable to mediation; which of the various practice models–public or private–were most viable in relation to the operating systems of attorneys, courts, and judges; whether mediation should be mandatory; and whether there were some generally acceptable goals and guidelines which defined mediator roles (Emery and Wyer, 1987a).

Design and methodology. The project allowed for a development stage in which the particular form of mediation to be used could be tested. The form of mediation used had the following characteristics:

> Mediation is based on an assumption of cooperation rather than competition.

> Mediation is conducted by mediators in the presence of whom communication takes place.
>
> The parties themselves remain explicitly in control of the decisions made.

While similarities and overlaps are recognized between the mediation process and psychotherapy, the two interventions differ in focus, in objective, and in style (cf. Kelly, 1983). In the particular setting and under contemporáry legal conditions, the mediator concentrates on child custody or visitation disputes, leaving financial issues to be resolved through the adversarial process (Pearson et al., 1983). In the Virginia panels, co-mediators were used (one male and one female on each panel). Although importance was placed on a close liaison with legal colleagues, the mediators were qualified mental health professionals who also received training in mediation techniques.

The experimental design for evaluating the mediation process once its form was established required comparing an experimental sample and a litigation control group. The design took care to allow for comparisons between mothers' and fathers' responses (neglected in earlier studies) and to measure systematically a number of outcome variables in relation to the parents which might affect subsequent well-being not only of themselves but of their children (Emery, Shaw, and Jackson, 1987).

From among families requesting a hearing concerning child custody or visitation issues, 20 were assigned to mediation and 20 for the regular litigation procedures. (The numbers were subsequently doubled.) Although these assignments should ideally have been randomized, ethical and practical considerations affected the choices, and the consequences were taken explicitly into account as much as possible. As the assignments could not be ordered, given the lack of mandated mediation in the state, a random selection was given the opportunity to participate in mediation or in what was described as an evaluation of the court's services (which meant, actually, litigation). It took only 23 offers of mediation to produce the required 20 for mediation; and 25 approaches to produce the litigation controls. No demographic or court-record differences could be found between the two groups.

Mediation was to be limited to no more than six two-hour sessions. Subjects in both groups were paid a modest sum for their participation, and following the resolution–by either means–a number of outcome procedures were applied about a month later. These included

> A *structured interview* to evaluate parents' experiences of their sense of rights being protected, and sense of having retained control of decisions made

An Acrimony Scale (AS), measuring persistence of conflict and bitterness

An Acceptance of Marital Termination Scale (AMT), self-administered, measuring a range of feelings about marital termination, using indexes developed by Kitson (1982) and Thompson and Spanier (1983)

The Beck Depression Inventory (BDI), assessing affective, cognitive, and behavioral components of depressive states. (Beck et al., 1981)

The goal of the measures was to compare outcomes of the two groups regarding subsequent litigation (and relitigation); satisfaction of mothers and fathers with the experience; and the impact of the procedures on the broader psychological variables of conflict over parenting issues, acceptance of marital termination, and the incidence of depression.

Course of the project. The following diary records some of the events that took place that were critical in the development of the project.

November 1981	Emery visited Los Angeles County Court and learned about their program.
January to July 1982	Emery sat in on custody hearings with Judge Zehler. They discussed at great length problems of litigation and mediation, and mediation as an option with local attorneys. Emery found this extremely helpful in terms of the university–court relationship, the projects relationship with the bar, and information gathered.
July 1982	Judge Zehler and Emery visited a judge in Arlington, Virginia, who was experimenting with mediation. Judge Zehler decided to go ahead with the project after this trip.
July 1982 to May 1983	Emery mediated a few select cases to continue relationship.
May 1983	William T. Grant Foundation gave support. Emery considered the quick turnaround and willingness of the foundation to risk the project as *very* important. Hetherington's support at the university was also critical.
July 1983	The county court and Emery hired a mediator *together,* joint ownership.
August 1983 to January 1984	Emery and Jackson worked on developing a mediation service prior to beginning the research. It was crucial to have this time to work out problems and establish service.
August 1983	Emery presented accounts of the project to the local bar, schools, mental health organizations, and statewide groups; established credibility and got the word out.
	Work of Joanne Jackson evolved on providing mediation service and administering it, public relations, and linking with university.
	Team of eight graduate students were involved in the evaluation study.

The project suffered some initial difficulties in the recruitment and training of mediators. Emery and his principal colleague attended a mediation training course in New York, and a graduate student assistant worked for a summer in a California court-mandated mediation service. In addition, the staff visited other mediation services around the state to gather information relevant to developing a viable mediation role. They used the technique of co-mediation to instruct novice mediators. As the team developed its technique, the decision was made to keep the co-mediation format. The two-person mediating team model became the regular procedure, one male and one female.

In the first year there was an additional problem in finding subjects for the research design. The number of subjects recruited for the experimental and control groups was less than expected for several reasons. There was a refusal rate of 27 percent, which, though not high in relation to others' experience with recruiting subjects from this group, was higher than expected. This may have been due to the fact that the service had not yet established a track record and reputation in the local community. In addition, a higher number than expected were ineligible for one reason or another, so that it look longer than anticipated to build the sample.

Results

The demographic characteristics of the sample are important. As a reflection of the population of court clients, the sample was predominantly blue collar, young, and racially balanced. Of those accepting mediation, about three-quarters settled their disputes without recourse to litigation (a slightly higher proportion among those referred from the courts as compared with those referred by lawyers). Among the litigation sample, one-quarter settled out of court, but overall they took three times as long to settle their disputes.

Preliminary findings only are available (Emery and Wyer, 1987a, 1987b; Emery, Joyce and Fincham, 1987). Initial results indicated that men expressed a greater benefit from the procedure than women. Feedback of preliminary results led the staff to examine how they were relating to women and to see if they were being insensitive to women's needs.

In addition, the difficulties experienced in homogenizing the sample led to the research team's increased appreciation of the predicament of families going through the dissolution process; the economic problems, residential mobility problems, difficulty in maintaining contact with parents, and so on, all contributed to the stresses they were experiencing. This led the team to enlarge their conception of the limitations of the mediation procedure. While appreciating that mediation could be helpful in decision making in custody, they recognized the impossibility of coming to grips with all of the postdivorce difficulties.

The content of the decisions varied in the two groups. While both showed the predominant pattern of female custody for most cases, the litigation group had one sole-father-custody decision and one split-custody decision; the mediation group had four joint-custody agreements. Significantly more joint-custody arrangements were made through mediation.

In the measures of satisfaction with the process, with the content of the decision, with oneself, one's children, and one's former spouse, fathers showed a greater satisfaction with the mediation procedure than with the litigation procedure, while mothers were more satisfied in some respects with the court experience. Emery interprets this to reflect the fact that mediation gave fathers a greater voice in custody than they would have been given in the court; in court they were virtually certain to lose. The finding that the mothers' greater satisfaction with their court experience and greater distress in relation to the mediation was contrary to expectations. The fact that mothers in litigation reported lower depression scores contributed to this picture. Mediation mothers showed high scores for assessing the positive impact of mediation on their children, though they were less satisfied for themselves (Emery and Wyer, 1987b). Also contrary to general stereotypes, fathers as a group reported significantly greater difficulty in accepting the termination of their marriage.

The initial hypothesis that mediation would produce reduction in parental conflict and acceptance of marital termination was only modestly sustained. Longer term results are being looked for, and it was noted that the high proportion of joint-custody decisions among the mediation group gave the experimental group a particular character not intrinsically related to the mediation process itself. That is, the mediation group differed from the litigation group not just in terms of the dispute resolution process, but also in the outcome of that process.

Parents' rating of children's adjustment was found to be related to marital conflict and acrimony, as shown in previous research. And, consistently with Rutter's (1978) cumulative stressor effect, it was found that adding maternal depression increased the correlation. However, contrary to expectations, the reduction in parental conflict associated with the divorce settlement did not show an early lifting of children's reported behavior problems. While additional passage of time may lead to this expected effect, the researchers suggested it may not in this case. This sample group, being biased toward low-income families, may experience a sufficient level of chronic stressors in their lives that mediation does not lighten the load sufficiently to show much of an effect (Shaw and Emery, 1987).

The finding that fathers are more satisfied with mediation than with litigation is taken to indicate that fathers are, by this approach, brought into the range of satisfaction hitherto experienced by mothers, the traditional winners in custody proceedings.

Dissemination of results, tentative though they were, began in the first year. In addition to notices in the local press and university publications, the investigators presented two papers at professional meetings, submitted articles for publication, and wrote several chapters for books on topics associated with mediation. Project staff conducted workshops and gave talks about mediation and children's experience of divorce to a range of local lay and professional groups. A meeting was held with court members throughout the state as well as state administrators (arranged by project mediator Joanne Jackson). Judge Zehler and Emery were featured lecturers. As a direct result, a statewide organization of mediators was formed and legislative efforts begun toward mandating mediation.

Discussion

In this project, as in the mentoring project, the empathy group, and the social skills curriculum project, the researcher was directly involved in the initial development of the intervention, which was subsequently put into action and studied. Many academic researchers regard this as a distracting activity, for which they will not be rewarded in the system – a waste of time and not necessarily well done by the researcher. It may be seen as a different order of activity, best performed and supported by others. In this case, the development of the mediator role was integral to the research design in order to test the implied hypotheses in the available research literature.

The nature of these hypotheses and the part played by the tests is worth discussing. For the action agency, the test of the hypothesis is that mediation served a number of positive functions for the court and its clients was in the results of the evaluation. If mediation works, the argument for its adoption is strengthened. For the researcher, a scientific proposition was in focus: namely, that conflicts could be reduced through this type of procedure. If mediation reduced conflict, then the theory was supported. The development of the procedure to be applied and tested is likened to a scientist's construction of experimental apparatus. The advantage of testing it in this kind of a setting is partly the need to gain access to the specific type of cases. Also there is the possibility that more valid data will be obtained through tests and interviews that are conducted by a court-sanctioned service.

The findings themselves, which the researchers continuously insist must be taken as highly tentative, given the small sample size and special project circumstances, are actually very interesting in a generic issues framework. The paradoxical finding that men get more satisfaction out of mediation than women do was surprising to the team initially, but in retrospect is understandable. Many reform-oriented women have tended away from litigation because the courts sometimes seem the male preserve, and the costs of litigation can be high. In addition, though the more gender-neutral "best interests of the child" concept is ideally more acceptable, it is vague and the 'tender years' principle has been discarded so recently that judges still tend to give custody to women. Emery and his colleagues suggest that custody mediation perhaps helps to achieve a better balance between the satisfaction of mothers and fathers in the disputes, as well as providing a more enduring and speedier form of resolution. For women, the immediate loss of leverage may be made up for in the long run by the recognition of a principle that many women stand for and by helping to bring about a more variegated pattern of resolution to situations which are less standardized than they have been.

Difficulties in conducting a project of this kind included the familiar political ones (i.e., opposing opinions by influential people) and the time lags in getting payoffs (i.e., overcoming obstacles to setting up and conducting such a project, including obtaining the cases and conducting the interventions, research follow-ups, data analysis, and report write-ups). These difficulties affect the academic staff in relation to the projection of publishable results, whereas conventional laboratory or clinical projects allow the completion of many small reports for rapid dissemination.

The time lag also affects the action agency in terms of its decision-making about commitment to the activity. These problems were partly dealt with in this case through the presentation of working papers, talks, and interim results. On the positive side, the time lags allow time to become immersed in the area of work, helping eventually with the work of institutionalizing the service.

The project has been very successful at stimulating new service development. It has become a model mediation program in Virginia. The court and the community are anxious to continue it (Scott and Emery, 1987). The team has had a great many outside referrals for mediation and academic/professional invitations. There is little doubt in the minds of the participants that this method of collaborative interactive development has been rewarding.

References

American Bar Association. 1982. *Alternative Means of Families Dispute Resolution.* Chicago.

Beck, A. T.; Ward, C. H.; Mendelson, M.; et al. 1981. An inventory for measuring depression. *Archives of General Psychiatry* 4:561–571.

Bienenfield, F. 1983. *Child Custody Mediation: Techniques for Counsellors, Attorneys and Parents.* Palo Alto, Calif.: Science and Behavior Books.

Burger, W. B. 1982. Isn't there a better way? *American Bar Association Journal* 68:274–7.

Coogler, O. J. 1978. *Structural Mediation in Divorce Settlements.* Lexington, Mass.: Heath.

Derdeyn, A. P. 1976. Child custody contests in historical perspective. *American Journal of Psychiatry* 133:1369–1376.

Emery, R. E. 1982. Interparental conflict and the children of discord and divorce. *Psychological Bulletin* 92:310–30.

Emery, R. E.; Hetherington, E. M.; and Dilalla, L. F. 1985. Divorce, children, and social policy. In *Child Development Research and Social Policy,* ed. by H. Stevenson and A. Siegel. Chicago: University of Chicago Press.

Emery, R. E., Joyce, S., and Fincham, F. 1987. The assessment of marital and child problems. In *The Assessment of Marital Discord,* ed. by K. D. O'Leary. New York: Lawrence Erlbaum.

Emery, R. E.; Shaw, D. S.; and Jackson, J. A. 1987. A clinical description of a model of child custody mediation. In *Advances in Family Intervention, Assessment and Theory,* vol. 4, ed. by J. P. Vincent. Greenwich, Conn.: Jai Press.

Emery, R. E. and Wyer, M. M. 1987a. Divorce mediation. *American Psychologist.*

Emery, R. E. and Wyer, M. M. 1987b. Child custody mediation and litigation: An experimental evaluation of the experience of parents. *Journal of Consulting and Clinical Psychology* 55: 179–186.

Fabricant, M. 1983. *Juveniles in the Family Court.* Lexington, Mass.: Heath.

Folberg, J., and Taylor, A. 1984. *Mediation.* San Francisco: Jossey-Bass.

Freeman, M. 1984. Questioning the de-legalization movement in family law. In *The Resolution of Family Conflict,* ed. by J. Ekelaar and S. Katz. Toronto: Butterworth.

Furstenberg, F. F.; Nord, C. W.; Peterson, J. L.; and Zill, N. 1983. The life course of children of divorce. *American Sociological Review* 48:656–88.

Glick, P. C. 1984. How American families are changing. *American Demographics* 6:21–25.

Goldstein, J.; Freud, A.; and Solnit, A. 1973. *Beyond the Best Interests of the Child.* New York: Free Press.

Goldstein, J.; Freud, A.; and Solnit, A. 1980. *Before the Best Interests of the Child.* London: Burnett/Deutsch.

Haynes, J. M. 1981. *Divorce Mediation: A Practical Guide for Therapists and Counselors.* New York: Springer.

Hetherington, E. M. 1980. Children and divorce. In *Parent Child Interaction: Theory, Research and Prospect,* ed. by R. Henderson. New York: Academic Press.

Johnson, C. T.; Bird, T.; and Little, J. W. 1979. *Delinquency Prevention: Theories and Practices.* Columbia, Md.: Center for Action Research/Westinghouse National Issues Center.

Kelly, J. B. 1983. Mediation and psychotherapy. *Mediation Quarterly* 1:33–44.

Kitson, G. C. 1982. Attachment to the spouse in divorce. *Journal of Marriage and the Family* 44:379–391.

Knitzer, J. 1982. *Unclaimed Children: The Failure of Public Responsibility to Children and Adolescents in Need of Mental Health Service.* Washington D.C.: Children's Defense Fund.

Kurdek, L. A. 1981. An integrative perspective on children's divorce adjustment. *American Psychologist* 36:856–866.

Landsman, K. J., and Minow, M. 1978. Lawyering for the child. *The Yale Law Journal* 87 (6): 1126–1190.

Lipson, L., and Wheeler, S. (eds). 1987. *Law and the Social Sciences.* New York: Russell Sage Foundation.

Minuchin, S. 1984. *Family Kaleidoscope.* Cambridge, Mass.: Harvard University Press.

Mnookin, R. 1975. Child custody adjudication: Judicial functions in the fact of indeterminacy. *Law and Contemporary Problems* 39:226–293.

Murch, M. 1980. *Justice and Welfare in Divorce.* London: Sweet & Maxwell.

New York Bar Association. 1984. *Law Guardians in New York State: A Study of the Legal Representation of Children.* New York: New York State Bar Association.

Parsloe, P. 1978. *Juvenile Justice in Britain and the United States.* London: Routledge.

Pearson, J.; Ring, M.; and Milne, A. 1983. A portrait of divorce mediation services in the public and private sector. *Conciliation Courts Review* 21:1–24.

Prescott, P. 1981. *The Child Savers: Juvenile Justice Observed.* New York: Knopf.

Saposnek, D. T. 1983. *Mediating Child Custody Disputes: A Systematic Guide For Family Therapists, Court Counselors, Attorneys and Judges.* San Francisco: Jossey-Bass.

Schlossman, S. 1977. *Love and the American Delinquent: Theory and Practice of Juvenile Justice.* Chicago: University of Chicago.

Scott, E. and Emery, R. E. 1987. The adversary process and child custody disputes. In *The Psychologist as a Consultant to the Court in Child Custody Determinations,* ed. by L. A. Weithorn. Lincoln: University of Nebraska Press.

Shaw, D. S., and Emery, R. E. 1987. Parental conflict and other correlates of the adjustment of school-age children whose parents have separated. *Journal of Abnormal Child Psychology.*

Sobie, M. 1984. *Legislative Proposal to Implement the New York State Law Guardian Study.* New York: New York State Bar Association.

Sobie, M. 1987a. *The Creation of Juvenile Justice.* New York: Charles Evans Hughes Press.

Sobie, M. 1987b. *Standard for Representing Children.* New York: New York State Bar Association.

Stapleton, W. V., and Teitlbaum, L. H. 1972. *In Defense of Youth.* New York: Russell Sage Foundation.

Thompson, L., and Spanier, G. B. 1983. The end of marriage and acceptance of marital termination. *Journal of Marriage and the Family* 45:103–113.

Wakefield, R. 1981. Family mediation: The wave of the future. *American Family* 4(4): 8–15.

Wald, M. 1979. Children's rights: Framework for analysis. *U.C.D. Law Review* 12 (2): 255–282.

Wallerstein, J. S., and Kelly, J. B. 1980. *Surviving the Breakup: How Children Actually Cope with Divorce.* New York: Basic Books.

Weithorn, L. S. 1984. Children's capacities in legal contexts. In *Children, Mental Health and the Law,* ed. by Repucci et al. Beverly Hills, Calif.: Sage.

Weitzman, L. 1981. The economics of divorce: Social and economic consequences of property, alimony and child support awards. *UCLA Law Review* 28:1181–1268.

Wilkins, L. 1985. Juvenile justice: Research and action. In *Children, Youth and Families: The Action-Research Relationship,* ed. by R. N. Rapoport. New York: Cambridge University Press.

5 Communities

The community provides the setting and context within which the influences of specific social institutions operate. In the early postwar years, community studies were fashionable in the social sciences, spanning the range from anthropological studies of village life to small town studies such as Lloyd Warner's Yankee City series, the Lynds's Middletown, and John Dollard's study of a southern town. John Seeley's Canadian study of Crestwood Heights and Margaret Stacey's English study of Banbury were of the same genre. Urban neighborhoods were studied as "natural areas" forming quasi-communities within which ethnic, class, and other subcultures flourished. There were studies at Chicago of the Gold Coast and the slum, of the little Italies, Chinatowns, and so on. Herbert Gan's study of the West End of Boston pointed up the social supports provided by urban neighborhoods and the importance for urban planners to recognize the human as well as the purely physical characteristics of local areas they were altering; and in Britain, Young and Willmott's Bethnal Green studies had a similar message.

These studies made it clear that the sense of community was not lost in modern society, despite the urbanization/industrialization upheaval of the eighteen and nineteenth centuries. Although the people in a modern urban locality do not relate to one another as in a small village, forming social ties in network patterns rather than tightly integrated groups, they do share elements of environmental experience and develop a sense of local identity. This is particularly true for growing children, whose travel and range of associations is more limited.

Neighborhoods tend to form characteristic environments which affect the quality of life within them. The type of youth groups on the streets and in local hangouts, the character of the local amenities, the nature of local associations and helping networks, all affect the character of the neighborhood. Different neighborhoods not only have different real estate values and demographic occupancy patterns, but they show different rates

185

of mental illness, crime and delinquency, school truancy, domestic violence, and so on.

Some of the neighborhood's physical and social characteristics are subject to forces outside its control. Even without wars or invasions to alter the patterns of life in a given neighborhood, the natural processes of change produce characteristic alterations. Familiar processes include migration of new settlers into areas around ports and railway stations; the succession of inhabitants, as established members of the group move up in society and make way for new immigrants. Synagogues become converted to churches, which become converted to Islamic or Buddhist temples, and then (with gentrification and the return from the suburbs) "distinctive condomimiums." Social service agencies are part of this process, both those formally provided by statute and those voluntarily devised by special groups. Settlement houses like the Henry Street house were outposts of charitable works established by affluent middle classes to help the down-and-outers. Their models were based on concepts of philanthropy. Later, their methods and staffing changed and they became professional service centers providing specific forms of counseling, therapy, and educational courses, as well as shelter and material help. Still later, they became nerve centers for outreach activities, the research and development laboratories for new methods of helping people to help themselves.

Most temporary theorists would probably argue that the search for a satisfactory pattern of life will not necessarily take the form of restoring tight-knit communities of previous centuries. But, both common sense and data support the idea that when elements of community are destroyed, people are at risk of being psychologically damaged. The creation of temporary, therapeutic communities has sometimes helped people with needs and experiences of this kind. The goal of therapy is to encourage in them sufficient self-esteem and competence to face the world and cope with its stresses, using such social supports as exist in the "real world" outside.

The larger, longer-term task of building new kinds of community support structures is something that is being worked out in various ways by different subgroups. There are those who believe that it is futile to provide small patchwork supports while the larger socioeconomic setting requires drastic revision, and those who believe in piecemeal changes based on specific solutions to particular problems of coping with stress. Whatever the grand strategy, there is general acceptance of the need to identify trouble spots in a changing world and to help create new modes of service delivery. Differences in sponsorship and control are involved in the long-term strategies, but there is considerable concurrence in the methods of work in countries with differing economic and political structure (Thursz and Vigilante, 1975, 1976). In countries like the United States, the dominant strategy is to develop solutions to problems as they emerge and, through creating and evaluating demonstration projects, to encourage others to follow suit.

The provision of social services such as health education, economic assistance, preventive medical treatment and rehabilitation, and personal counseling have become extremely complex, with many kinds of services emerging in response to different problems and attached to different institutions. There has been a growing realization of the interrelatedness of economic, psychological, and social factors associated with many problems, and this has led to experimentation through demonstration projects with new patterns of service delivery using interdisciplinary and integrative approaches (Cohen, 1975, p. 220).

The case studies presented here are three such experiments, chosen because their clientele are children and because the method through which they seek to develop their interventions represents the interdisciplinary integrative approach of action-research.

The projects describes represent the new generation of smaller scale innovations rather than the grand programs of the postwar period. They show the new emphasis on cost-sharing, devolution of decision-making to the local areas, and flexible redeployment of existing resources rather than building entirely new large scale programs. In the present dialogue within the social service professions and with the public at large is the theme of developing coping competence in children. The descriptions of the projects aim to contribute to the clarification of issues and to the task of assessing alternatives. Kamerman and Kahn identify these as generic issues:

Little progress will be made in improving social service delivery systems . . . unless there is prior clarity as to objectives . . . (and) in defining and testing alternative approaches. (Kamerman and Kahn, 1978, p. 95)

There is no attempt here to address the question of how a comprehensive system of personal social services for children in the community should be constructed. The cases presented concentrate on the workability of specific components that might go into the construction of such a system. Whatever form of integration and machinery for service delivery will ultimately evolve, the development of component parts proceeds somewhat autonomously. Though the success of specific experiments is effected not only by their efficacy but also by forces in the general ethos which help or hinder their functioning, eventual payoffs will depend both on the development of sound component services and on how the larger society sees fit to finance and organize their delivery. This is what Kamerman and Kahn refer to as *what* is being delivered, as well as *how* it is being delivered (1978, p. 113; cf. Froland et al., 1981).

The three projects focus on different types of intervention developed through different models of action-research. An analysis of their unfolding has contributed different sorts of lessons about the development of innovations and the conduct of action-research projects.

The parent/child mediation project originated as a demonstration project of an alternative form of dispute resolution in the juvenile courts. The actual intervention was a blend of a form of community hearings originated in Scotland and a set of American procedures for mediating disputes. A senior enterprising person, associated with a child advocacy organization and concerned with legal reform, liaised with a university professor concerned with mediation as a form of dispute resolution to set up the project. The actual conduct of the project was by a field director with a social work background and a young researcher working under the supervision of a professor experienced in mediation and conflict-resolution research (Merry, 1979, 1981). By the end of the project, the enterprising director had moved up into a senior post in the state government, the researcher's appointment and funding had expired, and the program was adopted statewide by a different agency (the social services rather than the juvenile justice department). The writing up was left to the professor and was accomplished with the collaboration of the field director and the researcher, though they were by this time busy with other obligations.

The community woman project was based on a new role that formed a component of a larger package of intervention measures. The larger package, Project Redirection, was designed by a manpower research and development organization for community settings across the country, to redirect wayward teenage mothers from a career of chronic welfare dependency into one of greater self-sufficiency. The package was field-tested and evaluated in a number of sites nationwide, and the specific component was studied in higher magnification but as part of this project. The research and development agency contained both operations staff, providing technical assistance to the field sites, and research staff, providing both formative and summative evaluations. All of the project staff were funded by grants, and programmatic continuities had to be arranged site by site on a local basis, after incorporating operational and monitoring skills from the developing agency.

The third project, also concerned with teenage pregnancy, had an entirely different character. The specific social intervention was The Door, a multiservice center for at-risk youths. The Door provides a range of alternative services, including those based not only on medical models (e.g., clinical services and contraceptive education), but also on a range of activities only indirectly related to health promotion, such as yoga, dance, drama, and tai chi. Using an implicit multiple-causes, multiple-effects conceptual model, the staff at The Door (many of who are volunteers or service professionals in training) take in and seek to help a wide range of at-risk youth, including teen parents.

The project originally was the work of a graduate student who was a volunteer at The Door and sought to use available data to develop a dissertation on teen motivational patterns associated with pregnancy and its aftermath. There was a rudimentary sense of collaboration with the clinical director and of the possible utility of the project for specific program development. But it was only through involving the student's thesis adviser, a professor at a neighboring university, that funding was obtained. From the professor's point of view, the project provided an additional set of cases for her larger study on motivational patterns of teen parents. In the course of the study, the clinical director left; the researcher, though completing her dissertation, left the larger project; the university department in which the professor was located was relocated, and both the overall project reports and the specific action-research yields were interrupted. However, a number of basic research reports emerged, with an eventual refocusing on site-specific elements for possible program application.

Case study: Parent/child mediation panels

This case study is an intervention which belongs partly with the legal institutions in that one of its contexts is the legal reform movement. Lawyers, as well as social workers, politicians, and others concerned with children, have continually worked for improvement in the way juvenile offenders are handled, particularly "status offenders," who are youth who engage in noncriminal misbehavior such as truancy, running away, or defying parental control. Lawyers, behavioral scientists, and concerned lay people have noted the rise in such offenses and the sometimes counterproductive effects of bringing them into the courts, with the attendant labeling and stigmatization that may occur.

Accordingly, there has arisen in the United States a movement comprising "alternative," or "diversionary" programs for handling disputes that might bring young people into contact with the law. A great deal of creativity has been poured into these programs from several directions.

One particularly interesting attempt by the Massachusetts Advocacy Center is the subject of this discussion. Elizabeth Vorenberg, then deputy director of the Massachusetts Advocacy Center, initiated the project, adapting the Scottish Children's Hearings Panels method to the somewhat different conditions prevailing in the United States. She was concerned with reforming legal policies affecting children. The cooperation of the district courts was obtained, as they too had an interest in improving the way they deal with children. Sally Merry, a professor of anthropology at Wellesley College, supervised the research, which was conducted in the field setting by Ann Marie Rocheleau. Merry's principal research interests have been in conflict resolution, both cross-cultural and in the urban community setting. Sandra Wixted was project director.

The research project was set up for two years, 1981–1983, under a grant from the William T. Grant Foundation. Grants to support the intervention program were from a consortium of foundations interested in legal reforms: the Ford, Edna McConnell Clark, Robert Sterling Clark, and Florence Burden foundations.

Background

The perception of at least four kinds of problems fed into the formation and execution of this project:

> Behavior problems of children, which their parents are unable to handle satisfactorily
> Problems of the juvenile courts in dealing with behavior problems
> Problems of applicability of a program developed in another country (Scotland)
> Problems associated with conceptualizing and using community-based mediation methods with children

The children's problems to which the intervention is addressed are encompassed in the term *status offender*. Although this term is now being replaced in some places by a less stigmatizing term, such as "children in need of service" (CHINS) or other variants (e.g., in New York, Persons in Need of Service [PINS]), it still conveys in a rough-and-ready way the kind of young person involved. The children may be habitual truants; they may be more of the "delinquency type" or engage in socially disruptive behavior; or they may be ungovernable by their parents. It is a category that overlaps with other categories used by police, social workers, psychologists, and others concerned with children's behavior.

One source book on status offenders notes that these young people may be considered a threat to themselves and society. They have tended, before the "deinstitutionalization" of correctional institutions, to be detained in settings where occasionally their deviancy was felt to become "amplified" through association with hardened delinquents or criminals, with subsequent escalation of their behavior from petty nuisance to more serious crime (Murray, 1979). They have increased in numbers and are increasingly of concern to the courts. Moreover, judges and lawyers have few guidelines to handling them. Many judges feel on firm ground in assessing guilt or innocence and applying available powers for punishment; but are less able to assess the welfare considerations of the troubled child.

In response to this rising problem, a large number of diversionary programs evolved in the 1970s, including a movement for "alternative dispute resolution." These programs are described in many publications of the Department of Justice's Office of Juvenile Justice and Delinquency Prevention. There were several reviews of dispute resolution programs directed toward juvenile offenders (e.g., Garofalo and Connelly, 1980; Vorenberg, 1982), which offered these conclusions:

- The extent of development of such programs reflects a widespread need.
- Many kinds of programs are apparently viable, with support in their local communities and reported successes.
- There is a great variety of foci and emphases:
  —type of youth served (e.g., truants, delinquents, runaways, neglected children)
  —methods used (e.g., rap sessions, service referrals, bringing together offenders and their victims)
  —staffing (e.g., lay vs. professional)
  —referral sources
  —ideology (on the use of coercive powers, on the relationship between diversionary modes of dispute resolution, and other "community empowerment" approaches)

Conceptually, diversionary dispute resolution relates to developments in different disciplines. Steven Schlossman, in a review of the history of the Chicago Area Project (1982), notes that the Chicago school developed an emphasis on social factors in the background of deviant behavior, from which stemmed the emphasis on the community as a focus for intervention. This contrasted with the approaches associated earlier in the century with the work of William Healey and other psychodynamic-oriented psychologists. Their conceptualization has focused on individuals and led to the formation of clinics as intervention sites. In anthropology, a number of scholars have looked at delinquency with a cross-cultural perspective, and at dispute resolution methods both in simpler and more complex societies (Nader, 1980; Merry, 1982). Dispute resolution processes must be understood in their larger social contexts, whether in simpler societies or in our own. Nader has noted that mediation as a method of dispute resolution requires linkages between the divided parts. In Lebanon, for example, making these linkages is difficult because of the schisms in that country (Nader and Todd, 1978).

To some extent the problem of disarticulation, if not schism, is endemic in modern, complex, plural societies, and thus affects the kind of social invention that will emerge and flourish. Philida Parsloe notes that our own society is divided not only in terms of subcultures associated with social groupings such as class and ethnicity but also in terms of conceptual approaches to issues relating to juvenile offenders. In analyzing the juvenile justice systems of Britain and the United States, she suggests that there are "three sets of ideas [affecting the structure of juvenile justice] . . . ideas of welfare, ideas of criminal justice, and ideas of community concern and responsibility" (Parsloe, 1978, pp. 9–16). Society's choice of emphasis among these sets of ideas affects how juveniles are handled. Justice Ketcham described the conceptual issue as follows:

One of the major issues of this decade will be whether the juvenile justice system should be controlled by law and legal concepts, by behavioral science and social principles, or by the citizen public in accord with principles of common sense and instinct. (Ketcham, 1978)

While some observers posit a movement away from the legal and toward the community basis for regulating children's misbehavior, the current picture is actually a merging and mixing of different emphases rather than an inexorable move toward community empowerment or juvenile self-care (Zatz, 1982). Seidman (1984) reviewed the diversionary programs that arose in the 1970s and concluded that though there was great variation, the tendency was still to concentrate on the individual - not surprising, given the individualistic values of our society. System-oriented programs, even those working with the youth's close network of family and peers, are unusual. Nevertheless, conceptualization aimed at linking individuals and social systems has advanced. Rosenheim, for example, has developed concepts of problem formulation ("problemization") for normalizing delinquency interventions through involving others in the community. Elizabeth Vorenberg, in her review of innovative programs for the American Bar Association (1982) noted among other things that there were few programs that went beyond the conventional tools of psychological or social work counseling to seek revision of the community structure, and few that emphasized the child's perspective (cf. Abel, 1982).

The Massachusetts Advocacy Center, taking up this perspective, concluded that what was needed was an intervention package which could replace the juvenile court procedure. Beginning by concentrating on status offenders, it sought a way to involve families and address family conflicts as a key underlying focus of mediation. Operating with the collaborative involvement of professional social workers and local persons, it developed a conception resembling the Scottish Children's Hearings Panels, which was being systematically observed and evaluated.

The Scottish system researched by Martin and his colleagues (1981) represents a radical change of the system. It is local neighborhood-oriented, uses volunteer lay people, and engages child and family. Children are brought before a hearing by a reporter if he considers them to be in need of compulsory measures of care (including protection, control, guidance, and treatment). The reporter is an official appointed for his knowledge of law or administration, who receives referrals, decides on their eligibility, and advises the panel. The panels were established in Scotland by the Social Work Act of 1968, which defined a child as a person under the age of 16 years, or between 16 and 18 if there is a supervision requirement in force.

A Scottish child may be subject to compulsory measures of care if he or she is beyond the control of his or her parents; is falling into bad associations or is exposed to moral danger; if lack of parental care is likely to cause him or her unnecessary suffering or to seriously impair health or development; or if any of the offenses mentioned in Schedule 1 to the Criminal Procedure (Scotland) Act 1975 has been committed.

Any person who has reasonable cause to believe that a child may be in need of compulsory measures of care can give the reporter information. Such information may therefore reach a reporter from sources such as a social worker, doctor, teacher, neighbor, parents, or police. Once the reporter decides that the child is eligible for a hearing, he makes necessary arrangements both with panel members and the child and family.

When a panel hearing is convened, three volunteers are assigned to a session and may hear from one to three cases during this time. One panel member is selected as chairperson in order to guide the process in a coherent and orderly fashion. Certain procedures are followed in all cases to ensure that the family understands why they are there and what their rights are. Other than this kind of formal procedure, the process is informal and panel members exercise care and concern in encouraging dialogue with the youth and family.

A reporter and a social worker sit in on every hearing. The reporter is responsible for keeping records, interpreting legal procedures, and providing administrative support as needed. If other professionals are involved with a case, such as school guidance counselors or child-care workers from a group residence, they are asked to attend. None of these people plays an active role unless addressed by the panel members.

The decisions made at a hearing are limited to whether or not a child needs "compulsory measures of care," that is, social service supervision and intervention, which may entail placement outside the home if considered necessary. The panel members make these decisions with input from the youth, parent, and social worker. If social services are not required, the case is dismissed by the panel.

Initiated in 1971, the Children's Hearings Panels attracted considerable attention, both in the United Kingdom and abroad, as a visionary innovation. Though many of its features resemble those of mediation panels generally, it was the specific application and the detail in which it was studied that merited special attention. American approaches to the mediation process differed in emphasis, as will be discussed below.

A number of evaluation studies revealed statistical patterns showing a general increase in numbers of cases referred to Scottish community reporters in the 1970s. Increases of referrals within certain categories were more marked than others, for example in parental neglect and truancy cases. More serious offenses, such as housebreaking, theft, and breach of the peace - for which offenders might be referred equally to the reporter or to the courts - remained relatively constant at high levels throughout the period, but proportionately fewer of them were referred to the hearings system in later years. More boys (1 in 7 in the population) than girls (1 in 20) were referred at some point to reporters. Of those referred to reporters, about one-third were made subject to compulsory supervision. Three-fifths of the cases subjected to hearings have not had repeat hearings. The statistical analyses were supplemented by a number of other studies, including interviews with reporters, social workers, and panelists; public opinion surveys; and observation of panels in action.

A great deal of material emerged from these studies. Though there are no simple conclusions about effectiveness of the panels, there is widespread feeling from all sides that they are doing a good job and should continue. But there is criticism of various aspects. Parsloe notes that the intention of having the panels made up of a cross section of the community does not in fact occur, because the criteria make it inevitable that the more educated classes (e.g., teachers) and those with more time to spare (housewives) predominate. Also, as pointed out by a number of observers, the methods of work (discussion, reasoning, analysis of relationships, and others) reflect values and modes of relating that are more middle class than working class. If deliberate efforts were to be made to include working class representatives of some of the rougher neighborhoods from which the offenders were drawn, the actions of the panels might be much more retributive in character. Local panels develop different subcultural emphases; for example, some give more emphasis to forming community pressure groups for children, others give more emphasis to learning about child psychology. Reporters are "gatekeepers" who, like social workers, probation officers, and policemen, screen children who come to their attention (Parsloe, 1978). This suggests that a key issue is how much discretionary action they should be given, and how it should be controlled. Too-broad guidelines allow for arbitrary disposition; too narrow, for insufficient individualization. Suggested changes have included adding checks and balances, guidelines, a broader community-based approach, and more community options that will blend children who have and who have not been in trouble.

Asquith reiterates another criticsm of the children's panels that was intrinsically present in the system, namely, that the children's minimal statutory rights may be ignored. In court, despite whatever else may be wrong with the procedure, due process is more surely observed (Asquith, 1983, p. 208). In Scotland the Children's Hearings Panels were designed to give emphasis to welfare considerations as distinct from judicial ones, but Asquith argues that too much emphasis in this direction puts the justice element at risk.

Whatever the resolution of these issues will ultimately be, the question arises as to what Americans found useful in this procedure and why they wished to adapt it to the United States. As a diversionary program, it would be likely to be subject to the criticisms of being unsystematic, inadequately implemented, and therefore difficult to evaluate. Some data suggest that the program does not divert real delinquents, but tends to draw in cases which would not have gone before the courts anyway, in effect expanding the judicial net, the opposite effect to their aim (Klein, 1979; also see Sarri and Bradley, 1980, for the Australian experience).

In favor of the intervention is the current interest in developing ways to reform the juvenile courts. Though the courts were developed in the early twentieth century to advance the welfare of children (as compared with the correctional institutions which preceded them), there was an increasing awareness that they were not dealing adequately with psycho-social problems which were possibly contributing to making children recidivists in delinquency and criminals in adulthood. Improving court procedures has been one line of reform (see the law guardian case in Chapter 4). At the same time, minor offenders and status offenders have increased in numbers, threatening due-process procedures by overloading the system. The idea of developing a simpler collateral system, complementing the work of the juvenile court, is appealing in this context. While there was no short-age of discussion of the Scottish system as an alternative to the juvenile courts, there was little on how it might work as a complement to the courts in the American context.

Elizabeth Vorenberg's conclusion to her "State of the Art Survey of Dispute Resolution Programs Involving Juveniles" (1982):

> Though there is evidence of widespread use of third-party non-judicial settlement in minor juvenile disputes, much of it existed before the "dispute resolution movement" of the 1970s. Juvenile mediation and arbitration in the current sense has not really been tested and, in many programs involving both adults and juveniles, it has even been avoided. Even some basic tenets of mediation programs - e.g. face-to-face contact between the parties to a dispute - are not present in juvenile "mediation" programs . . . Juvenile mediation and arbitration programs show promise in two major areas: they succeed in diverting juveniles from court and provide victims of juvenile crimes with greater satisfaction, especially where restitution and community service result from mediation and arbitration agreements.

Vorenberg recognized the risk of "widening the net," but indicated that it can be dealt with by following strict selection criteria, and in any case need not be considered as entirely negative if lasting behavior changes could be obtained.

With this background of issues relating to alternative responses to young offenders, it was characteristic of the work of the Mass. Advocacy Center to seek devices that would improve on some of the defects of existing approaches. The center had a history of supporting movements toward decriminalization of juvenile offenses and had been influential in the legislation to redesign status offenders (as the CHINS program), and to close reform schools. Vorenberg then became deputy director of the Mass. Advocacy Center and sought to develop improved ways of handling children under the new system. She and Sandra Wixted, the project director, visited the Scottish Children's Hearings Panels and discussed them with Sanford Fox, the Boston College law professor who had evaluated them for the U.S. Department of Justice's Juvenile Justice and Delinquency Prevention Institute. Also important in the intellectual, legal, and social service environment were Frank Sander and Daniel McGillis, members of the advisory board. Both had written about neighborhood justice centers, family law, and the role of alternative dispute resolution. This seems to have been one of those situations where if the Scots had not invented the Scottish hearings system, the Mass. Advocacy Center might have.

The pioneer American programs in alternative dispute resolution in the 1960s and 1970s did not focus on youth and family cases. They addressed the inability of courts to get to the underlying issues in disputes between adults, and they attempted to counteract the role courts play in escalating tensions, especially where those in conflict have had a prior relationship.

During the 1970s and 1980s the mediation movement gained ground as a way of dealing with a variety of minor interpersonal and property disputes. Dispute resolution programs using mediation, conciliation, and arbitration endeavor to provide more effective and enduring remedies for individuals involved in disputes with people with whom they have ongoing personal relationships. Their purpose is to discover the underlying issues in a dispute and explore ways of reaching some agreement about them. The disputants themselves define the problems and forge agreements, generally in explicit written form. Dispute resolution methods have been applied to a wide range of civil and criminal matters, including misdemeanor and felony complaints, small claims, landlord/tenant, domestic, and neighborhood disputes. These programs typically emphasize community involvement and train community volunteers to serve as third parties and to monitor the implementation of agreements. In view of the problems facing the juvenile courts in handling matters of this kind, the idea of using mediation methods for the resolution of disputes involving juveniles was both novel and appealing.

The action-research project

The fundamental issue addressed by this project was whether a workable device could be developed to resolve disputes involving status offenders and children in need of protection that would reduce family stress and avoid state involvement in the family, and child involvement in juvenile court. The Scottish Children's Hearings Panels served as a model, with the understanding that some of the conditions prevailing in Scotland were absent in the U.S., notably government financial support and powers of compulsory disposition of cases. The Scottish approach was innovative in the direction of replacing juvenile courts (for all but the most serious juvenile delinquencies) and involving the families of the offending juveniles. The project aimed to build on this approach, but considered that research was needed to help with evaluating innovative experiments.

The research part of the project proposed to "investigate to what extent, and under what conditions, the use of mediation in a hearings project . . . serves as an effective mode of resolving intrafamily conflict." It sought to increase understanding of effectiveness from two perspectives: that of the families and that of the state system (juvenile justice and social services). Measures of effectiveness for families were to include:

> The proportion of families reaching an agreement
> Reported satisfaction with the process
> Participants' sense that the process is fair and just
> Users' perceptions that the process is responsive, participatory, and
>   subject to their control
> Long-term resolution of disputes
> Acquisition of new skills in conflict management within the family
> Relative costs in time and money to users in comparison with alter-
>   natives, such as the courts

Measures of systemic effectiveness were to include:

> Cost of mediation hearings
> Impact of the mediation alternative on court caseloads and court costs
> Effect of the program on case loads in alternative agencies and their costs
> Impact of the program on the social service agencies
> Attitudes of referral sources (probation and other court officers, police,
>   social workers, school officials) on the effectiveness of the program

These measures were to be correlated with a series of variables indicating the nature of the conflict (e.g., truancy, parental control), the characteristics of the parties (their goals, networks), and aspects of the mediation experience (location, number of mediators, number of disputants, time expended, context in relation to threat of court coercion, alternatives available).

Initially the action agenda was paramount, with the research thought of as a service, useful in evaluation and dissemination. Eventually, a more interactive conception evolved, with a greater parity between the agency's goal of program development and the researcher's goal of increased knowledge.

Research design and methodology. The basic design had two components: a qualitative ethnographic component, which consisted of observations, interviews, and descriptive analysis of the experiment as it evolved; and a quantitative quasi-experimental component, which involved the systematic comparison of a series of mediated and nonmediated juveniles by a set of predetermined variables with structured instruments (some identical to those used by Murray and Martin in Scotland). True matching of the experimental and control groups by random assignment was not possible under the circumstances. However, an approximation of matching was obtained for two comparison groups: cases which were referred by the courts but for one reason or another did not go through with the mediation process; and a series of cases selected from court records as matching the mediated cases on several key variables, but which were not referred for mediation. Approximately 50 cases in each category were obtained during the research period. The qualitative methods included

>Observations of court proceedings involving juvenile offenders
>Observations of panel proceedings
>Interviews with juveniles, family members, panelists, social workers, school personnel, and court personnel

The quantitative methods included

>Analysis of court records
>A survey of panelists

In addition, the qualitative interview materials were subjected to quantitative analysis for selected variables. The interviews with juveniles and their families were conducted initially, one month following mediation, and six to eight months later.

Outcome variables to be assessed on the individual child's side were decided:

>The extent to which the mediation enhances the parties' sense of control over their lives, their ability to handle disputes, and their sense that they have some recourse for handling such problems
>On the community side, the social behavior and participation patterns of the individual and family
>In the family, changes in the strategy of handling disputes, both internally and in relation to the surrounding community

Course of the project. Several shifts occurred in the course of the Children's Hearings Panels (CHP) project, which affected the outcome. First, the researcher's role changes from a relatively detached model to a more interactive one. The project was initially conceived as an evaluation study. The more interactive action-research model began to evolve when "formative feedback evaluation" was requested, provided, and put to use. This took the form of an interim assessment of the difference three panelists (as in the Scottish hearings) would make, as opposed to two (as would be more feasible in America where achieving coordination among panelists was difficult). The analysis of observational materials on the panel hearings yielded information suggesting that there were no significant differences between two-person and three-person panels, so the structure of the panels was altered to make two the norm.

Another aspect of the development of more interactive roles was the researcher's functioning as a conduit of information. Rocheleau was the only person on the CHP project who was present in all phases of the process: observing the court proceedings, observing the panels in operation, and interviewing judges, social workers, panelists, and families. Others come into the chain of events only for one or another stage of the process. As she was being asked for information, Rocheleau had to work out a way of providing some feedback without unduly disturbing the phenomena she was studying or giving away confidences. The whole issue of confidentiality, and who was allowed access to what information, was a complex one and ways of handling feedback without violating confidentiality had to be worked out collaboratively between researchers and the field director, borrowing from the experience of other neighborhood justice projects. There were also issues about how much of what information the panelists were entitled to have. This point was important in relation to a second shift in emphasis, from the neighborhood character of the panels to a more interpersonal model.

At a later stage, when statistical data became available and was being analyzed, the feedback process was useful to check interpretations. It also came to be seen as an exercise in combining quantitative and qualitative analysis.

The second shift was the change from a neighborhood mediation model to an interpersonal model. Initially the neighborhood element was emphasized as part of the conceptualization associated with diversionary mediation models. But it became clear that clients and their families wanted anonymity and confidentiality. It also came from a "professional" bias of legal, social service, and psychological professionals involved in mediation who have introduced the "privileged communication" with the client issue. Any panelist who knew the family in question was therefore disqualified. This element was reenforced by the greater tendency in the American than in the Scottish panels to "uncover" family dynamics in the hearings, and by the greater degree of urbanization in the American setting.

The third change was from a focus on the courts to a focus on the social services. A number of issues arose in relation to the courts, which brought into focus the question of the place of the courts as the source of referral. While courts are concerned with keeping their case loads within manageable bounds and with seeing to the best interests of children coming before them, it became clear as the CHP project proceeded that there could be no assumption of automatic dismissal of cases after referral to mediation. The courts did not wish to give up their control over the course of events (and the administrative credits for handling the cases); they felt that they had the ultimate responsibility to oversee cases. The program began to take more cases directly from the Department of Social Services as this department became the major funding source after the end of the project.

With the coercive power of the courts in the background, an effort was made to understand how important the presence of this threat was for family cooperation and eventual outcome. The mediation liaison in the courts, when confronting a referral, stressed the voluntary aspect of participation in the hearings panels. It was clear that some parents, feeling that their children were out of control, wanted a show of force. The worker would then be faced with a dilemma: by knowing perhaps more than the parent about the potential exercise of force that was in the courts (e.g., to put the child into foster care), there was a temptation to reenforce that motivational element and to stress the project's link to the court. On the other hand, the conceptualization of the mediation process requires involvement or participation without the threat of coercion. Coercion was generally regarded as undesirable, because any agreement, if it is to stick, should come from the participants rather than be imposed from outside. Because of both the referral issues and the conceptual issues, there was a gradual reorientation of the project toward the social services. In the study almost 80 percent of cases were referred from court. (Subsequently it became fifty-fifty: half from court and half from social services.)

There was another shift in the study of mediation, from being a means of understanding family conflict to being the topic of study in its own right. It had been recognized from the outset that the American approach had more of a mediation style than the Scottish one, which was quasi-judicial in style. Although children were present in the Scottish situation, it was noted that they were not conspicuously active in the hearings. Steps were taken in the Cambridge-Somerville CHP project to involve the juveniles as well as the parents. Some of the American work in the mediation field had evolved with the view that mediation with children was impracticable. Vorenberg had been convinced that children as well as parents could and should be involved, as a distinctive element in the American adaptation of the panel idea. However, the sharpening of the emphasis on mediation - as distinct from family dynamics - was reenforced when Vorenberg left the project and Merry assumed responsibility for final analysis and write-up. Merry's focal professional involvement was in the study of mediation, rather than family dynamics.

Another change in focus was the issue of *career continuity* for the researcher as the project moved into its later stages. Rocheleau took another job when project funds were exhausted while continuing to participate in the final writing-up, which was taken over by Merry as research supervisor.

The issue of *program continuity* became salient when Vorenberg left. The project director, Wixted, assumed increased responsibility for continuity. The project had become increasingly known to the state social services department, and when it was introducing a statewide program of panel mediation, it asked CHP to take on a training role for the program. Wixted had constructed a manual for mediation in disputes involving children, and this was useful as a basis for program continuity.

Results

In the end, only three-quarters of the cases subjected to mediation through the CHP came from the courts. The rest came from schools, social service agencies, the police, and directly from families who had heard of the program. A final report of the project describes the court procedures, the children and their families, and the mediation process (Merry and Rocheleau, 1985). Quantitative data are presented in an appendix, while qualitative analyses constitute the main text of the report. The findings are described in four sections:

1. Descriptions of the types of children and families who were mediated, and how they compare with the comparison groups who were not
2. Descriptions of the mediation panels: how they are selected and function, and observations of how well they work as a dispute resolution procedure
3. Family issues and processes involved in mediation
4. American adaptations of the Scottish procedures (the "reinvention" process)

1. The children and their families. The general profiles of the child and family in mediated and nonmediated cases were roughly similar, both generally poorer, less educated, and more of them single parents than found in the demographic characteristics of the Cambridge-Somerville area. About 80 percent of the fathers in the mediated sample were in service or manual worker occupations, compared with about 40 percent of the local population. About three-quarters were Catholic and one-quarter Protestant, with small variations among the subsamples and a tiny proportion disclaiming any religion. About a quarter (22 percent of the mediated and 33 percent of the nonmediated) of the juveniles were from intact parental homes, with 4 percent of the mediated and 10 percent of the nonmediated representing remarriages, and 63 percent of the mediated and 70 percent of the nonmediated with divorced, separated, or single parents. The educational level of parents was relatives low but similar for the study samples; 35 percent of the mediated and 31 percent of the nonmediated mothers had more than 12 years of formal education and 22 percent of the mediated and 20 percent of the nonmediated fathers had more than 12 years of formal education, as compared with an overall rate of 47 percent for Cambridge-Somerville adults generally. Income levels, too, were similar with a disproportionately large percentage of nonmediated families who were referred but did not participate in the lowest (under $10,000 per annum) category, with a similar though smaller contrast between mediated (22 percent) and nonmediated (6 percent) parents in the higher income bracket (of $21,000 a year or more). The school grades of the children in both mediated and nonmediated groups were similar. About 25 percent from each group came from the eighth, ninth, and tenth groups. However, 14 percent of the mediated group and only 7 percent of the nonmediated group came from the higher groups, with the corresponding imbalances in the lower grades.

The most frequently used descriptive category among both mediated and nonmediated cases was "stubborn" (43 percent of mediated and 28 percent of nonmediated cases). This category represents a catch-all label for families in which the parents described their children who are at home as out of their control. Runaways came next (33 percent and 24 percent, respectively, and truants mentioned least for the mediated cases (24 percent but most for the nonmediated (46 percent).

The most frequent reason given for not participating in mediation after having been referred was that the family was not interested (26 percent). Fifteen percent felt that mediation was not the appropriate method when the problems were school problems, and 13 percent indicated that running away could not be solved by mediation.

An analysis of the cases coming to the court over the period of the study showed that about half were referred, and of these about half were mediated. Merry and Rocheleau concluded that mediation serves the court as an adjunct to their work, being a useful resource in reducing the work load, but *not* something that might replace it, as in Scotland.

2. The mediation panels. For those cases that were mediated, a "local culture of mediation" evolved in the project, and its characteristics were described in the final report (Merry and Rocheleau, 1985):

> The underlying theory of the CHP mediation is that family conflict can be helped by constructing concrete agreements about the management of everyday life. (p. 69)

They concluded that as small and concrete agreements are followed, trust develops, and if both sides understand the other's reasoning, compromises over differences can be negotiated.

The mediators, generally working in teams of two, listened to each person and tried to clarify issues of concern and identify ways the situation could be changed. Mediators were volunteers; ideally they were neutral and accepted the importance of maintaining confidentiality. The idea that the effectiveness of mediators lay partly in their being seen as local volunteers - a tenet of community-empowerment ideologies - was not supported in this research. The children showed little awareness of concern with this as an issue, and their parents only slightly more so. Though the mediators were volunteers and did live in the same geographical area, the hearings panels, like other voluntary groups, drew disproportionately from higher educated and more well-to-do members of the community, while their clients were of the obverse demographic bias. (Gaps within urban communities can be very great along these lines, despite geographical proximity of residence.) Clients tended to indicate that age, sex, and parenting experience were more important qualifications for the mediators. A few indicated they wanted the opposite of the community-empowerment ideology, namely, that the mediators should be outside professionals.

The report contains descriptive accounts of the mediators, why they do mediation, how they think it works, and what function they see it as playing in the whole system of courts, families, and the community. As has been noted, the mediators came from a relatively highly educated group of men and women interested in social and community values and in developing their own skills. Two styles of mediation emerged, without prestructuring from the case coordinators: those whose natural style gravitated toward what might be called an "exchange," or "bargaining" procedure, of trying to get each participant to give up something to get something else; and those whose style gravitated toward an *"uncovering" procedure,* of seeking to explore levels deeper than the presenting problems, to understand underlying motivations and processes and hidden agenda. The first, more confrontational, approach, in which resolutions were sought by trading things under pressure, is a more familiar one in other mediation experiments. The second, which sought to develop an appreciation of the needs and perspectives of those involved in order to reach a consensus, is more used in therapeutic groups and programs (Silbey and Merry, 1986).

3. Family issues and processes. Agreements were reached in 84 percent of the cases mediated. They consisted of written agreements about conflict-laden topics such as curfews, chores, staying out late, the child's social life, and school attendance. Agreements were described as fair and balanced by 85 percent of the children, 93 percent of the mothers, and 100 percent of the fathers one month after the mediation hearings. About two-thirds reported that it helped in the overall family situation, with a similar proportion indicating that it had been helpful in the follow-up interviews six to eight months later.

The most frequently mentioned element in the improvement was communication. Improved communication is reported to lead to improved understanding of opposing perspectives and to improved family functioning. Associated with this was the reported improvement in the way conflicts were handled as they arose. The task of formulating an explicit written agreement was considered important, but perhaps the key ingredient was *talking* rather than fighting; negotiation and reasoning were used to finish an argument with a settlement of the issue. The authors summed up the changes as follows:

Almost all changes from one (strategy of handling conflict) to another were from a confrontational (punishment, getting angry, using violence) to a non-confrontational strategy (talking, ignoring, avoiding, referring). (p. 142)

They argued that the shifts in conflict management strategies toward negotiation and disengagement are achieved not by any single feature of the process, but by the entire mediation experience, from the way it is presented in the first place, through the way it is handled by the case coordinator, the mediators, and by the method itself: of working out solutions in the mediation session itself and writing down agreements as they are reached.

4. Adaptation of the Scottish procedures. Comparing the Cambridge-Somerville panels with their Scottish prototypes, the report argues that Scottish panels have been able to develop an apparently totally new approach because they are set up under the state and have replaced the juvenile courts. However, this (Scottish) breakthrough has not worked out to be as totally radical a departure as was initially assumed. There has been pressure on the Scottish system to replicate the system it replaced, and it is coming to resemble it.

In the Massachusetts situation, in contrast, the courts would not dismiss cases referred for mediation, nor would they refer cases of child neglect and abuse. Consequently, the program developed an emphasis on the complementarity between the community-based mediation procedure and the court system. The ways in which it differed from the court's approaches were in its focus on the family rather than just the child and the panels' use of discussion and encouragement of the child to participate in a negotiation rather than make decisions by coercive behavior. The family discussion experience provided a model for the family to use subsequently in resolving their internal conflicts.

As for the efficacy of this short-term intervention with such long-term intractable problems, the project reports a modest sustained success. Also noted is that this type of intervention does not deal directly with material issues such as income or housing though it may contribute indirectly to their solution. The process was found to be most effective with complex families with poorly developed communication skills, such as reconstituted families with younger children behaving reactively (e.g., stubborn, running away). It is less effective with older children, who are in many instances thinking of leaving home soon anyway, with girls, and with truants. There is some indication that mediation is used more often by families with working mothers than those with full-time mothers, speculatively because the former need to have conflicts resolved in order to continue with their living pattern, which may be necessary for survival, particularly in single-parent families.

Discussion

A number of interesting points emerged from this project in the context of the larger field (Merry, 1982, 1984, 1988). One of the most impressive was the way a multifaceted formulation and structure created difficulties but also offered advantages. The difficulties were in achieving some balance among the various goals. Inevitably there were differences of opinion about which issues of the agenda should be paramount: the policy issues of legal reform, the issues of family dynamics, the issues of conflict resolution through mediation, or those of the applicability of the Scottish model. Among the advantages of this multifaceted approach was its flexibility, which was necessary for it to adapt to a changing situation.

As it became clear that the courts were not prepared to entertain as radical a set of reforms as the visionary project initiator had envisioned, it was inevitable that a shift in emphasis would occur in relation to the court procedures for status offenders. This was reenforced by the project initiator's (Vorenberg) change of job, which left the principal responsibility for writing up the project results with the others in the team. Another change, generated by an unanticipated uptake of the program in the social services area, diverted the attention of the project director (Wixted) to the new arena of action. A manual had to be written, training programs conducted, and the new application of the method monitored. This left the main brunt of writing up to the research staff.

The researcher (Rocheleau) was competent and effective, but relatively inexperienced and in need of continuity in career development. The fact that she had been hired by the advocacy organization meant that her prospects for career development would lie in other organizations. She took a job with a state agency in the corrections field and continued to help with analysis and writing up on a consultative basis. The research supervisor (Merry) was left with the job of writing up the overall report, and fortunately, she was supported in a regular academic post. However, with no funds allocated for the report, additional inputs had to be sought, and inevitably the job was prolonged through having to be done "on the side." The job of writing a report that had scientific value (beyond mechanically reporting on how well the intervention worked) required conceptualization, which in this case increasingly reflected Merry's interests in mediation.

In the end, the project contributed a case study for the growing field of mediation by adding to the recognized set of procedures and settings (cf. Folberg and Taylor, 1984). The case is an example of a community mediation approach and combines elements of family mediation mostly known in the field from the work of divorce mediators.

As for the interest in a social intervention which was transplanted from one sociocultural setting to another, the case contributes to our knowledge of such experiments. There are many attempts to transplant innovations, and they succeed or fail in part on how well the relevant issues and assumptions are understood and identified.

Conceptually, this project represents the shift toward an intermediate point of intervention. A focus on the individual *or* the community is replaced by a focus on the individual *in* a community context (particularly in the family, but also in the court and larger community context).

Technically, the action-research collaboration has shown the importance of resilience in weathering problems and changes that tend to characterize such projects. It has also reaffirmed the value of such an interactive relationship. Although research may function to deflate some of the imagery associated with an innovative effort, it provides substantive documentation of what is happening, which, in the words of the project director, can be "wonderful."

As a social intervention, the program was nurtured by "adoptive parents," but this did not require a fundamental compromise of principles or methods. The work emerged in the interstices of the two realms - legal and social services - to deal with shared problems. As a demonstration project, led by dedicated and charismatic persons, it will doubtless experience modifications that tend to accompany routinization and diffusion. But this experience, too, need not compromise its fundamental value.

Case study: The community woman

The community woman is a voluntary community-based support person for teenage mothers. The project was part of a much larger demonstration program conducted by the Manpower Demonstration Research Corporation (MDRC), designed to develop ways of reducing some of the damaging effects of early out-of-wedlock motherhood, particularly chronic welfare dependency. The demonstration program, Project Redirection, was national in scope and had two phases: the first demonstration project was comprised of programs at host agencies in four sites: New York (Harlem YMCA); Boston (El Centro del Cardinal); Phoenix (Chicanos por la Causa) and Riverside, California (Children's Home Society). This demonstration was conducted between 1980 and 1982, and it was on the basis of preliminary evaluations that the community woman component was selected for focal study. The first demonstration project was supported by the Ford Foundation, the Office of Youth Programs and of Policy Evaluation in the Department of Labor, and the national office of the Work Incentive Program (WIN).

In the second demonstration project commencing in 1983, seven additional agencies were added to the sample, in Albuquerque; Atlanta; Brooklyn; Cleveland; Greenville, Michigan; El Paso; and St. Louis, with the aim of assessing the program's capacity to be disseminated. In both demonstrations the goal was for the sites to find their own funding after the demonstration period. As the second demonstration coincided with a reduction of federal funding generally, this round of experiments received much less MDRC-controlled funds. Ford Foundation support continued, and some federal funds from the Office of Adolescent pregnancy Programs were forthcoming, but these funds had to be supplemented by local public agencies and foundations. The William T. Grant Foundation supported the specific study of the community woman as a significant social intervention that potentially buffered the stresses on the young mother and child. Alvia Branch, Janet Quint, and Jim Riccio had responsibility for the research, part of which was executed under contract by external agencies. Conceptualization and analysis within the MDRC was accomplished by the collaboration of MDRC researchers and operations staff. The research continued until 1985.

Background

The problem which Project Redirection addressed was the complex of risk factors associated with unmarried teenage motherhood. With the high rate of sexual activity among youth (rising in the seventies from 30 percent to 50 percent among metropolitan area females; Zelnick and Kantner, 1980) and an erratic use of available contraception, numbers of girls getting pregnant have inevitably risen. Though the birth rate of 15- to 17-year-old girls declined by 15 percent in the 1970s with the corresponding rise in abortion rates (from 11.4 per thousand 12–17-year-olds in 1976 to 12.9 per thousand in 1978), the rates still remained high, and 45 percent of the pregnancies occurring to women 17 years of age and younger resulted in a live birth. The recent tendency with such births is for the mother to keep the child rather than assigning it for adoption. Numerous studies have shown that there are many risk factors associated with this group of young mothers (higher risk of toxemia, anemia, and other complications) and their babies (higher risk of being stillborn, or premature, or with low birthweight or physical or mental handicaps).

Following the birth, the young mothers face additional risks of dropping out of school, of having additional children before they are ready, and being unsuccessful or poorly paid in the labor market. A disproportionately large number become dependent on public welfare. (According to one analysis, 71% of the mothers under age 30 receiving welfare in 1975 were teenage mothers.) A national survey showed that teen pregnancy is associated with numbers of school drop-outs, and for those girls who have their babies, the chances of returning to school are very low (Furstenberg et al., 1981). Moore et al. (1979) conclude that "an early birth seems to result in a lifelong loss of schooling" (p. 10). One estimate indicated that an average nonwhite high-school dropout who starts her welfare "career" as a single mother will average ten years of AFDC dependency (Bane and Ellwood, 1983). The cost to society in 1975 was estimated to exceed eight billion dollars (Burt and Moore, 1982).

These are, of course, statistical tendencies. Many young mothers cope well with their situation, and eventually marry, or if not, blend into the ordinary population as self-sufficient households. However, the risks to the individuals concerned and the cost to the public are so great that this subgroup has become a cause of national concern, with a wide range of federal and local programs addressed to one or another aspect of the problem. One prominent response to this phenomenon has been to emphasize the health problem. In keeping with the medical and public health model, teenage pregnancy has very widely been seen as a health hazard, particularly to the child, a helpless victim of the parents' behavior. Beyond this, the social welfare response has been prominent, together with a concern for the high costs to the public (Moore et al., 1979; Burt and Moore, 1982). In a review of basic research on the topic, McAnarney

(1984) noted that the issues were diverse and being dealt with in a very fragmented way. She identified the need for better integration between the scientific disciplines and between research and action.

Project Redirection, and the Community Woman Project within it, can be seen as an effort in this direction. The sponsor, MDRC, is a nonprofit corporation which develops *and* evaluates innovative social programs. Generally it operates with a combination of public and private funds, and the way it conceptualizes its work is very close to the action-research model, though it does not use that term. In some of its work it functions in the style of an R & D laboratory, in which researchers and operations personnel work together to develop a new model and then negotiate sites for field demonstration and evaluation; the model is then revised and disseminated if appropriate. The MDRC also evaluates existing innovations which others may have designed and brought into operation.

The background considerations underlying the development of the MDRC model were the following:

- Despite growing concern with the problems of teenage mothers and the development of a range of programs, there was a shortage of reliable information about their effectiveness. Many interventions seemed plausible, but little was known about whether and how they worked (Klerman, 1979, 1981)
- The diversity of motivations, settings, and influences called for a multi-disciplinary approach and a multisite field test, a situation currently lacking (Burt and Moore, 1982, p. 123)
- Because of diversity of values involved (e.g., regarding abortion, contraception, lone parenting, and public assistance), it made sense to concentrate on the objective of enhancing the young mother's capacity for self-sufficiency through education, training for employable job skills, and acquisition of life-management skills (including family planning, nutrition, and parenting).

The participating projects upheld the goal of eventual economic self-sufficiency for their clients. Integral to this was the emphasis on the continuation or resumption of education, preparation for employment, and also a conception of appropriate means by which these goals should be attained (a mixture of practical skills training, services brokering, peer and other social supports, and specific indoctrination in the areas of health, contraception, and parenting). Along with this package were practical supports and an attempt to build a community spirit, such as through recreational activities. At the core of the program was the Individual Participant Plan that enabled a tailored set of goals and ways of achieving them to be monitored for progress along the way. The community woman was a quasi-kin support role. As Kahn and Kamerman (1985) point out, the program as a whole and the specific role within it developed on the basis of ideas from social work practice, public administration, and counseling, rather than from social science theory.

For the first demonstration project, the program was advertised nationally and five sites were initially chosen from among applicants: Boston, New York (Harlem), Phoenix, Detroit, and Riverside, California. These sites had a useful range of differences, so that the generality of the model could be examined; and at the same time they had essential similarities, as urban areas serving high-risk populations. Teens under the age of 18 participated in all of the sites, and those offered the package of services lacked a high school diploma and most were either receiving welfare or living in a welfare-dependent home. Locating the service package in a community center rather than a clinic was a distinctive feature, as was the community woman informal support role and the individual participation plan (IPP), drawn up jointly between the teenager, the community woman, and the staff of the demonstration center.

The research design for Project Redirection had three major parts (cf. Quint and Riccio, 1985, p. 3):

> *Ethnographic analysis,* using field work techniques to describe diverse circumstances and background of teens in the program
> *Implementation analysis,* to describe the treatment program and assess the feasibility and cost of putting the program into place
> *Impact analysis,* to measure the effects of the project on teens' contraceptive practices, childbearing, educational, and employment-related behaviors

The action-research project

After a review of the project's early ethnographic report (Levy and Grinker, 1983) and an interim impact report (Polit et al., 1983), it was decided to develop a special research project focusing on the community woman component which had been part of the demonstration from the beginning, but had not been singled out for specific scrutiny. Fundamental to the rationale for a special substudy was that within the multifaceted approach of Project Redirection there was an interdependence between the skill training components (including health education, parenting, and employment-related skills) and the affectional, supportive components (including personal and peer counseling and the community woman relationship). Although the skill-training components were manifestly relevant, less was known about how the affectional components functioned. One suggestion from other research on teen mothers was that they functioned as a form of stress-buffering. The MDRC's interim implementation report noted that the teenagers themselves rated as most helpful first the practical training in parenting skills, and, as a close second, the community woman.

To explore the interrelationship of these components, a specific project was carved out of the larger program, beginning in the second phase of the first demonstration program.

The study of the community woman role also was seen as fitting the action-research model because it aided the development of an action role using research findings. The role had already been developed from its precursor role in the Sisterhood of Black Single Mothers in Brooklyn, in which low-income women in the community volunteered to help teenagers in a one-to-one relationship. The innovation in Project Redirection was in adapting this strategy to a comprehensive service program for teen mothers.

The community woman concept resembles various Big Sister and Big Brother programs, which are formalizations of fictive kin practices, often spontaneously developed in urban situations. The use of "uncle" and "aunt," "brother" and "sister" among urban dwellers lacking local kin ties has long been a familiar phenomenon, not only in the slum but among middle-class families. Specific roles like the community woman are examples of type II inventions. Examples also exist of type III inventions that use fictive kin imagery. For example, one community-based organization uses quasi-extended family imagery to form a surrogate family for youth at risk for delinquency involvements (Woodson, 1981).

The first demonstration project research reports documented the feasibility of putting the program features into place, the preliminary favorable impact impressions, and the weight given to the community woman by the teenagers. From the start, the community woman was conceptualized as one of the three "primary mechanisms through which Project Redirection attempts to reach and serve its participants" (the other two being the Individual Participation Plan and Peer Group Sessions). It was seen as a linking role to the larger society, a conception supported by qualitative data from the ethnographic study.

In the second demonstration project, the goal was not only to add a larger number and broader base of teenage mothers, but to study certain features in higher magnification, among them the community woman. Central to this was the question of how well the program could "travel." Would new sites be able and willing to take it over as a whole package and operate it with the help of local community foundations, but eventually with more permanent local support? Were component parts equally reapplicable?

The focus on the community woman was seen to have as a practical benefit the increased understanding of this program component. As with many comprehensive service programs, no site did exactly the same thing; none did the entire package, but most of the young women were exposed to most of the program elements, and some more than others. The community woman component had been added initially on the basis of the impression from the Brooklyn Sisterhood of Black Single Mothers that this kind of role might be a useful component. In the course of the first implementation study, that impression was strengthened. By adding a more focused research element to the second implementation stage, the program sought to better understand its reshaping of the role and thereby achieve a sharper definition of this role as a specific program tool. Relevant to the study was the importance of age, education, employment status, and personal values in developing the relationship between the community woman and the teen mother. What elements of the community woman and of matching her to particular types of teenage mothers were relevant to developing a viable relationship?

From an academic point of view, this role is of interest not only as an innovation based on a grass-roots revival of a traditional "quasi-kin" role but also as a relationship which constitutes a *social support structure* (McLanahan, 1981) or *stress buffer* (Thoits, 1982). The community woman has elements in common with the *mentor* and, in her relationship with the teenage mother on the one hand and the whole range of community agencies on the other, she may function as a *mediator*.

Research design and methodology. The research piggy-backed on the larger study, so it had to fit into the evaluation study being made of the programs as a whole. Of interest in the overall project design was the distinction made between *implementation* and *impact*. Evaluation of implementation related to the program's (and in this case the role's) feasibility; evaluation of impact related to the program's effect on the target population of teenage mothers.

The specific research on the community woman was designed, therefore, to dovetail with the program's sample of teenagers. In the four sites which completed the first phase (Detroit did not remain in the set), there was a total of 300 teenagers and 200 community women. In the second demonstration, the experimental teenager group was increased by 501, and the number of community women by 153.

The study of the community woman role was exploratory, raising broad research questions, such as, What was the relevance of their various demographic characteristics? of being mothers themselves? of being employed? of their personality and value orientations? of their skills? of their remuneration? of local conditions and availability? In the first demonstration project, the community women were of a wide age and ethnic range, but most of them (80 percent) had had some experience working with teens, and had held regular jobs (95 percent). Only one-fifth were currently employed, and there was a great deal of local variation in availability and in how much the agency targeted their recruiting programs. Over half had had their own first child before they were age 20, and over half had at some point been on public assistance. One set of questions was concerned with the relevance of these features, both the common elements and the diversities.

Another set of questions related the role in dynamic terms: What was the best match between particular teens and particular types of community women? What techniques or styles of managing the role lead to optimum outcomes? Would too little or too brief an involvement detract from the support element in the role? Would too much or too long involvement detract from the move toward self-sufficiency in the teen?

A final set of questions was concerned with how the community woman fit in with other relationships of the teen mother, such as her own family and the baby's father. As the biological father of the teenager's baby was often not on the scene, a concern of the overall program was with the issue of fathering and who might provide wanted fathering. How might the father figures impinge on the teen mother's relationship with the community woman? A parallel study to the second demonstration study was set up by the Bank Street Fathering Project. In this set of studies, the fathering issues were linked conceptually to the MDRC work but conducted independently in other sites.

In the larger framework of the second demonstration study, two quite distinct questions were salient: How well would the Project Redirection model "travel" (e.g., to other types of urban settings and to rural settings), and could it be institutionalized within the service delivery network? With the movement toward decentralization and the increased involvement of community foundations and local agencies, there was the need to forge new kinds of local relationships. This shift did not affect the salience of the community woman component as far as the MDRC model was concerned, but it had potential implications for the overall evaluation study if reduction of funds led to curtailment of the role (a paid volunteer role). If that happened, it would become difficult to determine whether it was being curtailed because of financial stringency or for other reasons.

Course of the project. In the first phase of Project Redirection, the central project funds were used partly to develop and evaluate the intervention, and partly to help the field sites to offset costs. Participating agencies could be helped financially, and their participation in the research was relatively easy to achieve as a quid pro quo.

In the second demonstration project, the situation changed. The focus broadened from a demonstration of implementation and impact to a demonstration of how a program model diffuses. The financial and political base shifted from a well-supported centrally organized project with operational funds to a diversified local one in which funds would have to be found locally. This stimulated a search for new sites (e.g., schools) and new modes of operation. There was the question of whether the same degree of research cooperation could be attained without the leverage of providing the funding. However, discussions with the local community foundations provided insight into what the grass-roots thinking was and helped to shape the direction of the research (Riccio with Council, 1985).

The emphasis on a more *active* intervention grew in the course of the project, particularly in relation to family planning education and the affirmation of the value of independence. It was based partly on disappointing impact results from the first demonstration study. In some sites the community women were pressed into a more active role in monitoring the individual participation plans and in drawing up the plans themselves, and more likely to be working.

Results

The findings of the community woman study provided answers to the initial questions and an improved conception of the nature of the role. The effect of the Project Redirection intervention was modestly better for the experimental group than for the comparison group, a finding which was blurred by the fact that the comparison group also experienced interventions, owing to the agencies' widespread interest in the problem of teenage pregnancy. This means that there was no "untreated" comparison group in the short-run, rather a group experiencing only Project Redirection intervention and a group receiving other community-based intervention. Nevertheless, of Project Redirection teens, a significantly lower percentage were subsequently pregnant at 12 months, a significantly higher percentage used contraception, and significantly higher percentages were in school or employed (Quint and Riccio, 1985, p. 19).

There was a positive relationship between time in the program and desired outcome, and a negative relationship between degree of initial disadvantage and outcome. By 24 months after program enrollment, almost half of both the experimental and comparison groups experienced a repeat pregnancy, which highlighted the importance of follow-through in effectively counteracting the long-term forces acting on the teen.

From a program point of view, the research both provided reassurance that the package could be effective relative to other approaches and emphasized the need for modest expectations and improvement in certain elements (e.g., the intensity of service delivery modalities and the attention to retention issues and to follow-through).

In regard to the community woman role specifically, the researchers found that from the start they had set a very broad set of guidelines for the position (availability for a minimum of five hours a week, ability to the necessary paper work as well as provide emotional support and guidance to young mothers, and willingness to work for a weekly stipend of $15 per teen, up to five teens). These guidelines were gradually sharpened following the first demonstration project.

In the second demonstration project, the community woman volunteers were more concentrated in the 25 to 34 age group (48 percent) or older (40 percent over 45); more were living in intact families, and their educational and occupational record was better than in the first demonstration. About half (47 percent) were currently married and living with their spouses, and 21 percent were widowed or divorced. Five out of six of the community women had had a high school education. Sixty-four percent were working at the time of of their recruitment, and most sustained active involvements in community organizations, particularly in church groups (59 percent).

In the first demonstration project, the Riverside experience revealed that the optimal situation would have been to have the distribution of the community women mirror that of the teens. In Riverside, 60 percent of the community women were white and relatively affluent, while the participants in the program were only 46 percent white (and poor), with 22 percent black and 29 percent Hispanic. This imbalance was recognized as problematic in Riverside, and active attempts were made to recruit community women in the same ethnic groups as the teens, but were not successful. In the second demonstration project, a more uniform degree of congruence betwen background characteristics of community women and teens was achieved, although the general educational level and occupational engagement level were higher than in the first demonstration program.

Improved descriptions of the role emerged, and the tasks performed by the community woman were grouped into the following categories:

> Instruction and problem-solving
> Serving as a confidante to the teen
> Reinforcing program objectives

Monitoring the teen's behavior
Performing general program responsibilities

The original conceptualization of the community woman role was that she would present herself as a role model and would also employ a degree of persuasion in discussing the positive value of the program elements as she herself had experienced them. For example, she would discuss the importance of developing life-management skills, formulating goals, and working to achieve them, all in relation to her own experience. A wealth of anecdotal material supported the viability of this conception; for example, one community woman said, "I keep talking about the importance of education, and after hearing me on the subject for a while, it begins to make more sense to them." Over the course of the project some new elements in the role conception emerged, for example, the idea of "shadowing" (allowing the teen to tag along and help, while the community woman raises her own children, shops, sews, cooks, and so on).

In both demonstrations the confidante role was found to be important. Teens reported such interactions as, "I tell her things I don't tell anyone else; we talk about how I feel." Frequent observations were that the community woman was easier to approach and talk to than program staff or others in formal positions. She was "like a big sister."

The *linkage* aspect of the community woman's role, between staff and the teen, came to be seen as perhaps the most salient element. The community woman reinforced program values to the teen by explaining why it was important to have education, to use birth control, and to prepare oneself for employment. In the other direction, the community woman let program staff know how the teen was doing and whether any problems were brewing that might, without intervention, lose the teen for the program. Key to the success of this linking role was the community woman's own "insider" status in the teen's social reference group ethnically, parentally, and in terms of the local community and social class values.

Though some community women sustained close and warm relationships with the teens (taking on mother-substitute role elements), most wished to avoid an authority relationship and preferred to act as advisers offering information and suggestions, rather than "laying down the law."

Examining the relationships between the community woman and her teen vis-à-vis the father of the baby, the general pattern was found to be one of coexistence. Generally there was little direct involvement of the community woman with the fathers, although sometimes community women took the teen's boyfriend along on outings or had them to her home. Occasionally community women influenced the boyfriend directly by getting him to take a constructive stance toward the teen (e.g., urging her to return to school).

The relationship with the teen's family was a more delicate one. In a few instances, the teen's mother felt that the community woman was too intrusive and wanted to take over elements of the mother's role. When this happened, indirect expressions of resentment sometimes thwarted the community woman's efforts. More generally, there was passive accept-ance. However, community women who took more active steps to work with the family conducted home visits and explained both to the teen and her family how the program might benefit both. These visits also served to provide the community woman with a more accurate picture of the mother, so that she could correct any tendency for the teen to exaggerate the problems in the maternal relationship, and thus avoid the polarization of the two women into good and bad figures.

Many community women made other contributions that went beyond the basic duties assigned to them. These included babysitting, organizing holiday events, canvassing local businesses, and conducting educational workshops for teens in the program. Many teens indicated the importance of the community woman relationship, sometimes giving it as a reason for joining the program. The role was, by that time, better known and teens could therefore state at the outset that they liked the idea of a community woman being "there for me" (Riccio with Council, 1985, p. 30).

In relation to the question of matching teens with community women, about two-thirds of the assignments were found to be workable. In about 10 percent of cases, no community woman was assigned, and in the remaining cases changes had to be made sometimes to improve the fit, sometimes to harmonize schedules, and sometimes because of a turnover in community women. The only site in which there were more serious difficulties of matching in the first phase of the program was Riverside, where the race and class mismatches proved to be a more serious impedi-ment than was envisaged. According to the first-phase final report,

> From knowledge accumulated over the course of the demonstration, the answer appears to be "yes" (the community woman has to reside in the same community as their teen in order to be effective) (but it is) a community of shared values and experience - not a geographical community - is the reference point. (In Riverside) many of these (higher socio-economic class) women did not understand the public assistance bureaucracy and could not help teens who needed assistance in manag-ing the system. (Branch, Riccio, and Quint, 1984, p. 76)

In addition, these busy, middle-class ladies often had relatively inflexi-ble timetables and were not able to be as responsive to their teens' needs.

"The world of domestic violence, housing projects, homelessness, and in many cases abject poverty, proved overwhelming." The first demonstration report further concluded that this traditional type of middle-class volunteer had a place in programs like Project Redirection, but unless the teens were of their own race and class, their best contribution would be as fund-raisers, workshop presenters, or administrators.

In the second demonstration phase, other problems were detected: in Brooklyn, the need for an efficient management element to keep contacts going in this complex setting; in Greenville, the need to think of activity bases for forming relationships other than the characteristic urban ones, of outings to zoos, amusement parks, and the like.

The remuneration issue was thoroughly explored. Many of the women who made stable community women needed some remuneration because they themselves were of the same relatively disadvantaged stratum as the teens. However, this was not found to be critical, except perhaps to low-income women, particularly in the second demonstration phase. However, their main reasons for participating were to meet their own needs and also for altruistic reasons (to do something useful, to help others, to take part in a program of activities in the community, and so on). Where both of these needs were recognized and supported (e.g., community woman committees, and recognition of service through "community woman of the year" awards) more stable and committed participation was obtained. Turnover in community women was seen to be inevitable and sometimes useful in providing new energies to a program, but its management was important, because the loss of a community woman to a teen who has developed a trusting relationship can be distressful. The length-of-stay record showed an average participation span of 13 to 14 months, considered high for this type of volunteer program.

In the second (replication) demonstration, the financial constraints were met in different ways which provided instructive information. In some instances reduction of the community woman's stipends led to a decline in the range of activities possible for the community woman, particularly for low-income volunteers. However, the project sites were able to achieve sustained commitment from many woman with minimum or no remuneration.

The overall project report concluded that the community woman role is a vital part of the program package:

Without the community women, [Project] Redirection would lack a range of valuable information about the participants and their life circumstances. This kind of knowledge, which most other programs lack, allows Project Redirection to make judgments and decisions about teens on a more fully informed basis. Community women are also helpful in conveying program objectives to participants . . . the community women counsel the teens informally on birth control and teach them parenting tasks. They also encourage good school attendance, and not only reinforce the program's philosophy, but do so in terms that the teen can understand. Moreover, the community women help to prevent the staff from becoming overextended . . . In addition, it appears that community women are important to the teens' perception of the program. In one site which did not have an effective community women component, teens drifted away a short time after enrollment. (Branch, Riccio, and Quint, 1984, pp. 128–9)

In the second demonstration, aside from the refinements in understanding and conceptualization of the role, as mentioned above, there was a more explicit recognition of the turnover process. The potential for positive as well as negative impact of such a turnover was recognized, and the need to plan for it as a natural inevitability. Of the 83 community women who left, nearly half (46.2%) did so because of conflicts between the demands of the role and their own family responsibilities, and a further 15 percent left because they lost interest. For 17.2 percent, their termination was at the request of the program staff. However, all of the sites were able to maintain a steady flow of new community women to replace those who left (Riccio with Council, 1985, p. 40).

Discussion

The Community Woman Project is of interest in several ways. It was part of a much larger project and consisted of the study of one element in a program in higher magnification. The innovative element, the community woman role, grew in prominence in the overall program partly as a result of participants' evaluations and partly as a result of the special attention given to it in the research. How much of that was rational building on results and how much as "Hawthorne effect," produced by the stimulation of the research itself, remains to be seen. However, the probability is in favor of the former, as the researchers were not very intensively involved at field levels.

In the course of this program's development, there was a major shift in political/environmental circumstances. This had several effects, including undermining the definitiveness of the quasi-experimental design, in that the "no-treatment" control group actually got considerable treatment because community concern with the issue of teenage motherhood produced a groundswell of community supports of various kinds. This affected the impact finding of the first demonstration phase. It also produced a new situation in relation to dissemination; the network of local agencies became more oriented to local sources of support as well as local sources of clientele. Because this usually meant a reduction, there were pressures to revise the program in various ways. Some of these were useful, and provided serendipitous findings. The search for new sites led to more collaboration with schools, demonstrating the feasibility of service delivery at school-based sites. The large number of school drop-outs among teen parents makes it inevitable that community agencies will be required even where there are effective school-based programs.

The action-research model used in this program development is different from that in most of the other projects in this book. The MDRC is an organization which is dedicated to research and development and contains within itself researchers and operations personnel who design innovative programs and arrange field trials for program evaluation and subsequent further dissemination. Another project using a similar model in the mentoring project (see Chapter 3). Another organization in the children's field using this type of model is the High Scope Educational Foundation. The fact that they are evaluating their own designs is a complicating factor, though rigorous attention to methodology has helped to counteract bias.

An advantage of this close interaction is in the synergism of social science and operational knowledge, seen at several stages in this project. The initial adaptation of the community woman idea benefited from the social science input (the conceptualization of role models). In later stages, the multidisciplinary character of the work allowed for applications in fields other than the social-psychological role-theory areas. The work was being used for teaching in courses on "human capital." This may have influenced conceptualization at later stages of the project, when the idea of "investing in oneself" appeared.

Another example of a shift of emphasis which emerged partly from intrinsic findings and partly from interactions in a changing environment had to do with the timing of the intervention. Some of the local projects that emphasized the establishment of an orientation toward employment had been concentrating on mothers with children in school or approaching school age. Project Redirection demonstrated the possibility of working with a broad spectrum of mothers with an employment goal, and their findings reinforced the importance of early intervention. In their relations with state and local agencies, considerable interest was generated in developing early intervention programs. A task force on adolescent pregnancy was set up with the American Public Welfare Association following the completion of the project.

These examples illustrate the way the eclectic, multidisciplinary approach characterizing projects such as this is subject to an organic growth process; they readapt to changing circumstances in the development and implementation of an innovation.

This type of demonstration project also illustrates the problem of continuity, once the demonstration program is over. The move toward self-sufficiency of local projects was achieved within both the first and the second demonstration phases. Uniform and uninterrupted continuity, requiring new sources of permanent support, are particularly difficult to achieve and present a problem for most social interventions, particularly those of national scope emerging in an era of reduction of federal program supports. This circumstance, however, presents a set of challenges in relation to which the MDRC responses have been instructive (Blum, in Riccio with Council, 1985, p. vii).

Case study: The Door – a model center for alternative services for youth

The Door is a multiservice center for inner city adolescents. It was established in New York in 1972. One of its programs is aimed at addressing the problems of teenage pregnancy, including its prevention. The action-research project in relation to this program, on risk factors associated with teenage pregnancy, was co-directed by Irma Hilton of Yeshiva University and Claudette Kunkes of The Door. The specific project was linked to a larger set of studies at the university directed by Hilton. The Door's clinical director, Loraine Henricks, was the administrative sponsor of the project from 1979–1981, and subsequently, Therese Nowlan, administrator of health programs.

Background

There are two fields relevant as background to this project: the teenage pregnancy field (cf. Ooms, 1981; McAnarney and Stickle, 1981, 1984; Hamburg, 1981; Hamburg and Lancaster, 1985; and the preceding case study, The Community Woman); and the field of alternative service provision (cf. Gordon, 1978; Lear, Foster and Wylie, 1985).

Alternative services began in the late 1960s, with clear dissatisfactions, concrete services and vague longings. Most were created by nonprofessionals in direct response to the needs of disaffected and homeless young people. Welfare departments, emergency rooms, and mental health clinics ignored these young people and their problems, gave service to them at the cost of condescension, labelling and coercion. In alternative services we tried to offer them what they needed –

medical care, information about drugs, counselling, a place to crash – in a respectful and loving way. (Gordon, 1978, p. 126)

Free clinics, runaway centers, group foster homes, hotlines, and outreach programs were the action armamentarium of this movement. Their approach is nonspecific, that is, they provide a range of helping services without labeling young people whose behavior is unconventional or who are in distress.

In relation to outreach efforts of major medical teaching institutions, the issues has focused on how better articulation can be developed between health care institutions and those with health-related problems who are for various reasons unreached by conventional methods. Youth at risk for socio-behavioral problems such as sexually-transmitted diseases, unplanned pregnancy, episodes of violence, and mental disorder are on the increase proportionately and are not well served by the major orthodox health care institutions (Lear et al., 1985).

The Door, as an example of the alternative services movement, began its development in 1970. A group of 12 professionals, all of whom shared an interest in youth problems, was brought together by the conviction that the critical needs of the adolescent population could best be met by a new form of human service facility. The basic philosophy underlying The Door's program is the total-person approach, which addresses each teen's physical, emotional, intellectual, interpersonal, creative, and developmental dynamics, as well as family, legal, educational, vocational, and other life issues and needs.

The Door's parent organization, the International Center for Integrative Studies (ICIS) originated as a research and educational institution concerned with the human-centered disciplines and sciences. Founded in 1962, ICIS brought together people from different disciplinary and professional perspectives to provide new understanding and also to help manage the already foreseeable rapid changes that would mark the rest of this century.

By the 1970s a number of programs were in place to scan for breakthroughs in concepts and applications in the many fields of human endeavor and for development of new concepts and knowledge. The Door and other projects became human service applications of ICIS's interdisciplinary holistic approach and of stress innovations and alternatives.

In The Door's developmental phase, the program aimed at creating an innovative center which would provide teens with effective services in a nonalienating way and with a sense of meaningful life alternatives. The explorations of how to make this ideal viable in the complex inner city environment of New York took the form of setting up informal interdisciplinary task forces, which met regularly and visited relevant local agencies and institutions serving youth. In the course of these visits to public health and youth service departments, public and private hospitals, community agencies, schools, courts, and residential and nonresidential programs (such as storefront facilities), an offer of a storefront facility was made. They used the space to provide a medical/psychiatric service for an outreach drug treatment unit during the day, and the new center for youth in the evening. This arrangement lasted for three years, operated mainly by volunteers working with the core professional staff. During this period The Door gained experience, developed programs and procedures, tested concepts in practice, and evolved a clearer set of ideas about what kind of an environment was wanted for its program. At the same time a sense of shared commitment developed among the staff, and funds were attracted by the dynamism of the new program.

The first major funding for The Door was in the drug abuse field. Eventually described in a publication of the National Institute of Drug Abuse in 1981, the program was introduced with the following quotation from an article in *New Physician:*

In many ways the Door's success defies explanation. It started without money, without staff – just with high hopes and some donated furniture. Now it receives federal and foundation support . . . The kids treat The Door with respect, and some of the volunteers seem more dedicated to it than to their full-time jobs. Most significantly, it has been adopted as a model for adolescent care by several groups, including HEW, the American Academy of Pediatrics, and the World Health Organization. (Henig, 1977, p. 34)

The disclaimer with which this description starts is deceptive. As the author goes on to describe, the acute crisis facing urban young people, the lack of effectiveness of conventional services for engaging youth's problems with drug abuse, violent crime, homelessness, disintegrating family situations, and a wide range of educational, vocational, and health difficulties made it apparent that something innovative was desperately needed, and funding agencies were searching for people with competence, commitment, and promising new ideas.

Several members of ICIS were involved in the initial development team of The Door, participating in it as an expression of an integrative ("holistic") approach to human services for adolescents, and with increased funding, ICIS was able to help arrange a larger and more autonomous premises and to expand the administrative structure to receive and manage public grant funds.

The Door was adopted as a model project by ICIS as a demonstration of a more effective, holistic, integrated human services approach for adolescents. . . .

ICIS. . . provided support services, space, management support, and ongoing encouragement for The Door. (National Institute of Drug Abuse, 1981, p. 2)

In the course of its growth over a four-year period, The Door developed from a storefront, part-time volunteer unit to the largest youth-serving agency in New York City with a mixed staff of employed and voluntary personnel and a range of youth-serving programs. The following aspects of The Door were developed concurrently during this period:

• Formalization of an ideology or philosophy of treatment;
• Formalization of a governing organization

The elements of the ideology grew out of the purposes of ISIS, as well as such concepts as Maslow's hierarchy of needs or Erikson's developmental stages and Rogers's client-centered approach.

These concepts were interpreted in the treatment approach for adolescents by a group of young professionals. Two of the founders of The Door, Loraine Henricks and James Turanski, developed some of these concepts in relation to an innovative center for youth which they had earlier helped to establish in Montreal at the time of Expo '67. They had been impressed with the gap between the needs of the adolescents and the services being provided. The Door's development team placed a strong emphasis on the importance of an open-access approach to youth, of meeting them on their own terms and providing a range of identity-exploring activities. This approach was related historically to the therapeutic community movement; the emphasis was on providing a round of life-like activities that served to make evident the nature of the problems to the clients, and that allowed them opportunities for developing more constructive patterns of social behavior. There were four therapeutic phases:

. . . 1) life stabilization, 2) confrontation and therapy, 3) reintegration and exploration of alternatives, and 4) autonomy . . . During this four-phase process, individual and group psychotherapy, drug and alcohol counselling, learning workshops, and rehabilitation and creative workshops are available to each participant.

In individual therapy, with the help, support and challenge of the therapist, the young person can explore and deal with anxieties, negative self-images, destructive behavior patterns and distorted perceptions of reality. Through the on-going therapeutic process, more constructive ways of functioning and relating, a healthier self-image and better reality-testing are established. The young person moves from a state of confusion, isolation, withdrawal, or destructive acting-out, toward a more resolved, involved and active life. (National Institute of Drug Abuse, 1981, p. 28)

The most all-encompassing statement of The Door's philosophy is on the notion of taking into account "the total person" (physical, emotional, intellectual, interpersonal, creative, and developmental) in the total life situation (family, peer group, school, work, legal, and community). This was termed "The Door's holistic approach" (National Institute of Drug Abuse, 1981, p. 3).

The Door's staff evolved a sense of being a leading innovative center to which professionals from all over the world came for training and inspiration. The Door was achieving recognition as a new model for adolescent service delivery. This contributed to the ethos leading up to the formation of the project.

Research at The Door

Most of the funds obtained in the development phase of The Door were clinical service and program funds. Very little money was available for research or evaluation. Initial energies were concentrated on developing new ways of meeting the needs of inner city youth, and later on developing a management/administrative and fund-raising structure to handle the associated fiscal and organizational issues.

A "utilization" survey was conducted by the staff in 1978 and again in 1980, the purpose of which was to determine the demographic characteristics of clients and their pattern of service utilization. In 1978, 535 young people were interviewed and in 1980, 500 were interviewed. A finding of considerable significance was that the clients surveyed had received an average of 5.3 services, indicating the importance of serving teens in a multiservice milieu. Data referral channels and clustering of subgroups in specific service areas were identified, and this stimulated internal discussion. For example, it was found that family planning service personnel referred more clients to psychiatric services than to other activities. Recreational and creative workshops attracted younger, minority males in significantly high proportions. Staff began to ask one another why. When satisfactory internal answers could be provided, alterations in practices were introduced. However, in cases where the questions were regarded as unanswerable with the available information, the idea of a more formal research investigation had to be deferred until appropriate resources were available.

There were, of course, varying opinions among staff as to the need for research and the extent to which The Door should try to attract more research funds. However, graduate students working among the volunteers at The Door were encouraged to develop research projects, which were sometimes associated with their thesis requirements. In one such study, an evaluation of the family planning program, it was found that an overwhelming majority of the clients continued to use contraceptives successfully over a two-year period after receiving sexual counseling and contraceptive services at The Door. This study raised the need to address many unanswered questions, why, for example, some clients did not continue using contraceptives.

A small grant from the National Institute of Drugs and Alcohol was made to The Door to look at the relation between drug use and the development of basic skills such as reading and math. This study documented and examined the inverse relationship: as clients' skills improved, their use of marijuana dropped off. A generic finding like this was useful to the staff, to administrators, and to program developers.

In considering a research project on teenage pregnancy, several things made the idea attractive to the clinical and administrative (host) participants. There was a genuine interest in learning more about the causes of unwanted teenage pregnancy, and it was recognized that additional funds would have to be generated. Also, staff hoped that they could learn from a teen pregnancy study that would identify risk factors associated with pregnancy. It was anticipated that the study would enable the early identification of clients who were at risk for pregnancy. Appropriate interventions could then be designed and implemented in order to prevent unwanted and unplanned pregnancies.

Claudette Kunkes, a clinical psychologist at The Door, conducted a research project on teen pregnancy which served as her Ph.D. dissertation (1978). Since the numbers were small, The Door encouraged Kunkes to develop a more extensive proposal that would look at a larger sample of adolescents so that risk factors could be more precisely identified. Kunkes and The Door approached Irma Hilton, who had been Kunkes's thesis adviser, for assistance in developing a successful research application. Hilton had received a request for applications from the National Institute of Mental Health (NIMH) for proposals in the area of teenage pregnancy, and she proposed to Kunkes that a project be developed to include The Door and Inwood House, a contrasting type of facility for pregnant teenagers. A proposal was submitted to NIMH in March 1979 with Irma Hilton as the principal investigator and Yeshiva University as the applicant organization.

While the proposal was under review at NIMH, it came to the attention of a trustee of the William T. Grant Foundation. The idea of an additional project was explored and submitted to the foundation for support from private sector funds; the proposal was reviewed and funded in July 1979.

The action-research project

The project had as its goal to understand why adolescents get pregnant in the face of all the risks. The formulation was a multicausal one: social, cultural, and interpersonal deficits lead to a series of psychological needs, which might be served by presumably unplanned and unwanted parent-hood. It hypothesized that if these needs were understood it would be possible to design services to help adolescents learn to meet these needs in other ways. The proposal submitted to the foundation stated the following objectives:

This study has four primary goals. The first is to identify those demographic and psychological characteristics associated with an increased susceptibility to unwanted teenage pregnancy and/or motherhood. The second is to support a hypothesis that these characteristics form a framework of psychological needs which are served by the pregnancy. The third is to develop intervention services to meet these needs. The fourth is to demonstrate that teenagers exposed to such interventions are less at risk for unwanted pregnancy and/or motherhood. (Hilton, 1979)

The theoretical orientation of the project was articulated by Hilton in her introductory remarks to the symposium on teenage pregnancy at the 1983 meeting of the American Psychological Association:

Although sufficient knowledge of the importance of contraception and an awareness of its availability are a necessary part of effective contraceptive use, they are not sufficient to ensure proper utilization. The psychological benefits of spontaneous sex without preparation, or the possibility of re-defining an ambiguous self-identity by becoming a mother, are motives which blur the perception of birth control information even when it is provided. Thus, understanding motives for pregnancy is an important part of ensuring effective contraceptive use.

Variables hypothesized to be important in the background of these motives included unsatisfying early parent-child relationships, poor relationships with peers, psychological immaturity (impulsitivity and poor frustration tolerance), low self-esteem, and tolerant attitudes towards sexuality and pregnancy. Kunkes's doctoral dissertation had pointed up some of the motivational factors behind a young girl's pregnancy. Girls who were pregnant would have lower levels of ego development.

It should be noted that from Hilton's point of view there was no explicit action-research (or site evaluation) intended. The intention in the formal design was to control for, rather than understand or evaluate, site differences.

Hilton's larger interest as a policy-oriented psychologist, however, required a focus on generalizations that could be made about antecedents of teenage pregnancy. Data from The Door was seen as contributing to the picture, but not defining the parameters. From The Door's point of view, shared to some extent by Kunkes, the study promised the possibility of designing and evaluating specific interventions to reduce the incidence of unintended pregnancy. The Door made available birth control counseling and methods, and exposed the teenager to alternative life options. The question was what kind of antecedent variables might limit or enhance the likelihood of internalizing and acting upon specific opportunities.

The project design, then, had two dimensions: a *generic dimension,* in which the aim was to increase understanding of the motivation to become pregnant, and a *specific dimension,* in which the aim was to understand the meaning of specific site experience on the course of the pregnancy and parenthood.

The target population was sexually active clients who came to The Door for service. The interviewees included young women who were sexually active and used contraception effectively, and young women who were pregnant and planning either an abortion or a full-term delivery. When possible, the male partners of these young women were also interviewed. The design was set up to make possible analyses on the basis of age and length of exposure to The Door's service.

An interview was constructed by the principal investigators to reveal family structure and relationships, peer relationships, school and work experience, and future plans. Access to birth control information and services, ego development, defensive structure, self-esteem, locus of control, sex-role orientation, and attitudes towards the role of women were assessed through measures with already established reliability and validity.

A follow-up interview to understand the effect of the pregnancy experience and motherhood on the attitudes of these adolescents toward effective family planning was developed for administration 18 months later. The physical, mental, and psychological well-being of the mother and baby were also assessed at that time.

Course of the project. At the end of the project's first year, when the data had been gathered but not yet analyzed, many changes occurred. Differences had been building up for some time among The Door's administrative staff, and in 1981 Henricks and Turanski left and become involved in international youth service projects.

The liaison between the university (Hilton and Fischler) and The Door (Henricks and Kunkes) also came under stress for a variety of reasons. Kunkes withdrew from the project after the data had been collected to establish a private practice and this created a gap in lines of communication between the university-based group and the administration at The Door. The relocation of the university group from Manhattan to the

Einstein Medical Campus in the Bronx also added to the problems because of the sheer logistical difficulties. Therefore, when the follow-up interviews were completed in the spring of 1982, a request was made to shift the project to the university because the task of data analysis was more logically suited to a university setting; besides which there were no longer any project staff on The Door's payroll. The separation, however, was made on amiable terms with the administrative staff at The Door and feedback was promised as soon as it was ready.

Analysis of results began in 1982 and has continued. Because the orientation of the university team focused on the causes and effects of teenage pregnancy, the early professional papers concentrated on considering these issues independent of the effects created by or encouraged by the performance sites. Built into the design, however, was the possibility for an examination of differences attributable to the effects of The Door. The research team wanted to know which of the variables hypothesized as linked to pregnancy risk were relatively impervious to site influence, and which might change after exposure to special interventions such as The Door.

Research results

The initial questions incorporated scientific and practical goals: What are the precipitating factors in adolescent pregnancy? What services would be effective to prevent it?

Early reports of results on the first question were, as noted, on common features that transcended site differences. For this analysis the 283 cases achieved at The Door were combined with 67 cases from Inwood House after a preliminary analysis revealed that there were no significant differences in key predictor variables for initial pregnancy risk. For the second question, the analysis required separation of the two sets of data to make site comparisons of the efficacy of the specific interventions. The findings are presented according to (a) precipitating circumstances, (b) preventive services, and (c) The Door's efficacy as a service facility.*

A. Precipitating circumstances. Five precipitating factors were highlighted for discussion.

---

* Based on unpublished draft materials by I. Hilton, 1985, and a paper for *Psychology Today* entitled "Psychological variables in the prediction of teen pregnancy risk and suggested intervention strategies" (from excerpts summarized by I. Hilton, personal communication, October 1986) and other working papers by Hilton, Kunkes, and others on the Yeshiva team.

1. Sex education and contraceptive knowledge are necessary but insufficient conditions for prevention of teenage pregnancy.

Though the data, as well as common sense, indicate that sex-education and increased knowledge about contraceptive practice are necessary if pregnancy is to be a chosen rather than unwanted event, the teens in this study did not necessarily translate this knowledge into more effective contraceptive use. Teens who were pregnant and planned to carry their babies to term did not know significantly less about birth control than a comparison group of effective contraceptive users.

2. The earlier the initiation into sexual activity, the greater the likelihood of a pregnancy.

This correlation is associated with the lower level of ego development (immaturity) of the early teenagers (their impulsivity; undeveloped forecasting and reality testing for such problems as having and rearing a baby). This means that though prior preparedness may have been available through contraceptives, teenagers do not make appropriate use of the available resources. They may fear the side-effects, they may be reluctant to acknowledge their sexual activity thus overtly, and they may be particularly susceptible to peer pressure. They may be unable to say "not now," or "wait."

3. Psychological needs other than those associated with immaturity may also be operative.

Many teenage girls become pregnant in a quasi-rational way, that is, to meet the needs that they recognize in themselves which they do not perceive to be getting met in other ways. If they are embroiled in a tense family situation or one that has become disrupted, leaving them with a sense of isolation, they may develop an overpowering need for companionship and for a sense of being needed and wanted by another human being. This may be accompanied by a feeling that because of what she has experienced, she can help the baby to have a better experience of being loved and supported.

4. Absence of social constraints against early sexuality is a factor.

The data indicate that when family and peers do not express disapproval of early sexuality, the teen is more likely to respond to the generally greater acceptance of unwed sexuality and pregnancy in today's social environment. Where there were also examples in the teen's own family of acceptance of unwed pregnancy, the likelihood of the girl becoming pregnant in her teens increased significantly.

5. Social disadvantage increases the chances of teen pregnancy.

A number of socio-demographic factors interact with the psychological needs described to increase chances of teen pregnancy: disintegrated family structures, ethnic minority status, and low socioeconomic status.

In summary, the findings confirm an interaction of psychological and socio-demographic factors. Early sexual activity in the presence of low ego development (personal immaturity), social permissiveness, family disruption, and socioeconomic disadvantage lead to heightened risk of teen pregnancy.

In considering preventive findings and their implications, it is important to note that there are two risk points: first, in relation to the chances of becoming pregnant while still in the teens, and second in relation to a recurrence. In both cases, resolutions may involve carrying the child to term or abortion. (The model developed by Hilton for this prediction appears in Fig. 5-1).

B. Preventive services. The data do not provide an evaluation of actual preventive services, except in relation to recurrence. However, by implication Hilton has drawn some tentative conclusions about how pregnancy may be averted.

Given the finding that permissive attitudes and lack of constraints in the child's immediate environment are involved, some conclude that it is important to consider ways and means to re-enforce the idea of postponing sexuality. Some media figures are advising against early sexual experimentation. Service agencies such as Boys Club and Girls Clubs have initiated programs to encourage young people to postpone sexuality. The YMCA/YWCA organizations are promoting pregnancy prevention programs which include encouragement for the teen to say no.

Sex education and contraceptive provision are more than ever seen as important, while the development of effective programs remains a continuing challenge. It has been demonstrated that these programs work best in the presence of a more mature person who is psychologically equipped to use these resources.

Given Hilton's finding that disrupted and permissive family environments are conducive to teenage pregnancy, it follows that improved parent-child relationships are needed. Learning to clarify values and develop skills in communication and conflict resolution may help. Faced with increased stress associated with divorce, reconstitution of households, and working mothers, families need supports to be able to provide the needed inputs of information, constraint, and modeling that children require.

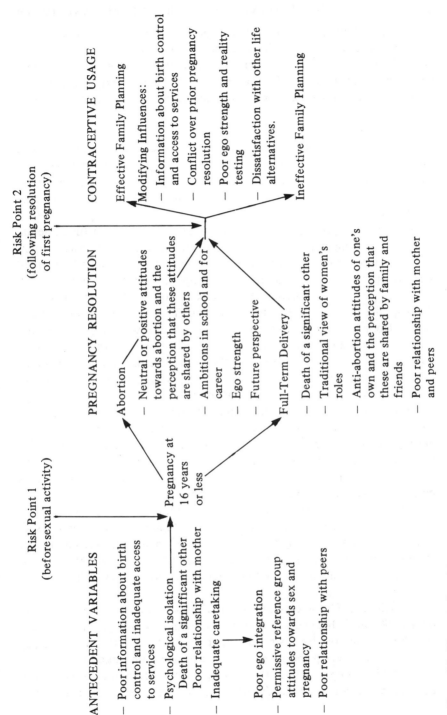

Risk Point 1
(before sexual activity)

Risk Point 2
(following resolution
of first pregnancy)

ANTECEDENT VARIABLES

— Poor information about birth
  control and inadequate access
  to services
— Psychological isolation
  Death of a significant other
  Poor relationship with mother
— Inadequate caretaking

— Poor ego integration
— Permissive reference group
  attitudes towards sex and
  pregnancy
— Poor relationship with peers

Pregnancy at
16 years
or less

PREGNANCY RESOLUTION

Abortion

— Neutral or positive attitudes
  towards abortion and the
  perception that these attitudes
  are shared by others
— Ambitions in school and for
  career
— Ego strength
— Future perspective

Full-Term Delivery

— Death of a significant other
— Traditional view of women's
  roles
— Anti-abortion attitudes of one's
  own and the perception that
  these are shared by family and
  friends
— Poor relationship with mother
  and peers

CONTRACEPTIVE USAGE

Effective Family Planning
Modifying Influences:
— Information about birth control
  and access to services
— Conflict over prior pregnancy
  resolution
— Poor ego strength and reality
  testing
— Dissatisfaction with other life
  alternatives.

Ineffective Family Planning

Figure 5-1. *Theoretical model*

The strengthening of family supports does not obviate the importance of also involving other social influences on the teen, such as peers, churches, and voluntary associations. Given the finding that a sense of isolation and alienation often underlies the search for fulfillment in sexuality and early parenthood, it is important to develop alternative ways of providing these social supports.

C. The Door as a service facility. The second research question relates to The Door as a distinctive innovation, invented to provide alternatives; the study had contrasted this agency with another facility concerned with the task of caring for the young mother and inculcating parental life-management skills.

The Door's explicit philosophy and approach aims at a fundamental reeducation using involvement of peers (including the male partner), counseling services, and the provision of a range of experiences that might serve to open up a sense of alternative life options to the premature parent. The first approach to isolating effects specific to The Door was to analyze the responses of Door clients by comparing those who had only registered at The Door but were not exposed to the full intervention program, and those who stayed and participated for at least six months. Those who participated will have experienced the impact of this supportive milieu with its counseling and other enabling services, and the invitation to experiment with alternative role conceptions.

Empirically, Hilton found that young women who had six months or more of access to The Door were more likely to have used birth control, to have used more effective contraceptive measures, and to have used them more often; they said, in significant proportions, that they had received birth control services from The Door. These girls with longer access periods to The Door were functionally more mature than those with minimal exposure; they also had more education, were more likely to be working, tended to be more assertive, and tended to have higher self-esteem. Hilton observes that there is no way of knowing if exposure to The Door program fostered the features described above, or whether there was a selectivity of the more "with-it" teenagers to seek out this kind of service and use it effectively.

Nevertheless, Hilton concludes that The Door does make birth control information available in a way that is used by those ready to make use of it, and the information itself is given impetus and strength through the array of services bolstering the teen's decision to avoid unwanted future pregnancy. This is important, as the sheer presence of contraceptive knowledge alone is not found to differentiate between the different outcome groups. Still more important, distinctive features of The Door's intervention are the provision of alternative role options and involvement of the male partner.

Those young women who had access to The Door over the six months or more period showed evidence of having benefited by these elements of The Door's program; their continued enrollment was associated with an increase in their internal locus of control and improvement in their self-conception.

Hilton notes that there is a substantial subgroup of The Door sample of older girls, functioning at a relatively high level of ego development, who report positive, albeit strict, parental backgrounds. These factors limit pregnancy risk, but in this population they are associated with an anti-abortion value orientation in themselves and their families; a traditional view of the role of women; a steady boyfriend and a history of prior pregnancy, all functioning in the direction of carrying the fetus to term. Though The Door allows the male partner to become involved, and thereby hopefully to recognize a responsibility in the potential consequences of sexual activity, changing the mindset of these young male partners is a challenge as yet to be effectively met.

In conclusion, Hilton pinpoints these areas for improvement:

- The need to reach teen women earlier, because the earlier the age of initiation, the more likely the occurrence of an unwanted pregnancy
- The need to improve retention of younger teens in the intervention situation, because those who sustained access fared better than those who did not
- The need to improve the effectiveness of involvement of the male partners, since many males abdicated responsibility
- The importance of dealing directly with parents. While The Door has always taken attitudes, values, and behavior of parents into account, concentration has been on the needs of the adolescent client who presents for service provision. Direct sustained attention to parents would represent a departure from early Door policy, which emphasized treating the adolescent as an individual and therefore de-emphasized providing services to the parents.

All of these points are in context of the overall conclusion that The Door provides an unusual mixture of emotional support, alternative life options, a role for the male partner, and the provision of technical/medical/educational services, all of which effectively reduce teen pregnancy risk.

From the point of view of The Door, the results could not be analyzed as quickly as the clinical staff would have liked. The program directors decided to seek funding in 1985 to address the problem of repeat pregnancy. The New York State Department of Health, Bureau of Reproductive Health funded a pilot project in 1986 designed to serve those at highest risk for repeat pregnancy. Hilton's results were incorporated into the development of a risk-assessment tool and the design of an intervention geared toward reducing the incidence of repeat pregnancy.

The three risk factors for repeat pregnancy identified by Hilton and Kunkes and used by The Door in program development were (1) unresolved conflicts over the outcome of the first pregnancy, (2) younger age at initiation of sexual activity, and (3) low level of ego development and psychological isolation. The program also incorporated other risk factors outlined by Hilton and Kunkes which correlated with incidence of pregnancy but not of repeat pregnancy: large family size, traditional concept of women, poor school performance, history of teen pregnancy in the family, and acceptance of pregnancy by family and peer group.

The pilot program will focus on recruiting high-risk young women, involving male partners, working through unresolved pregnancy issues, initiating contraception early after pregnancy resolution, anticipating possible interruptions in birth control use (contingency planning), exploring psychological needs and family relationships, providing continuous supportive counseling, addressing attitudes of peers and family regarding the desirability of teen pregnancy and teen parenthood, encouraging improved family communications, supporting education and career goals, and maintaining client-counselor contact on a monthly basis.

The Door is currently seeking funding to evaluate the usefulness of the risk-assessment tool and the effectiveness of the new intervention in its ability to delay the onset of and reduce the incidence of repeat pregnancy in the teen years.

Many positive features of an action-research approach have been demonstrated in this project in spite of delays and less than optimal communications. The Door will continue to use an action-research approach, assuming that financial support for its research efforts can be secured.

Discussion

As with many other social interventions, The Door experienced organizational turbulence as it grew from a small, innovative organization with charismatic leadership to a committee-managed organization with enlarged fiscal responsibilities. In addition the action-research component of the project (i.e., involving a continuous collaborative-interactive relationship between researcher and clinician) was disrupted with the departure of the clinical director and the site-based research associate, and the shift of the project from The Door to the university. The university-based researchers produced the findings reported above. These findings contribute to answers to the basic research questions raised initially and yield a revised theoretical model for predicting early pregnancy. There were secondary issues of site-specific effects and because of the larger comparative framework, Hilton was able to draw interesting contrasts between the two sites she studied. Hilton's policy discussions tended to be drawn on a larger canvas and were expressed in relation to public service bodies, professional journals, and action committees.

Amicable relations were retained with The Door staff, but the interactive development of site-specific practical implications of the analysis were less developed. The Door staff were pleased with the quality of the research, but staff needed reports and data on risk factors before results could be generated by the research team.

Kunkes produced a conceptualization of the action-research relationship based on early field experience (Fig. 5-2). When Hilton's findings began to emerge, she and others continued to discuss with staff of The Door issues of follow-through on implications for The Door. One implication was the development of a "pregnancy risk-assessment tool" based partly on the study findings. This would seek to identify high-risk clients so that intervention improvements might be directed toward reaching them earlier and more effectively, particularly adolescents who do not sustain involvement.

This study complemented an evaluation study of the functioning of The Door as a whole (Fink, Kosecoff, and Roth, 1985) in that it indicated that the kinds of approaches used at The Door helped young people to internalize contraceptive information to deal with conflicts associated with past pregnancies and helped to involve the males and to provide alternative role conceptions.

The Door delivers health-related services to adolescents who might not be as receptive to these services in a more formal and bureaucratic professional context. The use of an exciting ambience, presenting stress-reducing pursuits and pastimes, and promoting alternative behavior and lifestyles delivered in a supportive nonalienating way is helpful, not only as attested to by their own follow-up studies, but as indicated in follow-up studies in more orthodox facilities. The Door, too, has its less reached as well as its more effectively reached clients in terms of at-risk target groups. Of particular interest are the younger women and the hard-to-

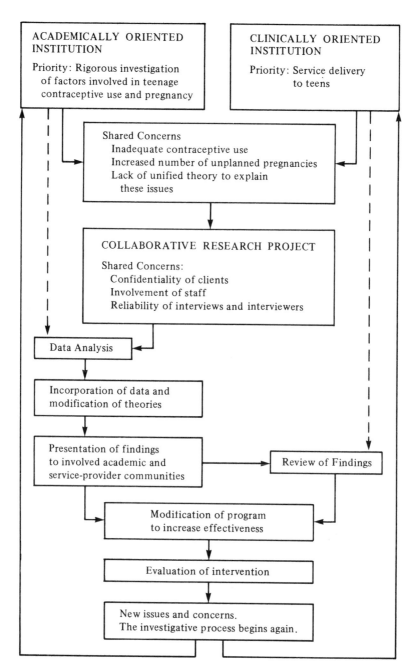

Figure 5-2. *A model for collaborative action-research* (Kunkes, C. 1983. A model for applied action research. Unpublished paper.)

reach males. For the young women, particularly challenging are problems of getting their families into collaborative relationships. For the hard-to-reach male, a greater effect may be achieved through an enlarged range of center activities.

In a review of comprehensive milieu programs for youth conducted for the William T. Grant Foundation early in this project, Anita King (1983) found that though there were many programs that had one or another element of The Door's multiservice milieu approach, few had evaluated them to pinpoint areas of strengths and weakness. She noted the twin spheres of infuence on youth – family and community (including peers) – and suggested studies of these differences (and possible complementarities) of approaches emphasizing one or the other.

The difficulties that this project experienced as an action-research enterprise has not led to rejection of the approach. On the contrary, The Door and the researcher have emerged from the experience with a renewed interest in the potentials of a collaborative interactive approach, having learned from the data as well as from the working-through of many organizational changes.

References

Abel, R. L. 1982. *The Politics of Informal Justice*. New York. Academic Press.

Asquith, S. 1983. *Children and Justice*. Edinburgh University Press.

Bane, M. J., and Ellwood, D. 1983. *The Dynamics of Dependence: The Routes to Self-Sufficiency*. Cambridge, Mass.: Urban Systems and Engineering.

Blum, B. 1985. Preface. In J. Riccio and D. C. Council, *Strengthening Services for Teen Mothers*. New York: MDRC.

Branch, A.; Riccio, J.; and Quint, J. 1984. *Building Self-Sufficiency in Pregnant and Parenting Teens: Final Implementation Report of Project Redirection*. New York: MDRC.

Burt, M. R., and Moore, K. A. 1982. *Private Crisis, Public Cost: Policy Perspectives on Teenage Childbearing*. Washington D.C.: Urban Institute Press.

Cohen, N. 1975. Changing perspectives on US Social Services. In *Meeting Human Needs I*, ed. by D. Thursz and J. Vigilante. Beverly Hills, Calif.: Sage.

Fink, A.; Kosecoff, J.; and Roth, C. 1985. An evaluation of The Door: Summary. Santa Monica, Calif.

Folberg, J., and Taylor, A. 1984. *Mediation*. San Francisco: Jossey-Bass.

Froland, C.; Pancost, D. L.; Chapman, N. J.; and Kimboko, P. J. 1981. *Helping Networks and Human Services*. Beverly Hills, Calif.: Sage.

Furstenberg, F., et al. 1982. Patterns of parenting in the transition from divorce to remarriage. In *Women: A Developmental Perspective*, ed. by P. W. Berman and E. R. Ramey. NIH Publication No. 82.2298. Washington, D.C.: NIH.

Garofolo, J., and Connelly, J. 1980. *Dispute Resolution Centers*. Hackensack, N.J.: National Council on Crime and Delinquency.

Gordon, J. 1978. *Caring for Youth: Essays on Alternative Services*. Washington, D.C.: NIMH.

Hamburg, B. A. 1981. Teenagers as parents: Developmental issues in school-age pregnancy.

In *Psychopathology of Children and Youth,* ed. by E. Purcell. New York: Josiah Macey Foundation.

Hamburg, B., and Lancaster, J. (eds). 1985. *School-Age Pregnancy.* New York: Aldine.

Henig, R. M. 1977. The evolving "Door." *New Physician* (March), p. 34.

Hilton, I. 1979. Teenage pregnancy: Causes, effects and alternatives. Grant proposal submitted to and approved by NICHD; funded by the W.T. Grant Foundation, 1979–1980.

Hilton, I. 1986. Quoted by Stark, E., in Young, innocent, and pregnant: Psychological variables in the prediction of teen pregnancy risk and suggested intervention strategies. *Psychology Today* 20(10): 28.

Hilton, I.; Hart, B.; and Kunkes, C. 1981. Teenage pregnancy: Causes, effects and alternatives: Is sexual restraint a solution? Presented at the First International Interdisciplinary Congress on Women, Haifa, Israel, December, 1981. Proceedings of the Congress.

Hilton, I.; Kunkes, C.; Fishler-Hedgepeth, P.; et al. 1983. Teenage pregnancy: Causes, effects and alternatives: Implications for social policy. Symposium presented at the American Psychological Association Meetings, Anaheim, Calif., Proceedings of the Meetings.

Hilton, I.; Montoya, E. C.; Sornstein, J.; Fishler-Hedgepeth, P.; and Kunkes, C. 1984. Teenage pregnancy: Crossroads on the route to empowerment loss. Presented at the Second International Interdisciplinary Congress on Women, Groningen, Netherlands, Proceedings of the Congress.

Kahn, A. J., and Kamerman, S. 1985. Personal social services and income transfer experiments: The research and action connections. In *Children, Youth and Families: The Action-Research Relationship,* ed. by R. N. Rapoport. New York: Cambridge University Press.

Kamerman, S., and Kahn, A. J. 1978. *Family Policy.* New York: Columbia.

Ketcham, O. W. 1979. Children's rights: The problem of non-criminal misbehavior. *State Court Journal* 3:22

King, A. S. 1983. Review of research on innovative adolescent centers. Paper for Grant Foundation Workshop.

Klein, M. W. 1979. Reinstitutionalization and diversion of juvenile offenders. *Social Problems* 22:292–303.

Klerman, G. L. 1979. Evaluating service programs for school age parents: Design problems. *Evaluation and the Health Professions,* pp. 55–68.

Klerman, G. L. 1981. Programs for pregnant adolescents and young parents: Their development and assessment. In *Teenage Parents and Their Offspring,* ed. by K. D. Scott, T. Field, and E. G. Robertson. New York: Grune and Stratton.

Kunkes, C. 1978. Adolescent pregnancy: Factors determining its causes and resolution. Ph.D. thesis, Yeshiva University.

Kunkes, C. 1983. A model for applied action research. Unpublished.

Lear, J.; Foster, H. W.; and Wylie, W. G. 1985. Development of community-based health services for adolescents at risk for socio-medical problems. *Journal of Medical Education* (October) 60:777–785.

Levy, S. B., and Grinker, W. J. 1983. *Choices and Life Circumstances: An Ethnographic Study of Project Redirection Teens.* New York: MDRC.

Martin, F. S.; Fox, S.; and Murray, K. 1981. *Children out of Court.* Edinburgh: Scottish Academic Press.

Martin, F. S., and Murray, K. 1976. *Children's Hearings.* Edinburgh: Scottish University Press.

McAnarney, E. (ed.). 1984. *The Adolescent Family,* Columbus, Ohio: Ross Laboratories.

McAnarney, E., and Stickle, G. (eds). 1981. *Pregnancy and Childbearing During Adolescence: Research Priorities for the 1980s.* New York: Liss.

Merry, S. E. 1979. Going to Court: Strategies of dispute management in an American urban neighborhood. *Law and Society* (Summer): 891–925.

Merry, S. E. 1981. *Urban Danger: Life in a Neighborhood of Strangers.* Philadelphia: Temple University Press.

Merry, S. E. 1982. The social organization of mediation in nonindustrial societies. In *The Politics of Informal Justice,* ed. by R. Abel, vol. 2. New York: Academic Press.

Merry, S. E. 1984. Anthropology and the study of alternative dispute resolution. *Journal of Legal Education* 34:277–284.

Merry, S. E. 1988. The mediation process: Myth and practice. In *Mediation in the Criminal Justice System,* ed. by M. Wright and B. Galaway. London: Sage.

Merry, S., and Rocheleau, A. M. 1985. The *Mediation Process in Parent/Child Conflicts: The Children's Hearings Project,* unpublished report.

Moore, K. A.; Hofferth, S. L.; Caldwell, S. B.; and Waite, L. J. 1979. *Teenage Motherhood: Social and Economic Consequences.* Washington, D.C.: Urban Institute.

Murray, K. 1979. Juvenile justice and children's hearings. In *Social Services in Scotland,* ed. by J. English and F. Martin. Edinburgh: Scottish Academic Press.

Nader, L. 1980. *No Access to Law: Alternatives to the American Judicial Systems.* New York: Academic Press.

Nader, L. and Todd, H. F. (eds). 1978. *The Disputing Process – Law in Ten Societies.* New York: Columbia University Press.

National Institute of Drug Abuse. 1981. *The Door: A Model Youth Center.* Rockville, Md.

Ooms, T. (ed.). 1981. *Teenage Pregnancy in a Family Context.* Philadelphia: Temple University Press.

Parsloe, P. 1978. *Juvenile Justice in Britain and the United States.* London: Routledge.

Polit, D. F.; Kahn, J.; and Stevens, D. 1985. *Final Impacts from Project Redirection.* New York: MDRC.

Polit, D. F.; Tannen, M. C.; and Kahn, J. R. 1983. *School, Work, and Family Planning: Interim Impacts in Project Redirection.* New York: MDRC.

Quint, J., and Riccio, J. 1985. *The challenge of serving pregnant and parenting teens: Lessons from Project Redirection.* New York: MDRC.

Riccio, J., with Council, D. C. 1985. *Strengthening Services for Teen Mothers.* New York: MDRC.

Rutter, M., and Giller, H. 1983. *Juvenile Delinquency: Trends and Perspectives.* New York: Penguin.

Sarri, R., and Bradley, P. W. 1980. Juvenile aid panels: An alternative to juvenile court processing in South Australia. *Crime and Delinquency* 26:42–62.

Schlossman, S. 1982. *The Chicago Area Project Revisited.* Santa Monica, Calif.: RAND.

Seidman, E. 1984. The adolescent passage and entry into the juvenile justice system. In *Children, Mental Health and the Law,* ed. by D. Repucci et al. Beverly Hills, Calif.: Sage.

Silbey, S., and Merry, S. E. 1986. Mediator settlement strategies, *Law and Policy* 8(1):7–32.

Thoits, P. A. 1982. Conceptual, methodological and theoretical problems in studying social support as a buffer against life stress. *Journal of Health and Social Behavior* 23:145–159.

Thursz, D., and Vigilante, J. 1975. *Meeting Human Needs I.* Beverly Hills, Calif.: Sage.

Thursz, D., and Vigilante, J. 1976. *Meeting Human Needs II.* Beverly Hills, Calif.: Sage.

Vorenberg, E. 1982. *A State of the Art Survey of Dispute Resolution Programs Involving Juveniles.* American Bar Association Dispute Resolution Progress Series, no. 1, July.

Woodson, R. L. 1981. *A Summons to Life: Mediating Structures and the Prevention of Youth Crime.* Cambridge, Mass.: Ballinger.

Zatz, J. 1982. Problems and issues in deinstitutionalization. In *Neither Angels Nor Thieves: Studies in the Deinstitutionalization of Status Offenders,* ed. by J. F. Handler and J. Zatz. Washington, D.C.: National Academy Press.

Zelnick, M., and Kanter, J. 1980. Sexual activity, contraceptive use and pregnancy among metropolitan-area teenagers: 1971–1979. *Family Planning Perspectives* 12(5):230–237.

6   Conclusions

The social interventions described in this book are of the intermediate type. They are neither at the large-scale (Type IV) program level, nor are they merely concepts (Type I), good ideas but untested in action. All involve the actualization of a new role or new group structure or small organization designed to help children or adolescents to develop coping capacities. Figure 6-1 locates the interventions in an ecological framework.

An understanding of the natural history of the case studies themselves and of other action programs operating in their fields underscores the point that the problems they address may be approached in various ways and at different levels. Having examined the cases in some detail, the three questions raised at the start of this book can now be discussed:

1. How do social interventions take form?
2. What are the issues in the use of action-research as a method for *developing* social innovations?
3. What do these action-research projects contribute to scientific knowledge about children's coping capacities?

Formation of social interventions

In the introductory chapter the many similarities between the invention process in technology and in the social-behavioral field were noted. Both processes benefit by a productive interplay between the scientist and the action agent; both increase when there is a surge of economic support and a perception of a payoff, although in the behavioral field the payoff is generally weighted more toward anticipated *noneconomic* benefits; both rely on enterprising individuals but have moved beyond the stage of requiring team efforts and specialist skills for different parts of the task; in both, inventors often experience resistance and rejection for innovations which subsequently prove their merit; and, conversely, in both there are

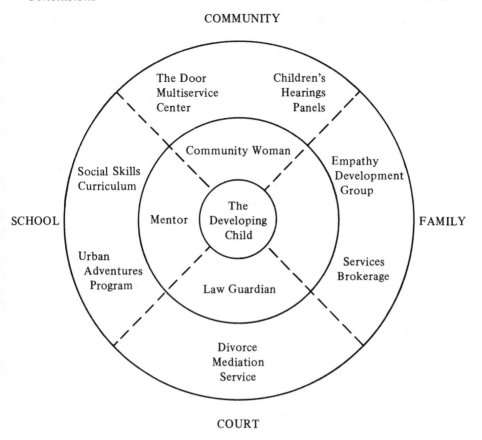

Figure 6-1. *The inner ring around the developing child contains the type II inventions (new roles), and the outer ring the type III inventions (new groups or organizations). The use of broken lines indicates the considerable permeability of the sectors. For example, one intervention (the Children's Hearings Planels) moved from the court sector to the community sector. Another (divorce mediation) moved from being a new solo role to a team procedure.*

disappointments in promising innovations. Risk-taking is important in both innovation processes.

Also noted were some of the differences, particularly the tendency for social innovations to develop *kaleidoscopically,* rather than advancing in a linear way.

Unlike the large-scale innovations of the 1950s and 1960s, which tended to be conceived "at the top," the innovations in this book are more grass roots-based. In the earlier large-scale programs, social scientists tended to be consultants rather than collaborators or inventors. But while many social scientists were favorably disposed to the large-scale scope of the great society programs, others were more cautious, even critical, of some of the side-effects of large-scale institution-building. In the juvenile justice field, for example, the concept of a "diversionary" program evolved with the aim of keeping young people out of the formal courts system altogether, though juvenile courts were established to avoid unsatisfactory aspects of the previous court system. In the mental health field, criticism was leveled at hospitalization, labeling, and iatrogenic illness, the undesirable consequences of programs which sprang from critiques of earlier programs. This is, of course, part of the dialectic process through which social changes occur.

Like the physical scientists who reacted against the war-time juggernauts which they had helped to create, some social scientists sought after the postwar era of massive program-building to reinstitute smaller scale, "primary" institutions and more person-oriented procedures. The "Small is Beautiful" movement is one example; alternative or "complementary" medicine and "quality of working life" are others. These are liberal reform ideas, seeking to rehumanize parts of society which may have become suboptimally effective through institutionalization/bureaucratization. The specific innovations reported here are not directly linked to these movements. However, they do reflect the newer emphasis on seeking solutions to contemporary problems through cultivating the capacity to cope with life's problems in a more direct and personal way, rather than looking for solutions at the level of total societal change.

This shift in focus is found both in conservative groups that emphasize the value of traditional modes of coping and liberal groups that emphasize the need to find new solutions with, perhaps, a larger component of social supports. In both instances, there is a need for reliable information on how the solutions can be developed and applied (Haggerty, 1985). Whether the solution is a traditional one or an innovatory one, research information inevitably becomes required as the need for evaluation makes itself apparent, and as further information is wanted. The cases presented illustrate the variety of agenda involved in attempting to deal with problems associated with children's development in a social context, and the role that research can play. They are all new "social interventions," but some are more based on traditional ideas and practices than others.

First, in examining the roots of these interventions, it was noted how the social field innovations tend primarily to be reinventions. Though charismatic innovators often stress the novelty of what they are doing, knowledgeable observers may experience a strong impression of *déjà vu*. They ask, Why do we have to continuously reinvent the wheel? Most, if not all, of the key elements in the social interventions that have been described have identifiable precursors, many with cultural elements known in antiquity. The mentor concept was well developed in Confucian teachings; marriage and family brokerage are widespread in preindustrial cultures; the advocate was a well-developed role in ancient Rome; the center-for-alternatives idea reflects the ethos of the bazaar; the idea of setting challenges for youth is seen in initiation rituals of youth in many simpler societies; the use of kin relations in creating social support groups is similarly widespread in earlier societies, as is the prescription of steps in decision-making.

However, there is a difference. The interventions in this book have not been applied automatically according to traditional formulae. They have drawn on traditional elements of knowledge and experience, but then have applied them in a new and tentative way to solve a problem that has been unsatisfactorily handled by the "automatic" social procedures in use. *Conceptualized* historical antecedents have been brought into action as part of a deliberate application of abstract ideas to concrete contemporary problems. The establishment of the new application depends partly on its assessed efficacy evaluation, and partly on economic, political, and other considerations.

The case studies confirm the general tendency for modern social interventions to evolve from a base of explicitly conceptualized antecedent models, while at the same time expressing a sense of novelty (Table 6-1). The family services brokerage, for example, used the idea of service integration, which was a recognized concept in the 1960s and 1970s, but added the new idea of a family services brokerage to empower families to maintain themselves. The Children's Hearings Panels derived from the Scottish and other neighborhood dispute-resolution models, but it had to be reinvented to suit its new social setting. The Urban Adventures program was explicitly based on the Outward Bound idea, but was adapted in a novel way to a metropolitan school setting with educationally at-risk ethnic minority children. In the mentor and the community woman roles, there was a self-conscious modeling of the innovation on conceptualized antecedents, but each had an element of novelty in regenerating specific lost roles important for specific, current child-development problems.

The kaleidoscopic aspect of the social change process is apparent in the

Table 6-1. *Antecedents of inventions*

Interventions	Recent antecedents (references to research reports)	Novel features
Family services brokerage	Service integration (Weissman)	Interagency brokerage function, Multilevel treatment model
Empathy development group	Group therapy (Slavson; Foulkes and Anthony)	Focus on empathy as intervening variable in transmission of violence
Social skills curriculum	Cognitive skills and awareness groups (Elardo and Cooper, Spivak et al., Cowen et al.)	Multilevel problem-solving model built into school curriculum for 9–10-year age group
Mentor role in schools	(Career) mentor (Levinson)	School setting; school–university linkage
Urban Adventures program	Outward Bound (Miner and Boldt)	Adaptation of challenge program for disadvantaged children in urban setting.
Law guardian	Children's Courts and Guardians (Landsman and Minow; Sobie)	Universal provision of an advocate for the child as a right
Divorce mediation as an alternative to litigation	Mediation and arbitration in other fields (Folberg and Taylor)	Adaptation to family court setting
Children's Hearings Panels	Scottish Children's Panels (Martin et al.)	Adaptation to American setting in conjunction with juvenile courts
Community woman	Fictive kin support roles in urban ethnic groups (Caplan)	Adaptation to program for teen mothers
Center for alternatives	Therapeutic community (M. Jones)	A holistic approach to providing service options for adolescents

restoration of functional equivalents for something perceived to be missing. In developing the empathy group, the innovators sought a different sort of restoration. They recognized that the normal capacity for empathy, generally developed spontaneously in the growing child, may be disturbed with disruption of the child's intimate social environment. They created a form of compensatory action to avoid the transmission of this defect from one generation to the next, much as a biogeneticist might seek to correct a genetic defect. A similar bolstering of normal developmental skills is seen in the social problem-solving curriculum. The law guardian role had been invented earlier but needed renovation to improve its functioning. The action-research project aimed to accomplish this by assessing the role as applied to the diverse requirements of a large state and through the implementation of its recommendations to provide what Ralph Linton (1936) called an "improving invention."

What is the source of the drive to innovate? Earlier it was noted that innovative thrust may come either out of a scientific concept or from practical experience (Rapoport, 1985). The ten cases in this book throw further light on the issue (Table 6-2). The initiative to create and develop a particular intervention can come from either direction, but in the cases studied, six out of ten were initiated from the action-agency side. In three cases, the researcher provided the concept on which the action initiative was based, and in only one case was the new intervention jointly conceived and developed.

Whichever side provides the initial thrust, the development of an action-research project requires the recognition of specialist expertise and a sense of interdependence. In the social problem solving curriculum, the mentor role, and the divorce mediation procedure, the researchers provided the concept underlying the prototype invention. However, to develop and operate it as an intervention required an active facilitating response from the action agency. Of the projects that were initiated from the agency side, the leaders tended to have had some social science background. Innovative social workers, judges, psychiatrists, and educators, exposed to the social sciences as part of their academic background, developed interventions amenable to adding a social research component.

There is no evidence to suggest that a new intervention has a better chance of occurring if it is designed conceptually in an academic setting and then applied, than if it is based on the concerns of practitioners and then explicated with research. Enterprising individuals, a stock of useful

Table 6-2. *Source of initiative*

Agency	Researcher	Joint
Family services brokerage	Social problem-solving curriculum	Empathy group
Urban Adventures	Mentor	
Law guardian	Divorce mediator	
Children's Hearings Panels		
Community woman		
Center for alternatives		

ideas, and recent precedents are the ingredients in the development of a modern social intervention. However, the further development of efficacy in programs such as those described is enhanced through action-oriented research.

The innovations studied suggest that there are generally precipitating factors which trigger and facilitate the formation of these innovatory alliances. In all of the cases studied, external precipitators were present in the form of public concern (Table 6-3); this concern was expressed as political uproar, critical media or publication exposure, or advocacy group pressures. These precipitators generally highlighted the consciousness of *negatively* valued situations for developing children, that is, situations which put children at risk for subsequent mental health problems.

The external precipitators stimulate funding bodies to support programs, though the interaction between funding bodies and project applicants is complex. Funding bodies tend to express societal values through program targeting. The applicants express current academic concerns as well as an effective level of professional competence. After some discussion between the two systems, the actual funding of projects emerges from the interplay of these factors.

Though there were marked social precipitators in the background of these interventions, they were not "inventions mothered by necessity represented by catastrophe." Nor were they created by autocratic fiat. Rather, they emerged out of the *confluence* of ingredients. Certain effective ingredients for project development were seen in the case studies:

- A *good concept* based on evidence of its scientific currency and relevance to a specific problem (e.g., in a recent antecedent)
- An *enterprising individual(s)* with basic competence, legitimate credentials, auspices, and persuasive skills
- A *precipitating circumstance,* such as an expression of public concern, or or widespread practice worries
- *Economic support* through foundation, government, or other public service agency

The formation of a viable project to develop a social intervention requires the orchestration of these elements.

Issues of action-research methods

All the projects are varieties of action-research, a method of work based on a partnership between researcher(s) and action agent(s). The aim of using this method is to accelerate the development of an action innovation, while simultaneously drawing on the learning opportunities in such a situation to advance science. Enthusiasts for the approach claim that its

Table 6-3. *External precipitators of new social interventions*

Social intervention	External precipitators
Family services brokerage	Negative effects of fostering
Empathy training	Negative consequences of family violence
Social problem–solving curriculum	Personal problems interfering with school performance
mentor	School drop-outs
Urban Adventures program	Social alienation
Law guardian	Inadequate legal representation
Divorce mediator	Parental conflict in divorce litigation
Children's Hearings Panels	Stigmatization in court proceedings
Community woman	Welfare dependency of school-age mothers
Center for alternatives	Adolescent behavior problems

distinctive advantage is in facilitating the development of new paradigms for understanding the processes of change.

First to be considered is what has been learned *about* action-research; then, what has been learned *from* action-research.

Diversity of action-research

First, these projects illustrate the diversity within the action-research "family" (as noted above) and the complexity of contemporary action-research settings, even small-scale grass-roots projects. Some of the ways in which they are diverse will be described.

Stage of development. Research can join up with program operation at various stages of program development. Innovative programs tend to develop through five stages:

> *Conception:* a "good idea" of how to deal with a specific problem
> *Actualization:* bringing into action a new role, group, or institution as a social instrument implementing the conception
> *Evaluation:* the objective monitoring and assessment of the innovation
> *Feedback* (and dissemination): publishing results of the evaluation
> *Institutionalization:* adoption of the innovation on a more permanent basis

In four of the interventions (the empathy training group, the social problem–solving curriculum, the mentor, and the divorce mediation procedure), the action-research project was initiated at the conceptualization stage. In the others, the program had been actualized and was in place before the action-research was introduced at the evaluation stage. The circumstances around this varied; in two instances (the family services brokerage and the law guardian), the interventions were institutionalized but considered to be in need of revision. In two cases, (the Urban Adventures program and the Children's Hearings Panels), the innovations were field trials that needed detailed scrutiny before the question of institutionalization could be considered. In the remaining two cases (the Community Woman Project within the larger Project Redirection and the teenage pregnancy study within The Door multiservice center), the action-research focused on a particular element within a larger program. These variations affected the methodology and the number of stages ideally to be traversed to complete the cycle.

Project structure. The projects are diverse in their structure. They indicate the necessity of going beyond the simple model of action-research as a collaboration between a researcher and an action agent, or a partnership between a pair of trusting colleagues with overlapping interests and values. This model of a core collaborative relationship is a necessary but insufficient condition for the successful conduct of action-research. The core cast-of-characters involves researcher and agency director, but also a number of other parties. On the agency side, there are agency staff, service users, governing bodies, and a variety of networks and constituencies. On the researcher side, there are academic and professional associations and employing organizations. For both, there is "the public."

Funding agencies. Funding agencies for the two parts of the enterprise are likely to differ. Depending on the specific history, a particular action-research project involves different arrays of participants and audiences. A project concerned with the actualization of a new concept has different, though overlapping, requirements: the evaluation and readaptation of an existing invention, the dissemination of an invention into new settings, or the solution of problems to make possible the institutionalization of an innovation.

Other project differences. Most of the projects described involved three or more core participants and various levels of organizational structure, rather than the classical partnership of the complementary pair within an autonomous unit. They also varied in the degree of complexity of the environments within which they took form, and toward which they aimed their results. The participants themselves set their sights at diverse targets, changing a particular institution, improving a statewide system, generating a national demonstration, making a conceptual breakthrough.

Beyond this, the projects differed in terms of how much they focused on specific versus generic issues. The mentor role, for example, was introduced as an adjunct to the teacher role in schools under stress, but it was conceived in more general terms in relation to stress-buffering roles and to the structure of teaching and learning in schools. The empathy group was developed to find a way to avoid recurrent violence in families, but it contributed insights into general problems of therapeutic groups that include children.

All of the projects are intrinsically multidisciplinary, linking diverse colleague networks, just as the diverse concerns of action and research and the problem-solving at both individual and social levels are recognized as relevant. Reference groups are multiple, but usually include a basic science or professional discipline and a substantive problem area, such as social skills development, mediation, or teenage pregnancy.

The complexity of project organization is not, however, directly related to the stage of development of the intervention. Of the four projects which started from initial conceptualization, two had simple structures, and two complex structures. The divorce mediation and empathy development projects involved a simple collaboration between researcher and agency director. The mentoring project involved not only the researcher and the school principals and classroom teachers, but also a city volunteer agency and a larger set of educational institutions. The social problem-solving project involved not only a community mental health center researcher and a school principal, but also an academic psychologist, additional schools, and parent organizations. However, even in the simplest partnerships there are various organizational levels involved. In the court-linked mediation project, the judge delegated development work to the court services officer; in the social skills project, the principal delegated development work to specific teachers; and in the empathy project, the social agency director delegated group development tasks to therapeutic group leaders. In all projects the relationships with subjects had to be taken into account and the research role distinguished conceptually from the intervention role, even though sometimes the two were self-consciously merged in action.

Among the projects where research was added later in the development cycle, when established operations were in place, there was also diversity. Some (the Urban Adventures and community woman projects) had relatively simple structures, while others (the Law Guardian Program) had extremely complex ones. All of the projects had to incorporate alterations of various kinds, even those in which considerable preparatory work had been done before going into the field. In Project Discovery, for example, in which the researcher and action agency director established a firm collaborative relationship from the outset, new formulations had to be worked out about the role of each in relation to the school and its staff once field work commenced.

The conclusion that emerges is that there is no simple fit between the type of action-research structure and the development stage of an innovation at which research should be joined to action; the structure of the project depends on the subject and the action setting. Action settings vary both with type (schools, courts, family service agencies, community service agencies) and level (local, state, or national). On the research side, different numbers and types of researchers become involved, according to the research methodology selected.

Entrepreneurship

As noted in the introductory chapter, entrepreneurship is important in the development of innovations. Drucker (1985) noted the particular difficulties found in public service organizations, and the *Harvard Business Review* extended the analysis to nonprofit organizations generally. The cases studied here contribute some further insights into the problem.

A special feature of the environment of entrepreneurship in the social sciences and social services is a conspicuous sense of ambivalence. When a project director is said to be "a real entrepreneur," there is a sense of uncertainty about whether this is an epithet of praise or of condemnation. Readiness to undertake a bold, uncertain, risky line of work is a sine qua non of the innovative process. There are numerous obstacles to overcome, a lack of models to guide the work, and problems of mobilizing support and participation. Yet, the kind of entrepreneurial orientation that is instrumental in taking on these difficulties continues to be considered a phenomenon more appropriate to the world of business and commerce than to the academic and professional life. The observation that an individual is a real entrepreneur carries with it doubts and suspicions about motivation.

What do the case studies show about these social entrepreneurs? In six of the cases, the principal entrepreneur was located in the action agency; in one case, this role was filled by a partnership between researcher and operator, and in three cases, it was the researcher who developed the innovation interactively with a responsive action-agency leader (e.g., a school principal or a judge). Five factors emerged as important elements in the way these persons exercised entrepreneurship:

1. *Basic competence* in their fields. Though some were regarded as somewhat marginal or maverick, all had impeccable credentials and had had their work favorably assessed by established peers.
2. *A high degree of commitment* to the new idea they were proposing and a certain tunnel vision about the importance of this particular solution for the perceived problem. The amount of energy they needed to find support and overcome obstacles without giving up attests to this.
3. *Some degree of flexibility.* Paradoxically, when the inevitable obstacles were encountered, ways had to be found to get around them. There was generally more than one way to do what they were committed to, and if the initially conceived way encountered obstacles – as frequently occurs with innovations – they had to be capable of making adaptations. To give some examples, when a school closed which provided some of the research cases for the trials of the problem-solving curriculum, the project leader accepted it as a challenge with a useful increment to the design, rather than as a crippling disaster; when the flow of subjects was interrupted for the empathy training group trials because of a client sit-in at the urban family shelter, the project turned their attention to constructing in-depth case profiles, and extended the timetable of the experimental design; when the city contract for a mentoring program went to another organization that had a different conceptual orientation and was not involved in the development of the mentoring role, the principals continued to develop the concept they had evolved in the pilot study, but for a wider application. The cases show how the entrepreneurs found alternatives when frustrations occurred, sometimes turning them to advantage without compromising basic integrity.
4. *An organizational problem-solving capacity.* In addition to basic competence (referring to the technical field of work), the entrepreneur needed an organizational problem-solving capacity in relation to the organizational field of forces in which the basic work operated. An enterprising psychiatrist must, accordingly, not only be competent as a therapist, committed to the new method and flexible in adapting it to specific circumstances, but also be able to solve problems of an organizational kind: arranging the physical facility, developing professional and financial accountability procedures, and dealing with government agencies, foundations, and the public. The same holds true for the enterprising social worker, teacher, lawyer, or social scientist. These organizational problem-solving skills include leadership, advocacy, public relations, and communications skills, and are not automatically inculcated in professional training.
5. *A sense of the complementarity* of the diverse contributions to the overall effort of thought and action, research and policy, science and human service. Successful interdisciplinary collaboration is marked by a sense of *trust*, an *overlap* in moral and ethical values, and a capacity and willingness to *communicate*. For example, the potential for distrust if some members of an agency fear that the researcher's findings could have a destructive effect can be countered if there is a core of trust between the principals. Or, if a researcher feels the agency will misuse the findings, misunderstanding can be avoided if communications are kept open.

Are there career risks that entrepreneurs take when they branch off into new ways of doing things? In the six instances where the original initiative came from the agency side, two of the original entrepreneurial directors (family services brokerage and Children's Hearings Panels) moved up into more senior positions with enlarged scope and responsibility by the end of the project, and three (Project Discovery, Community Woman Project, and the center for alternatives) moved out without a career advance. In the case of the law guardian project, there was no individual entrepreneur, the intervention having been developed interactively with the Legal Aid Society, the family courts, and the bar association involved. To the extent that there was an entrepreneur, it was the State Supreme Court judge who chaired the bar association committee; he remained in place.

In the case where the action agent and researcher developed the intervention jointly, the enterprising agency leader moved up, taking on the directorship of the larger organization overseeing the innovative unit and the researcher remained in place as a full professor.

In the three cases where the researcher originated the intervention in its current setting, one (the mentor project) became the type of case that Drucker described as a "displaced" development. That is to say, the researcher got credit for a good idea and early development work, but subsequent development of the intervention was taken over by "the system" with its own people and procedures. As the researcher was a tenured professor, this experience did not affect his career development. In the other two instances where the researchers were the entrepreneurs (the social problem-solving curriculum and the divorce mediation project), the principal investigators began the project at a more junior level, but moved upward as the projects succeeded. In both cases there was academic recognition in the form of a tenure appointment, although this unorthodox procedure caused a certain amount of anxiety. Both cases stressed the importance of rigorous research methodology using conventional standards. Both of these cases were characterized by strong *team* spirit with local agencies and by attention to dissemination and public relations.

Social entrepreneurship, then, while it carries a sense of risk and of being maverick, can lead to career advancement under contemporary conditions. However, in most cases, it involves stress and turbulence, and examples were encountered both in the reported series and in other projects in which creativity and innovation were not rewarded. Everyone concerned in the series of cases reported here felt the presence of career risks but also of potential payoffs. They varied in terms of how necessary they felt it was to weigh up the risks against the safer, more conventionally acceptable ways of doing things and advancing careers. In many cases there was a commitment to the idea with only secondary concern with the risks, and in some cases it was the risk that provided some attraction. In these cases there was an acceptance of political factors in project development and dissemination and little acrimony about the "triumph of mediocrity," or the "unwillingness to make radical changes." Nor did the action agencies express irritation at the "arrogance and impracticability" of researchers.

The cases generally suggest the importance of looking at social entrepreneurship in greater detail.

Role overlap

In the projects described, one of the concepts that emerged as contributing to the success of the action-research enterprise is *role overlap*. Wider discussions in the professional literature also emphasize the need for new integrations between practice and theory. Argyris and his colleagues (1985) have emphasized what can be learned by researchers taking a more interventionist role. Richard Price and his colleagues (1985) have emphasized the importance of working out explicit trade-offs to allow the diverse participants to collaborate in an undertaking of mutual interest. Reason and Rowan (1981) have emphasized the importance of a cooperative orientation, one that acknowledges the value of observations and analyses of clients and subjects as well as those of the professionals providing the services and the scientists studying them.

Flexibility

Another prevalent impression from the case studies is that because successful results can be produced in various ways, *flexibility* to meet the challenges of particular situations is important. Sometimes what has been considered as an ideal structure fails to produce results because of external factors, such as an unfavorable political climate or a change of regime. In other cases, a viable action-research relationship may founder for internal rather than external reasons. The various participants may fail to develop a shared sense of values or recognition of one anothers' goals; or there may be insufficient feedback or communication; or the diverse requirements and shared elements in one anothers' roles may be insufficiently recognized.

The use of a merged model of action-research (i.e., in which the researcher is also the action innovator) seems to be useful in the pilot stages of an entirely new intervention. In such a situation, learning through doing sometimes is facilitated when one person or a small team is involved. The more differentiated model seems to be most useful when an intervention is already in place; then specialist skills are required to produce persuasive technical information that might lever changes. This model is particularly applicable to dispersed situations involving many sites, such as an entire city school system, or the statewide system of family courts.

Continuity

Continuity is an explicit concern in most of the projects, partly as a matter of continuity in sponsorship and funding, but partly as a matter of continuity in involvement. Results are produced and digested at different rates in the various systems. The time required to complete research writing may not mesh well with the needs of the action agency if they require a report of findings for their next step (e.g., in obtaining support or approval). If the agency is a relatively autonomous one and not so pressured by external forces and deadlines, it can more easily tolerate the kind of delay. On the researcher's side, the delay while a report is being absorbed may be difficult if funds have run out and there is no source of support to fall back on. Decisions on publications, continuing agency support for further applications for funding, and so on, often take time that is not provided for in formal project schedules. If delays occur early in the researcher's career, they may hold up advancement. Protective support structures are important in providing the required continuity. At a university, these may be teaching; at a research institute, these may be other projects in related fields.

Other methods in innovation development

The action-research participants themselves expressed a positive valuation for it as a method for developing innovations. They perceived its value in relation to *cross-fertilization of ideas*. For example, in the family services brokerage, the researcher introduced to the agency a new perspective on the agency's service model and on its operating procedures, and in return got a renewed understanding of family issues in disadvantaged ethnic groups; in the empathy development group, the researcher's data on family profiles gave the service staff a new dimension of clinical awareness and the researcher in turn enlarged his understanding of methodological problems of researching children in group therapy contexts; and in the mentoring project, the pilot work introduced data helping the school program innovators to confront the need to clarify the various role conceptions of mentoring. And conversely, the researcher modified his conceptual focus on the place of mentoring in schools.

Disseminating information about the intervention was also emphasized by the participants. In the children's panels, research results helped with formulating training programs for wider adoption by the social services. In the law guardian study, the data increased consciousness about the problem leading to specific measures to improve the role, albeit short of the specific recommendations. In the social skills curriculum, the research helped to codify and communicate the elements of the invention for wider adoption.

Providing research information for advocacy programs was another valuable method. The projects fed their findings into movements such as those advocating widespread application of mentoring, mediation, social problem-solving, and social supports for buffering stress.

Though obviously not an unbiased sample, most of the participants – both on the action and the research side – stated that in future they would choose this way of working for developing innovations, in spite of the problems involved. Where there was a collapse of an initially formulated research design, or disappointing results in relation to an initial hypothesis, the joint participation element seems to have helped with the discovery of serendipities (see discussions of the Project Discovery, empathy group, and mentoring projects). Even where there was considerable turbulence (as in the center for alternatives project, in which changes occurred in both action and research personnel), there was an avowed interest in trying to restore aspects of overlapping interests in the action-research collaboration.

Researchers felt that this approach made data available that they might not otherwise have been able to obtain, and that the cooperative style of work was compatible with humanistic research values. Action agencies were convinced that this·way of working made research results more accessible and relevant, and that having a research project was stimulating and informative.

Conclusions about children and stress

We can now ask what contributions these action-research projects have made to the scientific understanding of the development of children's coping capacities. The individual case reports provide summaries of substantive results. They affirm the importance of a well-integrated and satisfactorily functioning family; of social support structures when traumatic life events occur, such as family violence or loss; of schools that provide instruction in social problem-solving skills as well as the "three R's," through the supportive inputs of a mentor as well as the more formal instructional lessons from an authoritative teacher, and schools that allow children to extend their experience outward into the larger social environment; of courts which provide a legal advocate for the child and a mediator for the parents in child-custody conflicts; and of communities that provide mediation for conflicts between the growing child and the family and neighborhood, and that provide confiding and supportive figures and multiservice facilities so that choice may be made among alternative pathways to a helping relationship.

At a conceptual and theoretical level, the projects taken collectively suggest two additional contributions: a multiple outcomes–multiple interventions model and a multiple systems model.

First, the intervention-outcome model. It seems from consideration of the various cases (in the context of the larger literature of which they are part) that an appropriate intervention model is one analogous to the "multiple problems–multiple causality" model described in the introduction. This might now be called the "multiple outcomes–multiple interventions" model, which is shown in Table 6-4.

Specific projects tend to be based on the particular approach of their principals and use formulations which are current in the particular discipline and in the language of the particular school. While specific interventions may be more suited to specific outcomes (e.g., cognitive instruction for problem-solving skills, group therapy for emotional development), it is clear that the efficacy of specific interventions depends to some extent on mediating factors such as social class, ethnic subculture, gender, and age. The implications of this are that different combinations of intervention may be optimal for producing a given outcome for different groups. Cognitive instruction may be more effective in the presence of practical assistance or group therapy or role support for specific categories of people.

At present, the conceptualization of interventions ranges between a "parochial" pole (advocating a particular intervention as the only or best way to achieve the desired effects) and an eclectic pole (trying various combinations as expedient). Ultimately, the goal is to be able to specify the combinations and conditions which are more efficacious, probably something between the two poles.

The second model emerging as important in these projects is the multiple-systems model. This emerges from the ecological orientation, which requires that events and persons be seen in a socioenvironmental context; action-researchers from psychological and sociological backgrounds

Table 6-4. *Multiple outcomes–multiple interventions model*

Interventions	Outcomes
Practical assistance	Improved self-concept
(e.g., home economics,	
service brokering)	Self-esteem
Cognitive instruction	
(e.g., problem-solving)	Interpersonal competence
Psychotherapy	
(e.g., affectional insight)	Problem-solving skill
Group therapy	
(e.g., empathy training)	Social sensitivity
Behavior modification	
(e.g., activity program)	Respect for authority
Role support	
(e.g., fictive-kin, mentor,	Family cohesiveness
advocate)	
Mediation role/panel	Academic performance
Transitional community	
(e.g., alternative services	Value clarification
center)	

share this orientation. When the variable in focus was at a sociological level (a role or institution), the analysis of its functioning was partly in terms of the implications for the individual child's development. When the focus was on the individual child (development of self-esteem, empathy, or competence at problem-solving) the analysis included a consideration of social context.

However, in examining the different ways in which the multiple-systems approach may be applied, we can discern instructive contrasts. Where the approach simply involves creating an interface between people working the different systems (social and psychological), the results seem less productive than when there is an integrated approach (i.e., variables in both system combined in a single conceptual framework; or concepts and data from both systems used by a single person). Examples of the latter approach are the two family services projects, the Project Discovery, and the mentoring and mediation projects. In these five the presence or absence of a correlation depended not only on the characteristics of the particular variables, but also on the state of the system in which the variables were imbedded. It is for this reason that the lack of a correlation between mentoring and academic performance, for example, was not taken as a negation of a relationship. Rather, the conditions under which the mentors were recruited, trained, and functioned were taken into account, and also the conditions under which the students were engaged. Subsequent formulations sought to improve these conditions before conducting another field trial.

In Project Discovery we find perhaps the best statement of a multisystems perspective. A modest correlation was found between improved self-esteem, academic performance, and participation in the program. But this correlation was recognized to be a result of the balance sustained between program staff, school staff, and students, all of whom affect the outcome of any given field trial depending on systems dynamics. If the program staff experience too much turbulence in their own system, the experimental stimulus being studied will be a different one than if they are in a steady state and have high morale. This is what Emery and Trist (1973) meant in their discussion of the "causal texture of the environment." The linked systems model in Figure 6-2 gives an account of the various systems scenarios that could affect outcomes.

Interventions can be used at social or individual levels, and in any of the component subsystems. Both the intervention model and the systems model suggest that there are many ways to achieve the goals of children's health and well-being, and many ways to add to knowledge in this field. Those who choose to work in the action-research mode give up a modicum of design purity and some of the satisfactions that come with contributing to the confines of a specific discipline. They gain, through engaging in the more turbulent world of action, a sense of drama and relevance in their work and the possibility of using their knowledge to benefit humanity. In doing so, they may take on both supports and criticisms.

The experience reported reenforces the observation of Robert Hollister (1974), a pioneer in the community health field. He observed that early enthusiasm about an innovation must be regarded warily. Those who take it up rapidly may have unrealistic expectations of quick payoffs. When skeptics attack the approach, its faint-hearted supporters may fall away. Sarason (1983) has also noted this polarization tendency, of seeking salvation and, when it fails to materialize, of finding scapegoats. Hollister warns innovators to beware of this kind of initial support and to anticipate the backlash stage when the innovation is achieving a measure of recognition but is still technically unproven. He advises innovators to know the opposition and suggests early attention to evaluation and to developing effective incentives for efficiency. Similar observations are applicable to research as an enterprise.

In the projects described, various approaches have been tried and varying degrees of success have been experienced. Some have been more

LINKED SYSTEMS MODEL

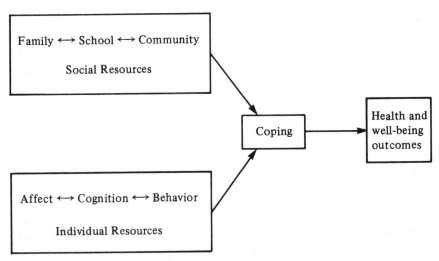

Figure 6-2. *Linked systems model*

efficacious and cost-effective than others and have reaped the rewards of recognition and application that are hoped for in a rational society. Luck has certainly played a role in dissemination and institutionalization, which depend partly on the confluence of political, social, and personal factors beyond the control of the project. But however irrational oppositional factors may seem, an action-research approach requires a sustained rational response in order to improve research design and methodology, to strive for better dissemination of findings, and to learn from failures as well as successes. It requires perseverence in meshing the standards of "normal science" with an acceptance of an "untestable" element in the development of new knowledge.

The general response of participants was positive. The findings are probably not major breakthroughs but they constitute discernible contributions to knowledge which, as Inkeles (1986) has stressed, should not be underestimated in assessing how a field advances. Perhaps the most impressive element in the findings had to do with serendipities. In the LESFU study, for example, the results anticipated by the design were forthcoming and discussed, but it was some of the other, unanticipated findings that were in some ways more interesting both to the agency and the researcher. The challenges of developing new management data systems and learning more about urban ethnic family cultures were not focal initially, but in the end they provided much stimulation. The empathy development group project stimulated discussions on the various possible interpretations of inconclusive results; but more important both to the agency and to the researcher was the identification of violent family profiles. In the social problem-solving project there was a linear course of development of findings bearing on the initial hypothesis and its subsequent extension into new settings; but in addition, the team enjoyed serendipitous findings. For example, when unexpected parent demands to participate occurred, a new dimension of insight into out-of-school influences was brought into focus. In the mentoring project, the development of a new conceptual orientation about learning styles was a serendipitous outcome. Though it did not feed directly into the development of the mentoring role in the New York schools, it contributed to a general understanding of how new support roles for students may be conceptualized. In Project Discovery, the unanticipated importance of the affectual dimensions of the experience enriched the eventual conclusions. In the Law Guardian Program and Community Woman and The Door projects, the additional findings were not, properly speaking, serendipities, but rather a "thickened" pattern of findings made possible by the action-research orientation. The interest in working back and forth between different dimensions of the problems enriched the projects. The Children's Hearings Panels project experienced a shift of emphasis which produced serendipitous results. Although the projects' goals had always included an element of seeking to understand the mediation process as well as the specific conflicts of family and community being mediated, the process ultimately received the greater emphasis. The resulting contribution to the understanding of mediation dynamics was greater than anticipated and enlarged the project's range of interest.

As noted in the introductory chapter, scientific advances have often come through serendipities. Many discussions have occurred about whether these can be produced deliberately and the general consensus is negative though keeping an open as well as a technically prepared mind are widely recognized as a sine qua non. On the basis of experience with these and related projects, action-research, with its exposure to turbulent real-life situations and its multidisciplinary problem-solving approach, offers a particularly fertile seed bed for serendipitous discoveries.

Donald Michael (1973) told corporate planners that they would be well advised not only to learn to plan, but also to "plan to learn." To take a leaf from Michael's notebook, action-researchers and their colleagues and funders should perhaps not only test the expectable, but expect the untestable – and learn from it.

Personal postcript

There are many impediments to advancing social science knowledge. There are also many difficulties in the way of designing and executing new social interventions. Expecting a project to contribute to both – to do action-research – is asking a lot, particularly in a world of uncertain and ambivalent support. Formidable institutional and professional obstacles make the marriage between research and intervention a difficult one to sustain. The requirements of dedicated service provision and of quality research may be in conflict, and individuals with gifts in one or the other direction may not be compatible with one another in an interdisciplinary team.

Nevertheless, I have come out of working in this way, and studying the experiences of others, with a reinforced conviction of its merits. At core, the action-research family of approaches is governed by common sense and a dedication to gathering nontrivial information to apply to humanitarian purposes. If the knowledge gained is only partial, the evaluations inconclusive, and the interventions only semi-effective, it is a challenge to do better – not a condemnation.

Dreaming the impossible dream, reaching beyond the comfortable span of the easily feasible – these are ingredients for innovative development.

References

Argyris, C.; Putnam, R.; and Smith, D. McC. 1985. *Action Science*. San Francisco: Jossey-Bass.

Caplan, G. 1974. *Support Systems and Community Mental Health*. New York: Behavioral Press.

Cowen, E.; Gesten E.; and Weissberg, R. 1975. *New Ways in School Mental Health*. New York: Human Sciences Press.

Elardo, P., and Cooper, M. 1977. *Aware-Activities for Social Development*. Reading, Mass.: Addison-Wesley.

Emery, F., and Trist, E. 1973. *Towards a Social Ecology*. London: Plenum.

Folberg, J., and Taylor, A. 1984. *Mediation*. San Francisco: Jossey-Bass.

Foulkes, S. H., and Anthony, E. J. 1957. *Group Psychotherapy: The Psychoanalytic Approach*. Harmondsworth: Penguin.

Haggerty, R. J. 1985. Annual report of the president. William T. Grant Foundation, New York.

Hollister, R. M. 1974. Neighborhood health centers as demonstrations. In *Neighborhood Health Centers*, ed. by R. M. Hollister, B. M. Kramer, and S. S. Bellin. Lexington, Mass.: Heath.

Inkeles, A. 1986. Advances in sociology – A critique. In *Advances in the Social Sciences, 1900–1980*, ed. by K. W. Deutsch, A. S. Markovits, and J. Platt. Lanham, Md.: University Press of America.

Jones, M. 1953. *The Therapeutic Community*. New York: Basic Books.

Landsman, K. and Minow, M. Lawyering for the Child. *Yale Law Journal* 87(6): 1126–1190.

Levinson, D. 1978. *The Seasons of a Man's Life*. New York: Knopf.

Linton, R. 1936. *The Study of Man*. New York: Appleton-Century.

Martin, F. S.; Fox, S.; and Murray, K. 1981. *Children out of Court*. Edinburgh: Scottish Academic Press.

Michael, D. 1973. *On Learning to Plan – and Planning to Learn*. San Francisco: Jossey-Bass.

Miner, J. B. and Boldt, J. 1981. *Outward Bound USA: Learning Through Experience in Adventure-Based Education*. New York: Morrow.

Price, R., and Burke, C. 1985. Youth employment. In *Children, Youth and Families: The Action-Research Relationship*, ed. by R. N. Rapoport. New York: Cambridge University Press.

Rapoport, R. N. (ed.). 1985. *Children, Youth and Families: The Action-Research Relationship*. New York: Cambridge University Press.

Reason, P., and Rowan, J. 1981. *Human Inquiry*. New York: Wiley.

Sarason, S. B. 1983. *Schooling in America: Scapegoat and Salvation*. New York: Free Press.

Slavson, S. R. 1956. *The Fields of Group Psychotherapy*. New York: International Universities Press.

Sobie, M. 1981. *The Juvenile Offender Act*. New York: Foundation for Child Development.

Spivak, G.; Platt, J.; and Shure, M. 1976. *Problem-Solving Techniques in Child Rearing*. San Francisco: Jossey-Bass.

Weissman, H. 1978. *Integrating Services for Troubled Families*. San Francisco: Jossey-Bass.

Index

Handicapped children, mentors in
education of, 109, 111–112, 114, 116,
118
Head Start Program, 12, 20–21, 89–90
initial evaluations of, 20–21
Ypsilanti studies on, 21
Hedaa, Maryann, in Urban Adventures and
Project Discovery programs, 122, 125,
126, 127, 130–131, 132, 133, 134
Henricks, Loraine, in The Door
multiservice center project, 222, 225,
229
Henry Street Settlement, 59, 186
Urban Families Center and empathy
development group of, 59–86
Herbert, Alfred, in Lower East Side Family
Union project, 38, 48, 57
Hilton, Irma, in The Door multiservice
center project, 222, 227, 228, 229, 232,
234, 235–236, 237
Hispanic clients
in empathy development group, 74
in Lower East Side Family Union, 52, 54,
56
in Project Discovery, 125, 138, 139
Housing problems of clients
in Lower East Side Family Union, 54, 55
in Urban Families Center of Henry Street
Settlement, 62, 63, 64, 65
Humm, Andrew, in mentoring role project,
108, 111, 115, 117, 119

Indians, American, action research on, 15,
19–20
Information system
of Lower East Side Family Union, 57, 58,
261
of Urban Adventures and Project
Discovery, 133
Institutionalization of inventions, 83, 249,
250
Integration of schools, action-research on,
18–19
International Center for Integrative Studies,
The Door project of, 223, 224
Inventions
antecedents of, 245, 246
breakthrough type of, 5
case study approach to, 25–26
comparison of social and technical types
of, 1–2, 4, 10–11, 242–244
differences in, 250–252
dissemination of. *See* Dissemination of
information
diverse structures of, 250
economic factors in, 7–8, 13, 250
of entrepreneurs, 6, 252–255

expansion and devolution of, 12
external precipitating factors in, 248, 249
improving type of, 5
initial support of, and backlash stage, 260
institutionalization of, 83, 249, 250
kaleidoscopic nature of, 5, 58, 244, 245–
247
of Lower East Side Family Union, 43–44,
49, 58
of mentoring role, 110–111
motivating factors in, 7–8, 10
multiple independent occurrence of, 8
national differences in, 7
of Outward Bound program, 122, 245
process in development of, 4–10, 249–250,
251–252
receptive environment for, 8
and reinventions, 5, 11, 245
related to advances in social theory, 11
research in development of, 6, 248–257
resistance to, 7, 9–10
role of chance in, 9
role of individuals and corporations in, 5–
6
social impact of, 5
social type of, 4, 10–13, 242–248
source of initiative in, 247, 254
team effort in, 6, 11
of Urban Families Center, 62–65, 83
volatility of, 11

Jackson, Joanne, in divorce mediation
program, 169, 178
Johnson administration, action-research
during, 17–18

Kennedy administration, action-research
during, 18
Kin imagery in Project Redirection, 212,
213, 246
Knitzer, Jane, in Law Guardian Program,
151, 156, 160, 166, 167, 168
Kronenfeld, Daniel, in Henry Street
Settlement projects, 59, 65, 72, 83
Kunkes, Claudette, in The Door alternative
multiservice center, 222, 227, 228, 229,
236, 237

Lash, Trude, in Lower East Side Family
Union project, 40, 41, 42
Law Guardian Program, 150, 151–169, 246–
247, 254
antecedents of, 246
appellate actions in, 158, 163
assignments of law guardians in, 153
background of, 151–155
caseloads in, 153–154